www.photoshop.imageready

Greg Simsic

QUE

201 W. 103rd Street
Indianapolis, Indiana 46290

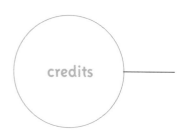

Executive Editor
Beth Millett

Development Editor
Sarah Robbins

Project Editor
Heather McNeill

Indexers
Kelly Castell
Sheila Schroeder

Proofreader
Maribeth Echard

Technical Editor
Caroline Collins

Team Coordinator
Julie Otto

Interior Design
Greg Simsic
Katy Bodenmiller

Cover Design
Greg Simsic
Anne Jones

Compositor
Greg Simsic

Production
Heather Miller

www.photoshop.imageready

International Standard Book Number: 0-7897-2551-7

Library of Congress Catalog Card Number: 2001087296

Printed in the United States of America

First Printing: June 2001

04   03   02   01   4   3   2   1

Trademarks

All terms mentioned in this book that are known to be trademarks or service marks have been appropriately capitalized. Que cannot attest to the accuracy of this information. Use of a term in this book should not be regarded as affecting the validity of any trademark or service mark.

Warning and Disclaimer

Every effort has been made to make this book as complete and as accurate as possible, but no warranty or fitness is implied. The information provided is on an "as is" basis. The author and the publisher shall have neither liability nor responsibility to any person or entity with respect to any loss or damages arising from the information contained in this book.

Thanks

Thanks to everyone at Que books for your help in putting this project together—most especially for the deadline extensions and exploding Christmas goodies. I extend those thanks to everyone appearing in the credits, where I once was listed.

Thanks, Beth (again), for the opportunity to write this book and for trusting my judgment.

Thank you, Caroline, for improving this book through your valuable input as technical editor.

Thanks, Katy, for getting me through the book's design.

Thanks, Mom, for the use of some images, and, you know, raising me.

Finally, I thank a small group of friends who called to make sure that I was still alive.

Table of Contents at a Glance

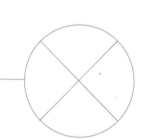

Table of Contents

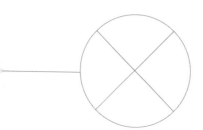

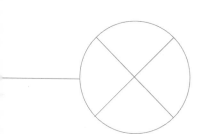

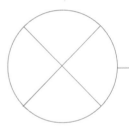

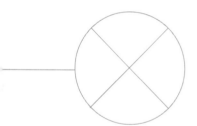

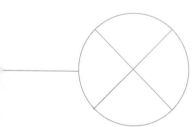

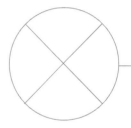

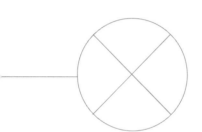

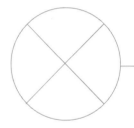

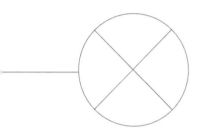

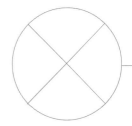

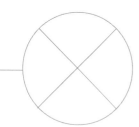

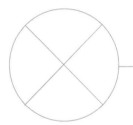

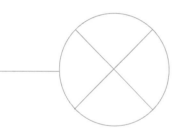

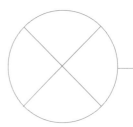

Introduction

Now that you're inside the covers of the book, let's get started. What you've got in your hands is a nuts-and-bolts guide to using Photoshop and its companion application ImageReady for creating and preparing Web graphics. It's no-nonsense. It's visual. It's blue.

This application duo, simply put, is the best package there is for creating and preparing graphics for the Web. It combines the power of Photoshop's image-editing tools with ImageReady's powerful Web graphics tools. The chapters break down the issues surrounding Web graphics and, through many step-by-step examples, show you how to to conquer them with these applications.

The book is intended to work both as a tutorial for those who are introducing themselves to the topics, and as a reference for those who just need a place to look up specific tasks. Photoshop users seeking an introduction to using it for Web work, personal Web page enthusiasts looking to improve their sites, professionals shifting from print to Web work, or just those seeking a reference for Web graphics production will benefit from this book.

Thanks for picking it up, and I hope you find it useful.

Hey! Get the Files from the Web Site

Step-by-step examples fill this book. In many cases, you can follow the steps either with a new image window open in Photoshop or by using a miscellaneous image appropriate to the exercise. However, some of the time, it will be helpful to work on the same file used in the example. These files are available from the book's companion Web site, at the following URL:

www.quepublishing.com

Follow the link to this book. Then, simply download the files and open them in Photoshop or ImageReady. They are copyright free and yours to keep.

Also, on the Web site are the links listed in Appendix A, "Web Resources" (page 360). From the site, you can jump directly to these links. Use them as a base from which to explore the many Web-based resources and to continue your Photoshop education.

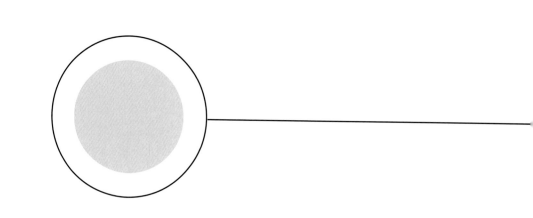

Part I

Jumping In

1

About Photoshop 6 and ImageReady 3

Welcome! Here you are at ground zero—the takeoff point for this book. This chapter introduces Photoshop and ImageReady as tools for Web design and fills you in on what they can do for you and what they are best used for. It covers the features new to these versions of the applications, and offers advice on working your way through this book.

Why Use Photoshop for Web Graphics?

You could break down the design/build process of a Web page into three phases: creating graphics, preparing them for the Web, and assembling the final HTML document in an editor. The thing to realize is that Photoshop and ImageReady play a role in all these phases. You will use them to create initial graphics, lay out a design, and even write HTML. The Photoshop/ImageReady combination might become the heart of your Web design operation. When a Web design is your final goal, they are best used in tandem, jumping back and forth as necessary.

This book is going to tell you what you can do with Photoshop and ImageReady. It will show you how to do these things and illustrate concepts with examples. But what it won't do is tell you what to do.

Photoshop, along with its Web partner ImageReady, is simply the most powerful graphics production program available, and the reasons to use it fill this book. With each new version, it becomes even more indispensable. It now can handle everything from the creation of graphics from scratch right through to dividing a design into discrete images and putting them back together again in an HTML document that it generates itself.

The New and Improved ImageReady/Photoshop Combo

Creating an entire Web page in Photoshop and ImageReady is now not only possible but easy and intuitive. And you won't sacrifice a thing—it can include sophisticated content and effects. ImageReady 2 broke ground with its integration with Photoshop, but with Photoshop 6 and ImageReady 3 these applications' production of Web graphics has reached a polished stage. It will surely bring sophisticated Web graphics production to a wider audience.

From initial design to a usable HTML document, Photoshop and ImageReady are involved in the entire process.

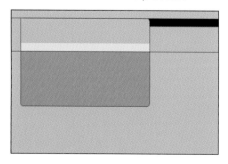

Exactly What Do These Applications Do?

Photoshop has many applications, but this book is limited to discussing its use in aiding the creation and preparation of graphic images for the Web. A quick scan of the table of contents gives you a good idea of what this dynamic duo does for you. This book is divided into five parts:

Jumping In: The section you're in now introduces you to Photoshop 6 and ImageReady 3, and covers their basic features.

Web Essentials: This section covers the issues which all graphics displayed in browsers must deal with. Knowing these chapters is essential.

Web Graphics: This section deals with creating basic graphics for Web sites: background images, type, buttons, and more.

Web Elements: This section details the creation of graphics specific to the Web: rollovers, image maps, animations, transparent images, and slices. This is where all the fun is.

The Bigger Picture: This section pulls away from creating specific graphic elements and deals with broader issues: using styles and effects, automating tasks, and, as a culmination, creating an entire Web page.

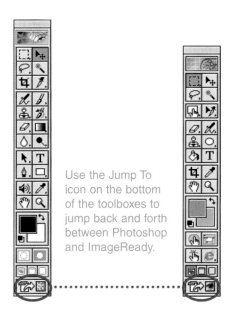

Use the Jump To icon on the bottom of the toolboxes to jump back and forth between Photoshop and ImageReady.

Together Photoshop and ImageReady can manipulate images; create graphics from scratch; adjust any image with powerful editing tools; save files in any common file format; produce HTML documents; create and coordinate the production of special Web elements such as rollovers, background tiles, image maps, slices, and animations; deal with Web browser color issues; and compress files into Web-compatible formats. This book concentrates on ImageReady operations because it is the application with the best tools for Web work.

What They Don't Do and What's Not in This Book

This book does not teach HTML, nor does it teach Dreamweaver or GoLive. This book does show you how to create and prepare graphics for use by those applications. ImageReady and Photoshop produce HTML files; however, in most situations this code will be a useful starting point, not the final document. Just as ImageReady and Photoshop work in tandem, so can these applications work in tandem with an HTML editing application.

You cannot expect these applications to be the final step in creating Web pages, despite their capability to write HTML documents. They are solidly in the middle of the process, after the concept creation and initial design stage and before the pulling together of all the elements and assets into a fully operational Web site.

Photoshop Versus ImageReady

At first it might seem strange that these applications are separate because so many functions overlap. But after you discover how extensive each of their functions is, you come to understand that if all these functions were combined into one application, it would be quite unwieldy. Photoshop menus are getting longer and longer as it is. Some differences between these two applications are major—Photoshop has no capability to create rollover effects, image maps, or animations. And, although ImageReady includes many of Photoshop's same functions, they are often less fully featured. In a few cases, such as creating repeating tiles, ImageReady has the better overall tools.

Other differences are minor. The same tool might work differently in one application than it does in the other. Right up there with the mismatched number of hot dogs in a package to the number of hot dog buns in a package is why you can choose Pattern from the Paintbucket options in Photoshop but not in ImageReady. In that case, the advantage goes to Photoshop, but that is not always so. The Offset filter, key to making seamless tiles, in Photoshop shows you a preview of its effects before you choose whether to accept them. ImageReady does not. In ImageReady, you can choose to offset the selection or image by a percentage or by pixels, but you don't get the preview. Throughout the applications, minor differences such as these are found.

Photoshop Is Better at	ImageReady Is Better at	Use Either for
General image manipulation and graphics creation	Web-specific tasks such as creating rollovers, defining image maps, creating animations, and creating background tiles	Saving optimized files in Web-ready formats
	Detailed Web color work and more convenient optimizing tools	Automating tasks
	Slicing images	

What If I Have an Older Version of Photoshop?

If you are using Photoshop 5.5 and ImageReady 2.0, almost everything that is demonstrated in this book is achievable in those versions of the software. However, you will have to supplement the instructions here with your own knowledge or some other source in order to discover the location and workings of various features. These applications have not changed significantly in terms of the types of things they can accomplish, but they have changed significantly, and for the better, in terms of how these things are accomplished. To make the instruction in this book as easy as possible to follow, the details of using the applications have been followed closely. If you use Photoshop and ImageReady often then springing the $199 for the upgrade is well worth it. I'm not getting paid to state that (although I've got my ears open); I'm just an enthusiast.

New to Photoshop 6 and ImageReady 3

Photoshop 6 and ImageReady 3 have not significantly increased their capabilities from their previous versions, but they have made performing the same tasks significantly easier. ImageReady has graduated to become a full-fledged application that alone is worth the price of Photoshop. If you judge an application by how well it facilitates its results, ImageReady scores high. Preparing Web graphics for the Web is now a relatively painless and streamlined process aided by an interface that eases you through the tasks. Here's a rundown of what's new in both Photoshop and ImageReady that pertains to Web graphics.

Interface

The Options Bar: The Options bar is covered in Chapter 3, "Photoshop and ImageReady Basics," (page 30). This new floating palette contains parameters and other features associated with the currently selected tool. This feature greatly improves the way you use these applications and will increase your efficiency. It makes tool settings a lot easier to find.

The Options bar while the Magic Wand tool is selected

Type Features

Photoshop Type Tool: Photoshop's Type tool now works similarly to ImageReady's Type tool—it is used right on top of the image for direct editing. Gone is the old Type dialog box. All typing, attribute selection, and editing is done in the main image window via the Type tool, its Options bar settings, and the new Character and Paragraph palettes. Use it and love it.

Paragraph Options: More is new than just the Photoshop Type tool's freedom from the dialog box. The Paragraph Type tool allows you to define a box within which the type is contained. In addition, you can set paragraph formatting such as indents and hyphenation options. All in all, Photoshop's type capabilities have taken a significant leap forward, which will enable you to use it for a greater variety of type operations.

Type Warping: Accessed via the Type tool Options bar, this feature lets you warp Type layers in various ways while the text remains editable. It works similarly to layer effects.

Layer Operations

Layer Sets: The Layers palette now has folders, called *sets*. Layers can be dragged into sets just like files in folders. Those 99 layered files can now be organized.

Layer Palette Modifications: Layers can now be color-coded. You can also lock several aspects of a layer independently: its position, its transparency, its pixel content, or all of the above.

Fill and Gradient Map Layers: Two new kinds of layers (Photoshop only), accessible from the Layer Effects menu, add new ways to mix and adjust layers. A *fill* layer can contain a solid color, a pattern, or a gradient. *Gradient Map layers* map a color gradation to match the values in the layers below it.

Layer and Rollover Styles: There is a new Style palette where Styles, which are sets of layer effects, can be saved for future use and applied with a single click. ImageReady supports rollover Styles that can contain layer attribute and rollover state information.

Extras

Vector-Based Graphics: There are new vector-based layers. Although the real power of these layers pertains to files being prepared for print, these tools can be useful in the creation of images. With the new Shape tool, for example, you can create lines, polygons, and custom shapes that can later, if desired, be turned into normal layers.

Annotations: This is Photoshop's (it is not available in ImageReady) built-in "stickies" feature. With it, you can place color-coded notes on top of an image. There is also an audio version to record and play back spoken comments. This is great when you're passing files around.

Photoshop Droplets: Photoshop actions now can be turned into *droplets*—small applications that apply an action to any file that is dragged on top of it. This feature was already available in ImageReady.

Web Features

Tool-Based Image Maps: In ImageReady, you now have the ability to create image maps of virtually any shape by using the Circle, Rectangle, and Polygon image map tools. Layer-based image maps are also still featured.

Photoshop Slicing: Photoshop now carries its own Slice and Slice Select tools. Now, images can be sliced right in Photoshop. Although slicing options are more fully featured in ImageReady, Photoshop does support slicing and, in the Save for Web dialog box, assigning different optimize settings to different slices.

Layer-Based Slices: Additionally, you now can create layer-based slices. Like layer-based image maps, these slices change dynamically as the content of a layer is altered.

Rollover Previews: Rollover effects now can be previewed right within ImageReady's main image window.

Weighted Optimization: This feature enables you to use an alpha channel to selectively adjust the compression of a file. It is available for adjusting GIF dithering, the lossy GIF setting, and JPEG compression.

Cascading Style Sheets: You now can choose to save Cascading Style Sheets within the HTML documents that both Photoshop and ImageReady produce.

Learning Photoshop and ImageReady

The chapters of this book are intended for use both as lessons and as references. Working through them from beginning to end will give you a well-rounded understanding of the topic at hand. But, step-by-step tasks as well as other useful information are pulled out from the text so that they can be accessed independently and quickly.

Working through the entirety of the chapters and the examples contained therein will give you a command of ImageReady that will enable you to work quickly through Web graphics preparation. Every possibility of every situation cannot be contained here, but hopefully through the course of all the chapters, a well-rounded knowledge of these applications can be achieved.

This book contains chapters that teach tasks and chapters that discuss subjects. You might need this book for both. Sometimes it will just be a reference—that's what the step-by-step instructions are for. However, reading a chapter in full will give you a more well-rounded understanding of a subject. Some chapters, such as the Web Color chapter, spend more time discussing the topic, because the most important skill in this case is being aware of the issues. Equipped with that knowledge, you'll be able to create graphic elements with the right goals in mind. In order to eliminate endless repetition of the same material, the book includes a certain of amount of cross-referencing. If you're including an animation as a rollover state, this is discussed in the Animations chapter, but you might need to refer to the Rollovers chapter in order to fully understand how to make this effect work.

SIDEBARS

These boxes appear in the margins and enhance the discussion of an issue by providing additional information, and defining terms.

Give Me More

These floating circles highlight important information or provide additional tips about the subject at hand.

step-by-step exercises

Figures, sometimes supplemented with callouts, provide visual aids.

title.psd @ 100% (photoshop.,RGB)

www.
photoshop.
imageready

100%

1. Numbered instructions appear here.

   They often are followed by additional information.

Interacting with the Web Site

Every chapter of this book contains examples that put to practical use the topics discussed. Reading these exercises without working through them will give you an idea of the features of these applications, as well as, introduce you to what it takes to get things done. However, working through them as you read will be of greater benefit, because nothing beats practice. Some of the exercises contained in this book use files that have been prepared ahead of time. This allowed me to get to the subject at hand without unnecessary setup. If you have these files at hand then working along with the example will be easier. These files are all available from the companion Web site for this book. To get these files, use a Web browser to go to www.quepublishing.com and follow the link for this book.

To access files used in this book, go to www.quepublishing.com and follow the link to this book.

Purge

Color Setti
Preset Mar
Preference

2

Helpers
Jump T
Fire
Jump To H
Dres
Previe

Cursors

Preparing Photoshop and ImageReady for Web Work

In this chapter, you learn how to configure Photoshop and ImageReady for Web graphics production. Getting things set up ahead of time will save plenty of time and headaches down the road. Many common Photoshop and ImageReady commands work according to preferences, and this is the place to get them set up correctly.

Why Bother with This Chapter?

Photoshop, being the versatile monster that it is, is used by many industries for many kinds of tasks. By paying attention to the settings discussed in this chapter, you can bring it into line with your specific needs. For the purposes of this book, that means creating a more Web-friendly working environment. Proper setup will make your Web work quicker and smoother. For example, if you set the Color palette to display only Web-safe colors, you'll always choose a Web-safe color in the heat of battle.

Macintosh Photoshop General Preferences

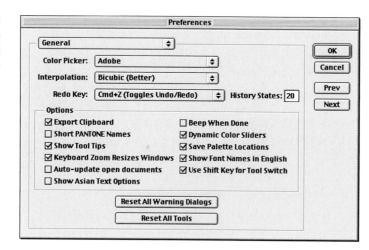

Note the similarities and differences. Set up these two applications to work as similarly as possible.

Macintosh ImageReady General Preferences

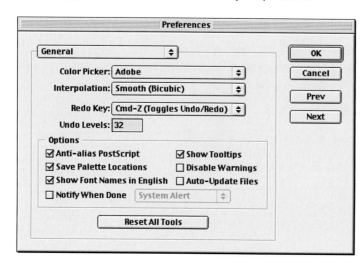

Photoshop and ImageReady Synchronicity

Of course, Photoshop and ImageReady are compatible and work well together, but you can ensure that they work even better together if you take the time to be sure to set them up as similarly as possible.

Although these two applications have many things in common, mysteriously some of those things don't work the same way. You can't change that, but for the settings you can control I suggest making sure they are the same in both applications, because you'll be jumping back and forth between the applications often. Of course, if Web work is not your only Photoshop activity, you'll want to keep that in mind before going wild with all the preferences for Web work. Note that not all preferences are shared by both Mac and Windows systems.

At the Bottom of the Edit Menu Lurks . . .

. . . the key setup helpers: Color Settings, Preset Manager, and Preferences. Within these three options you will find a number of ways to add convenience to your Web image and page production. Let's work from the bottom up.

Preferences

Preferences are application-specific settings (not file-specific settings) that are retained and used with all files until you change them. Photoshop and ImageReady both have Preference settings that work independently of each other. Setting the Undo key preference in Photoshop, for example, will not set the Undo key preference in ImageReady. Here's a rundown of important preferences to take care of.

Photoshop and ImageReady Preferences: General

Redo Key: (Edit>Preferences>General)
This setting is changeable in both Photoshop and ImageReady. Whatever you choose, make sure it is the same in both applications. I suggest selecting one of the top two options because (Command-Y) [Ctrl-Y] is assigned to other commands in both Photoshop and ImageReady. This chart breaks down how the Redo Key choice affects Undo/Redo operations. (The History palette is discussed further on page 38.)

	Redo Key Choice		
	Command-Shift-Z	*Command-Z*	*Command-Y*
Undo/Redo Toggle Key	Command-Option-Z	Command-Z	Command-Option-Z
Step Forward (through History states)	Command-Shift-Z	Command-Shift-Z	Command-Y
Step Backward (through History states)	Command-Z	Command-Option-Z	Command-Z

Windows users substitute Ctrl for Command and Alt for Option

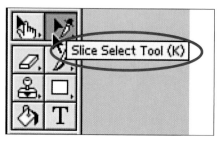

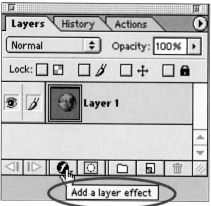

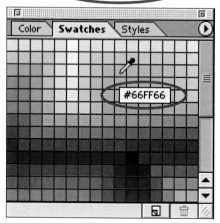

Tool Tips give useful information about Tools, Keyboard Shortcuts, palette icons and options, and more.

Show Tool Tips: (Edit>Preferences>General)

I recommend always keeping this turned on. This option turns on those little yellow boxes that appear on the screen when you hover the pointer over a tool or icon. On the tool box they tell you the name of the tool and its shortcut key. These labels are a great way to learn the tools. They also provide other useful information. They provide short explanatory notes about palette options in the Optimize palette, for example. In Photoshop, on the Swatches palette, they display the hex value number of color swatches (or whatever name they've been given). Use them as a learning aid. If they won't show up, move the pointer off the tool and then back on top of it.

Use Shift Key for Tool Switch: (Edit>Preferences>General)

Keep this setting on. Many tools in the toolbox are arranged in groups, and only one tool from each group is displayed at any one time. Each group has a keyboard shortcut assigned to it. This key selects the currently displayed tool from the group. By holding Shift as you press the shortcut key, you can access the other tools in that group. It's great, for example, for running through the Marquee tools and finding the Single Column Marquee Tool.

Interpolation: (Edit>Preferences>General)

When you resize elements in Photoshop and ImageReady, the pixel data that the image is made from must be reinterpreted to maintain, as best it can, all the other characteristics of the element. This setting tells Photoshop or ImageReady which method to use for this and similar types of transformations. Photoshop must do calculations to decide which pixels will end up in the newly resized image—not only which stay and go but what colors they will be. This is the way Photoshop fudges things at the pixel level to make it look the best at the "what-you're-seeing" level. For most purposes, it is best to leave this setting at its default: Bicubic.

The original image (left) was rotated while the interpolation method was set to Bicubic (center). You can see that a diagonal line that exists in the world of pixels cannot have the same crispness as a horizontal or vertical line. Pixels of various levels of opacity were added to make the edges look smoother at the macro level (right).

However, sometimes switching it to Nearest Neighbor could aid Web graphics production. You might guess that when Bicubic interpolation is used, new colors are added to the image as Photoshop picks a new color to place between two original colors. This is sometimes undesirable when you're trying to limit yourself to the colors in your GIF Color Table. It could ruin the palette. But if you choose Nearest Neighbor for the Interpolation method before resizing then Photoshop will not create new colors, but only choose a pixel's color from a pixel near it. You effectively limit Photoshop's color choices to colors that are already in the image. Take a look at these images:

The original image.
(shown at 700%)

Resized to 200%
using Bicubic
interpolation.
(shown at 350%)

Resized to 200%
using Nearest
Neighbor
interpolation.
(shown at 350%)

The resized image that used Nearest Neighbor interpolation (right) is nearly identical to the original. Notice the softening result in the middle image that is the result of adding new in-between colors.

Photoshop Preferences: Saving Files

Previews: (Edit>Preferences>Saving Files)
Files saved by Photoshop and ImageReady can have thumbnail previews added to the file. These smaller versions can be displayed from outside these applications, in file folders, as icons attached to the filenames. They are also displayed in the Open dialog box, and can be invaluable when skipping through an Open dialog box looking for something in a mess of vaguely named image files. (Then again, properly naming them might work as well.) Here's the downside—they increase the size of the file. It is generally advisable, for those working with Web images, to choose Never Save unless you know you'll need them. The file savings here, which is substantial, does not affect download time because the preview is eventually stripped from the file anyway, but it will save time as you work with these files in the meantime and helps you keep track of their true sizes from outside Photoshop and ImageReady. Or, keep them on while in the initial creative process and then turn them off as you switch into a production phase.

**Memory
Hogs**

*Previews can add
25%-30% to the
size of a file.*

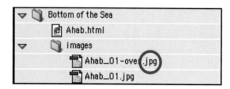

The file extension is added to the end of the filename.

WHAT IS AN OTHER CURSOR?

Here is a breakdown of how cursors are divided into two groups.

Painting	Other
Airbrush	Color Sampler
Blur	Crop
Burn	Eyedropper
Dodge	Gradient
Eraser	Lasso Tools
Paintbrush	Line
Pencil	Magic Wand
Rubber Stamp	Marquee Tools
Sharpen	Measure
Smudge	Paintbucket
Sponge	Pen Tools
	Slice

File Extension: (Edit>Preferences>Saving Files)
Turning on this option forces Photoshop to always add a three-character file extension to the end of every filename. The extensions are needed by non-Mac systems, and you might as well have the application. Make sure you don't forget to add them later because they are necessary for files to be used on Web pages. Also turn on the Use Lower Case option—for best compatibility with Unix systems.

File Compatibility: (Edit>Preferences>Saving Files)
Turn off this option unless your files will be used with a pre-Layers–capable version of Photoshop—versions 2.5 and earlier.

Photoshop and ImageReady Preferences: Display & Cursors

Pixel Doubling: (Edit>Preferences>Displays & Cursors)
Turning on this option causes Photoshop to use a lower-quality preview when performing some tool and transformation operations. This has no effect on the actual pixels—just the temporary preview. I turn on this option because it speeds up these operations. It is not available in ImageReady.

The following settings determine which icon is displayed for various tools. Refer to the table at left to see how the tools are divided into two categories. Changing the icon is potentially confusing because you lose a visual clue that reminds you which tool you're using, but you can always refer to the Tool options bar for that information.

Painting Cursors: (Edit>Preferences>Displays & Cursors)
I recommend using Brush Size. This option replaces the tool icon with an icon that is the exact shape of the current brush. It is necessary for any kind of precision brush work.

Other Cursors: (Edit>Preferences>Displays & Cursors)
I recommend Precise. This is particularly important for tools such as the Eyedropper. The tool icon is replaced by crosshairs that let you know precisely what you're aiming at. This can save you time and eye-strain because you might not have to zoom in as far to be as precise.

Photoshop Preferences: Units & Rulers

Rulers and Type: (Edit>Preferences>Units & Rulers)
The pixel is the base unit of both Photoshop and ImageReady graphics, and monitor display. Thus, it is important for Web graphics. You should measure everything in pixels when working on files for the Web. Setting both of these options to pixels enables you to make precision judgments while working. To change the units without opening the Preferences dialog box Control-click (Mac) or right-click (Windows) on the Horizontal ruler to access a menu of options. *ImageReady uses pixels for all measurements.*

The Almighty Pixel—by which all things Web are measured

**Break Rules;
Use Rulers**

Keep Rulers on while working so you can keep track of EXACTLY how large your graphics are (Cmd-R)[Ctrl-R].

Photoshop Preferences: Guides & Grid

Grid: (Edit>Preferences>Guides & Grid)
If you use Grids for anything, you will certainly want them spaced by pixel dimensions. As a default, I set the Gridline Every to 100 pixels and the Subdivisions to 2. This way, if I want a quick size reference, I can just use the shortcut key (Command-Option-') [Control-Alt-'] to turn on the Grid and up pops a line spaced every 50 pixels. Because you also can snap to Grid lines, you might have other uses for this feature—such as positioning evenly spaced elements.

The grid provides some orientation when laying out a design.

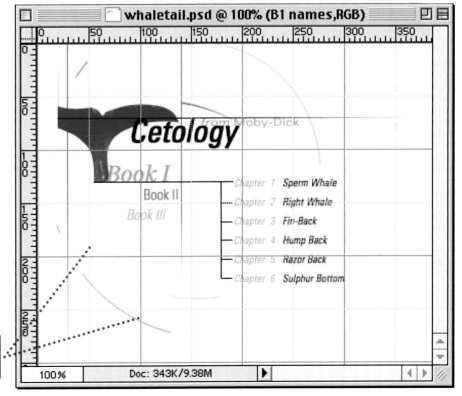

How Slices preview with the default settings.

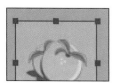

How Image Maps preview with the default settings.

ImageReady Preferences: Slices

These settings affect the appearance of slice guides. Increasing the size of the icon can make the slice numbers easier to read. However, these icons also can get in the way of viewing the image, particularly with smaller slices. Turn off the numbers if necessary. Changing their color can also make them stand out against a background and keep you from confusing them with other elements, such as guides. In Photoshop, these options are also available on the Slice tool options bar.

ImageReady Preferences: Image Maps

Again, these settings affect only the display of image maps. Unless you're having difficulty with seeing them, there is no reason to change them.

ImageReady Preferences: Optimization

Here you can choose the Optimize settings ImageReady automatically uses when you switch to the Optimize, 2-Up, or 4-Up views. If you work with the same kind of images all the time then this ability could come in handy for some production operations. If you commonly work with nonphotographic images that are saved as GIFs, you might change these settings to always show three custom GIF settings that you have determined work the best.

That's it for the preferences. You might have noticed that some of them have not been covered here. That is becuase they do not pertain to Web work. Next, let's turn to Photoshop and address the other two items at the bottom of the Edit menu.

Help ?

No man is an island. Take all the help you can get. Use the Help menu for quick information and a second opinion on difficult issues.

Preset Manager

With the Preset Manager you can set up and save Sets of libraries that include Brushes, Swatches, Gradients, Styles, Patterns, Contours, and Custom Shapes. For an ongoing project that you work on intermittently you could create a set that included all the common libraries necessary to that project. Another set of favorite libraries might be saved for general use.

Color Settings

The much-agonized topic of color rears its ugly head. Fortunately, for Web work easy guidelines exist that generally produce good results.

Do colors really need managers? Color management is an attempt to control color so that it is consistent across media and platforms. The promise of color management is that you can send an image through Hell and back—it will still look the same. No matter whether a particular image file is on a monitor, printed by an inkjet, or on a Mac or PC, it will always look the same. This work is acheived by embedding color profiles in the image files. The color profile contains information that each platform can either use or ignore.

Although color profiles can improve consistency while working on an image, they are not used by browsers. And this information will be stripped anyway on its way from upload to download, so why keep it to begin with? For Web work, you don't want this extra information increasing the size of your image files. Let's look at the Color Settings dialog box.

> ### Is This Color Info Too Gray?
>
> *Jump to Chapter 5, "Web Color" (page 72), to learn more about color terms and issues specific to Web graphics.*

The Color Settings Dialog Box

This is a very intimidating dialog box indeed (shown on the next page). There's a lot here. These settings control the way that Photoshop (this is not an ImageReady feature) handles color, and how or whether extra color information—the profiles described above—is embedded in your files.

At the top of this dialog box are a number of Presets that Adobe has supplied and named according to use categories. You'll notice one named Web Graphics Defaults. This setting and Emulate Photoshop 4 are the best presets for Web work. As you switch between them, you see that the only differences are in the Gray Gamma and the RGB (color space) settings. The Web Graphics Default selects RGB and Gray (or Gamma) settings that are the most common to the most people using the Web. Emulate Photoshop 4 emulates the way that Photoshop handled color before the days of color profiles.

Mac users must be aware that the great majority of Web users are running Windows. If you set the Gamma to 2.2 (the Windows standard), you can see a better approximation of how most users will view your images. Otherwise, you can alter them manually.

> ### ADOBE ONLINE
>
> *Built in to the Help menu are the Adobe Online features. These features offer a direct link to Photoshop resources on Adobe's Web site. The first time you use it, it will configure itself based on your input. The offerings are along the lines of automatic downloading of software updates, information on plug-ins, additional help, and connections to some online service bureaus. If you are a power user, Adobe Online might keep you up to date with the latest Photoshop news. By the way, if you click the icon at the top of ImageReady or Photoshop's toolbox, it jumps to the Adobe Online interface.*

This color space reflects the color space that is common to a wide variety of displays.

The Gray setting affects the lightness and darkness of the middle values. The Windows standard is 2.2, and the Mac standard is 1.8. Choose the setting that reflects your target audience.

Turn off all Color Management Policies.

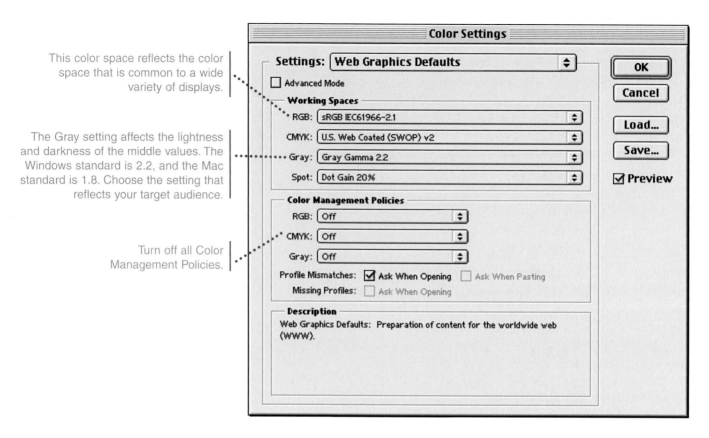

Turn off all the Color Management Policies options. These options add unnecessary data to files that is not relevant for Web work.

Calibrate Your Monitor

Color is all about perception. And everything affects your perception. So, the color you see on your monitor is affected even by things such as level of brightness and color of the light in your room. Calibrating your monitor is a way of adjusting it so that it displays colors within an acceptable approximation of other monitors.

On a Macintosh, open the Monitors control panel, click the Color icon; then choose your monitor from the list, or click Calibrate to adjust the monitor manually. Alternatively, open the Adobe Gamma control panel. On a Windows machine, use the Adobe Gamma utility found on your hard drive in the following folder: Program Files>Common Files>Adobe>Calibration.

Palettes

Info Palette

As you work on your images, do not neglect the Info palette as a source of information about selection sizes, cursor positions, and color values. Properly set up, it's very useful. To change the settings in Photoshop, choose Palette Options from the Info palette menu. (ImageReady's Info palette is not adjustable.) Set one of the Color Readouts to Web Color. I like to set the other to Opacity. As always with Web work, Pixels is the correct choice for Mouse Coordinates. Notice the Info box has another Color indicator named Index (Idx). This option displays information only when the Optimize file type is set to GIF or PNG-8 (ImageReady) or is in Indexed color mode (Photoshop). The index number is the place number of the current color in the Color Table. Color Tables are discussed in Chapter 5, "Web Color" (page 72).

Information. Cheap.

Check the Info Palette for size, color, and coordinate information as you work.

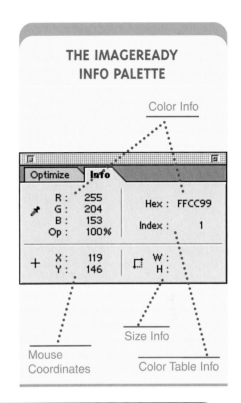

THE IMAGEREADY INFO PALETTE

Color Info

Mouse Coordinates

Size Info

Color Table Info

---

change the color of Photoshop's background

works in ImageReady, too

You can quickly change the color of Photoshop's background—the gray (by default) area that surrounds the image area when you pull the sides of the window away from the bounds of the image.

1. Set the foreground color to the new color.

2. Select the Paintbucket tool and hold the Shift key while clicking the background area.

Use this feature to surround a graphic file with the color it will be surrounded by in the final design to get an idea of how it will look in context.

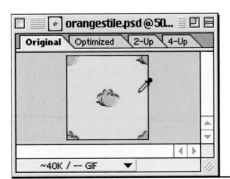

The background remains this color for all subsequent images during this and any future sessions until it is changed.

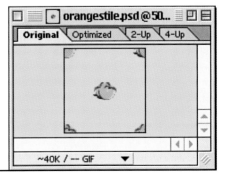

Color Palette

To limit color choices in the Color Palette to Web-safe colors only, choose one or both of the Web Color Sliders and Make Ramp Web Safe options from the palette menu. Keep in mind that even though you might always choose Web-safe colors, it doesn't mean that all colors in your image are Web safe. For example, if you chose a Web-safe color for some added type that is antialiased (blurred at the edges) then there certainly are non–Web-safe colors present in the image. These colors are added to maintain the smooth edges of the type. Many operations in Photoshop and ImageReady cause new in-between colors to be added to images. For more on this, see the Interpolation section earlier in this chapter.

Current Colors Ramp

Use the Current Colors Ramp to quickly find varying values of the current color.

The ImageReady Color palette

Click this icon that appears when a non–Web-safe color is selected to snap the color to the nearest Web-safe color.

Swatches Palette

The Swatches palette can hold sets of colors. To load a set of swatches, choose Load, Replace, or Append Swatches from palette menu (accessible by clicking the arrow in the upper right). Also, in the palette menu, Photoshop and ImageReady have five preset Web-safe swatch set choices: Visibone, Visibone2, Web Hues, Web Safe Colors, and Web Spectrum. You can also rearrange, rename, and save your own.

The ImageReady Swatches palette

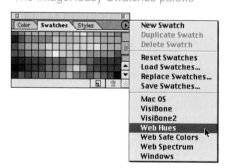

In Photoshop the Swatches palette can be reshaped to show a swatch library in various arrangements. This image shows the Web Hues library.

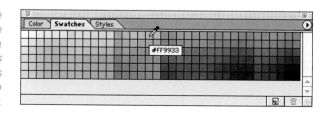

Palette Icon Sizes

The Layers, Animation, and Rollovers (in ImageReady only) palettes all display thumbnail previews. The default size (selected in this figure) is probably best for most situations, but you always have the option of increasing the icon size. That big preview can come in handy, especially if you're dealing with someone else's Photoshop file whose layers weren't labeled so well. To change the icon size, choose Palette Options from any of the palette menus.

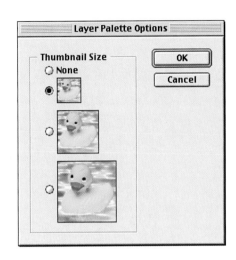

Get Your Ducks in a Row—Reset Palettes

If you can't find a palette or they've just gotten out of hand and you find yourself constantly tapping the edges of barely visible palettes to bring them forward, here's a way to get them back in line.

Go from
this
to
this.

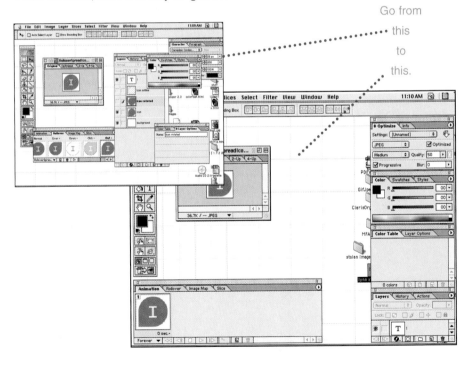

reset palettes

Photoshop:

Choose Window>Reset Palette Locations.

ImageReady:

Choose Window>Arrange> Reset Palettes.

More Setup Info

ON THE TOOLBOX

The Jump To ImageReady button in Photoshop.

The Jump To Photoshop button in ImageReady.

You can jump to other graphics programs, HTML editors, and Web browsers by placing aliases (Mac) or shortcuts (Windows) in the appropriate folders shown here.

Jumping to Other Applications

From ImageReady, there are three types of applications that you can jump to: another graphics application, such as Photoshop; a Web browser such as Internet Explorer; or, an HTML editor such as Macromedia's Dreamweaver. From Photoshop, you can jump to other graphics applications and Web browsers, but not HTML editors.

You'll always be able to get back and forth between Photoshop and ImageReady easily because of the Jump To buttons on the bottom of the toolboxes. You can't change where that button jumps to, but you can add other graphics programs to the Jump To menu found near the bottom of both applications' File menus. Here's how you do that: Make an alias (if you're on a Mac) or a shortcut (if you're using Windows) of the graphics application and drag it into the Jump To Graphics Editor folder inside the Helpers folder in the Photoshop folder (Photoshop>Helpers>Jump To Graphics Editor).

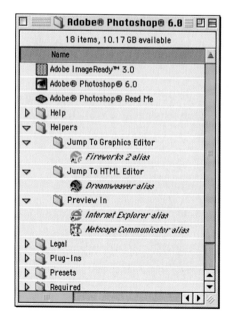

Also in the Helpers folder is a folder named Jump To HTML Editor for adding HTML editors to ImageReady's Jump To menu. There is also a Preview In folder for adding browsers to ImageReady's Preview in Browser list accessible on the toolbox. In Photoshop, these browsers are accessible from the Save for Web dialog box. If you're reading this book then you're probably using some kind of HTML editor. Photoshop does not set these up automatically like it does for the browsers. I recommend adding your normal HTML editor to this folder. It will be helpful to access ImageReady's HTML code easily while working in ImageReady.

Setting the Preview Browsers

Browsers also are easily accessed in ImageReady via the Preview in Browser button on the toolbox. Use this to preview images and designs. Whichever browser was last used for previewing becomes the default browser. Click and hold the button to access a menu of all available browsers. You can add more browsers to this list by adding shortcuts or aliases to the folder shown on the previous page.

Setting ImageReady As the Default Image Editor

Outside of ImageReady you might consider setting up your Web page authoring application to automatically use ImageReady as the default image editor. This aids the process of jumping back and forth between these applications as you build and edit pages. In Dreamweaver, do this by changing the External Editors (in the Preferences) for GIF, JPEG, and PNG files to ImageReady. Afterward, simply hold down the Command (Mac) or Ctrl (Windows) key while double-clicking the image to jump to ImageReady. In GoLive, ImageReady is already the default editor.

Reset Tool Defaults

To reset a tool to its default settings, click the tool icon on the Tool Options bar.

Making the Eyedropper Behave

It might seem silly to worry about the settings for this one tool before getting into some work on an image. However, knowing how the Eyedropper samples colors is important. Have you ever zoomed in really close to grab a color from a specific pixel and no matter how many times or how hard you clicked, the foreground color would not change to the color you were looking at? This was because the Eyedropper setting was not set to Point Sample. If it is set to 3x3 or 5x5 (the only other options), it averages the colors from a small section of pixels around the tool rather than selecting the exact color of the pixel that the Eyedropper is on top of. For general editing work in unmagnified views, the 3x3 or 5x5 samples work best because the sample averaging is probably best at picking up the color you're seeing. But for precision color work, such as the kind you will need to perform on Web graphics, set the Sample Size to Point Sample. Set this tool in the Options bar when the Eyedropper is selected.

Eyedropper results depend on its Sample setting:

Point Sample

3x3 Sample

5x5 Sample

Greg

3

Photoshop and ImageReady Basics

This chapter is intended to dust off some of your basic Photoshop skills with an emphasis on features that are important for working with Web images. It concentrates on features that will help you get around Photoshop and ImageReady with ease. Hopefully, you will pick up some tips to make you a more efficient user. Some cool new features of Photoshop 6 and ImageReady 3 also are mentioned. This is a useful, but by no means complete, guide to Photoshop.

Opening a New File

When you open a new file, some basic settings lay the foundation for the image. They are all changeable as you work on the image, but you might as well set them when you open the new file. The most important thing for Web graphics is that pixels be used as the image size unit. In ImageReady you have no other choices, but in Photoshop you have several. The mode should be RGB. Again, in ImageReady it is the only option (and for that reason, it is not actually displayed in the New dialog box).

The New dialog box

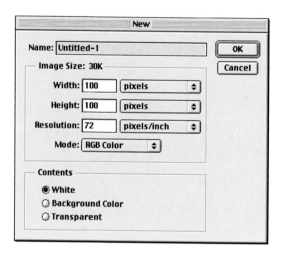

Opening an Old File

Photoshop is very versatile and can open virtually any image format. ImageReady, on the other hand, is limited to opening RGB images. When you attempt to open a non-RGB image in ImageReady, one of the following messages might appear. Open the image in Photoshop first, and choose Image>Mode>RGB to convert it. After resaving it, you can open it in ImageReady .

Files opened in ImageReady must be in RGB mode.

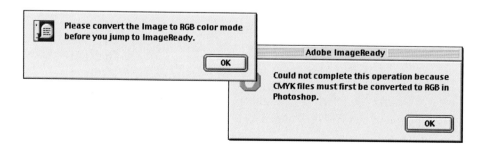

Image Size and Canvas Size

Of course, a file's image size can be changed at any time. There are actually two variables that you can change. Changing the image size resizes the current image, enlarging it or reducing it according to the size you choose. In these cases, calculations are performed to determine the new pixel content because pixels must be added or subtracted. The other size-changing operation is the canvas size. The *canvas* is the area in which the image sits. Changing the canvas size does not alter the image; it only alters the bounds of the image. If you enlarge the canvas area then space is added around the perimeter of the image. If you reduce the canvas size, the image can be cropped and you will be asked to confirm the operation.

Remember that whenever you resize an image, Photoshop and ImageReady must perform calculations to determine the new pixel content. If you enlarge an image to include twice as many pixels, Photoshop must perform calculations to determine the colors of the new pixels. When it does this, it uses an interpolation method. Photoshop has three interpolation methods, and ImageReady has two. See pages 18-19 of Chapter 2, "Preparing Photoshop and ImageReady for Web Work," for more about how interpolation affects the pixel content of a resized image.

> **IMAGE SIZE COMMANDS**
>
> *To resize an image:*
>   *Choose Image>Image Size.*
>
> *To resize the canvas:*
>   *Choose Image>Canvas Size.*
>
> *To reveal hidden image areas:*
>   *Choose Image>Reveal All.*
>
> *To trim unwanted areas:*
>   *Choose Image>Trim.*
>
> *To crop an image:*
>   *Make a rectangular selection and choose Image>Crop or draw a rectangle with the Crop tool (in the toolbox) and press Return.*

Automatic Canvas Resizing: Reveal All and Trim

Two commands feature automatic resizing of the canvas area: Trim and Reveal All. It is possible in Photoshop and ImageReady to paste an image that does not fit within the bounds of the canvas. When this happens, the parts of the image not seen are not deleted. They remain, and if you move the layer, you can see the rest of its contents. The Reveal All command (Photoshop only) enlarges the canvas size of a file so that all of these hidden image parts are seen.

The Trim command does the opposite. When the image is smaller than the canvas size, you can automatically crop the canvas to the size of the image. Be careful. This command also deletes all image areas of all layers not appearing within the bounds of the canvas.

Applying the Trim command to the image on the left has this result.

Viewing Environment

You can control a few of the most basic aspects of the applications' environments to streamline your working process.

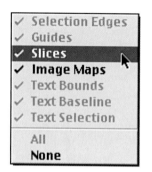

Extras can be turned on and off in the View>Show menu. This is the ImageReady menu; the Photoshop menu differs slightly.

Screen Mode: (Press F to cycle through the three modes)
On the bottom of the toolbox is a very useful viewing feature that is helpful in isolating an image that you are working on. It gets rid of the desktop and all other applications' windows, and centers the isolated image on a black screen. It's great for getting a quick look at the image without all the clutter. Also, press the Tab key to temporarily hide all palettes.

Show/Hide Extras: (Command-H) [Ctrl-H]
There are a number of elements that these applications display to help you work and make sense of the parts of an image that are not part of the actual image data. Most of these elements are guides of some sort. There are two steps to turning these features on and off. You must first select them from the View>Extras menu (or use a shortcut key). Afterward, all the elements checked in the Extras menu are turned on and off by using the Show/Hide Extras shortcut key listed above.

Rollover Preview Mode: (Press Y to toggle on/off)
In ImageReady, you can switch into a rollover preview mode that emulates the action of rollovers in a browser (ImageReady only).

Snap To: (Command-;) [Ctrl-;]
Snapping features help you quickly align elements. This is especially helpful when slicing images. Both guides and slices can be snapped to. If any tool gets close to a guide or slice when snapping is turned on, the tool jumps to that element. This also can hinder intricate work, so it's important to know how to turn off snapping.

Guides: (Command-') [Ctrl-']
To create a new guide, click one of the rulers and drag a guide into the image area. Drag them back to a ruler to get rid of them. To reposition them, use the Move tool. The keyboard shortcut is for ImageReady only.

Rulers: (Command-R) [Ctrl-R]
To turn Rulers on and off, press (Command-R) [Control-R]. The zero axes point can be changed by clicking and dragging it anywhere within the image. Double-click the origination point of the ruler to reset the axes to the upper-left corner of the image. The Info palette displays current ruler stats on tool and selection positions.

IMAGEREADY EXTRAS

On the ImageReady toolbox are buttons dedicated to controlling Slice and Image Map visibility. Click them to toggle these features on and off.

(A) ... *(Q)*

Or, use their shortcut keys indicated above.

Palettes

A lot of Photoshop work is done on floating palettes. Here are a few tips on working with them.

Opening Palettes

To open a palette, choose it from the Window menu. To compress the palette without removing it from the screen, double-click its title bar. For some palettes, doing this activates various palette display options.

Palette Menus

All palettes have a palette menu that has various features, some of which are not found elsewhere. To access palette menus, click on the right-pointing arrow in the upper-right corner of the palette. Many palettes have a command called Show Options. Choosing this reveals additional adjustable parameters on the palette. Palettes with this menu command have an ◆ icon in their title. Clicking this icon toggles the Show Options command.

Double-click the title bar to condense the palette to titles only.

Closes the palette

Cycles through Show/Hide Options variations

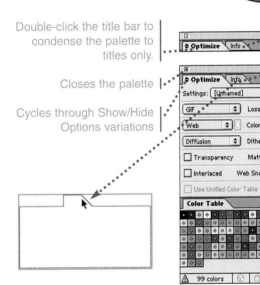

Palette Pier

Photoshop's Options bar has an area in which you can "dock" palettes. Drag palettes there that you use occasionally but don't need all the time.

Click the palette name to bring it forward.

Click and drag the title bar to separate this palette from the Info palette.

Click the arrow to open the palette menu.

The Color table palette has been attached to the bottom of the Optimize palette.

Rearranging Palettes

Palettes are arranged in groups by default. For example, the Color, Swatches, and Styles palettes are all contained within the same floating box. Click each title tab to bring the palette forward. To pull a palette away from the group in which it resides, click its title tab and drag it away from the current palette. You will see an outline of the palette as you drag. The new isolated palette pops up wherever you release the mouse button. You also can attach a palette to the bottom of another palette. To do this, drag the top of a palette to the bottom of another palette until a dark line appears at the bottom of the target palette; then release the mouse button. To place a palette in a group with another palette, click the title bar of one of the palettes and drag it onto the target palette. When a black border appears in the target palette, release the mouse button. Palettes also snap to each other, which makes them easier to align.

Palettes Be Gone!

Press the Tab key to hide or show all palettes, including the toolbox and Options bar.

The Toolboxes

You will use the toolbox constantly. To access hidden tools (marked by an arrow next to the tool), click and hold the mouse on the tool to access a menu. Here's a break-down of the tools.

● Indicates a Photoshop-only tool. Some ImageReady Tools are not in the same menus as they are in Photoshop. (The red dots are my additions, and do not appear in the actual toolbox menus.)

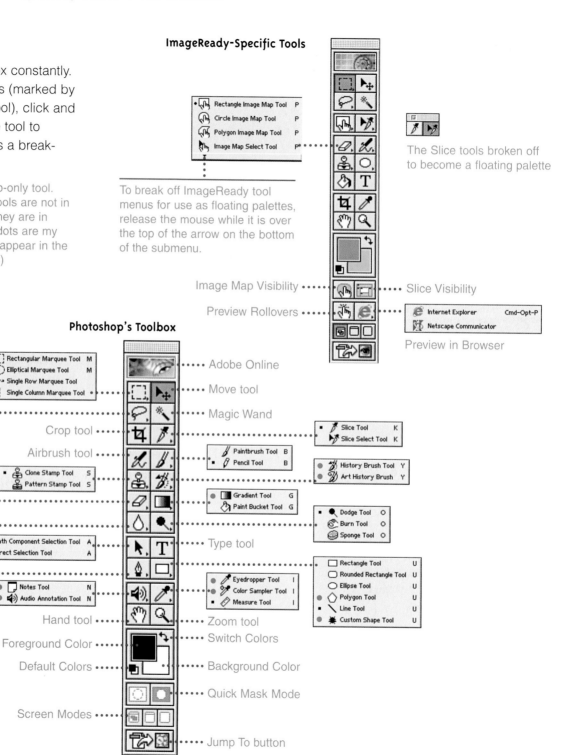

ImageReady-Specific Tools

●	Rectangle Image Map Tool	P
	Circle Image Map Tool	P
	Polygon Image Map Tool	P
	Image Map Select Tool	P●

To break off ImageReady tool menus for use as floating palettes, release the mouse while it is over the top of the arrow on the bottom of the submenu.

The Slice tools broken off to become a floating palette

Image Map Visibility

Preview Rollovers

Slice Visibility

	Internet Explorer	Cmd-Opt-P
	Netscape Communicator	

Preview in Browser

Photoshop's Toolbox

Adobe Online
Move tool
Magic Wand
Crop tool
Airbrush tool
Type tool
Hand tool
Zoom tool
Foreground Color
Switch Colors
Default Colors
Background Color
Quick Mask Mode
Screen Modes
Jump To button

●	Rectangular Marquee Tool	M
	Elliptical Marquee Tool	M
	Single Row Marquee Tool	
	Single Column Marquee Tool	●

●	Lasso Tool	L
	Polygonal Lasso Tool	L
●	Magnetic Lasso Tool	L

●	Eraser Tool	E
●	Background Eraser Tool	E
	Magic Eraser Tool	E

●	Blur Tool	R●
	Sharpen Tool	R
	Smudge Tool	R

●	Path Component Selection Tool	A
●	Direct Selection Tool	A

●	Pen Tool	P●
●	Freeform Pen Tool	P
●	Add Anchor Point Tool	
●	Delete Anchor Point Tool	
●	Convert Point Tool	

●	Notes Tool	N
●	Audio Annotation Tool	N

●	Slice Tool	K
	Slice Select Tool	K

	Paintbrush Tool	B
●	Pencil Tool	B

●	History Brush Tool	Y
●	Art History Brush	Y

●	Clone Stamp Tool	S
	Pattern Stamp Tool	S

●	Gradient Tool	G
	Paint Bucket Tool	G

●	Dodge Tool	O
	Burn Tool	O
	Sponge Tool	O

●	Eyedropper Tool	I
●	Color Sampler Tool	I
●	Measure Tool	I

	Rectangle Tool	U
	Rounded Rectangle Tool	U
	Ellipse Tool	U
●	Polygon Tool	U
●	Line Tool	U
●	Custom Shape Tool	U

The Options Bar

The Options bar is a great new feature of Photoshop 6 and ImageReady 3 that contains the settings for tools. Whenever you select a tool, the Options bar automatically switches to reveal the options for that tool. This is the place, for example, that you set the tolerance of the Magic Wand tool and choose a font for the Type tool. To reset any tool's options to the defaults, click the tool's icon on the Options bar and select Reset Tool from the menu.

The Magic Wand Options Bar

Click the tool icon to access a menu to reset a tool to its defaults.

Set the Wand tolerance here.

The Gradient Tool Options Bar

Access the menu of preset gradients here.

Choose a gradient type.

The Move Tool Options Bar

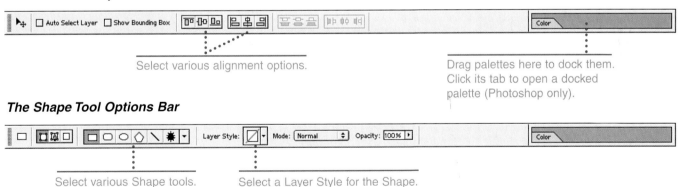

Select various alignment options.

Drag palettes here to dock them. Click its tab to open a docked palette (Photoshop only).

The Shape Tool Options Bar

Select various Shape tools.

Select a Layer Style for the Shape.

The Marquee Tool Options Bar

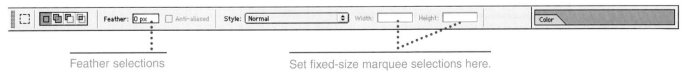

Feather selections

Set fixed-size marquee selections here.

The History Palette

Photoshop and ImageReady both support multiple undos and store the undo states in their History palettes. The number of states stored in the History palette is set by the number of undos selected as a preference. Preferences also enable you to change the shortcut keys that allow you to move forward and backward through the states in the palette (see page 17 of Chapter 2, "Preparing Photoshop and ImageReady for Web Work").

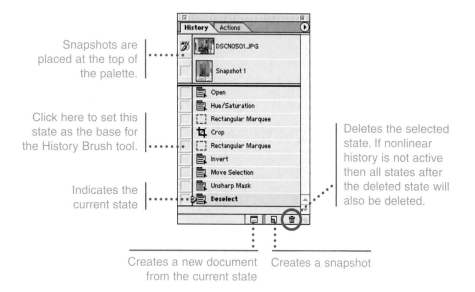

Snapshots are placed at the top of the palette.

Click here to set this state as the base for the History Brush tool.

Indicates the current state

Deletes the selected state. If nonlinear history is not active then all states after the deleted state will also be deleted.

Creates a new document from the current state

Creates a snapshot

Snapshots

Photoshop's History palette has the ability to create a *snapshot* of any current state. Creating a snapshot saves the current version of the image as a state in the upper part of the History palette, where it remains until it is deleted or the file is closed. You can revert to that state simply by clicking it. As a default, Photoshop automatically creates a snapshot when you open a document (new or old). To change this default, choose History Options from the History palette menu. If you ever need to revert to the file as it was before you started working on it then click this state. If this option has been turned off, you can always use the Revert command (File>Revert). Create a new snapshot whenever you're about to perform a series of commands that you are unsure of.

Linear and Nonlinear History

In Photoshop, you can choose between linear and nonlinear history. When linear history is activated, the History palette operates as a straightforward list of commands in the order they were performed. If you jump back to a previous state, that previous state becomes the current state. Afterward, if you perform any new operations, all history states after the current one are cleared.

What Did I Do?

Can't recall the operations you performed to make a certain effect? Check the History palette.

In nonlinear mode, you can jump back and forth between states, and states are never erased from the History palette (unless you delete them). Sometimes this is great, but it also can be confusing because the states in the History palette will no longer maintain a sequential record of the steps that led to the current state of the image. Breaks in the linear history are indicated by a solid line between commands. Use this feature with caution.

To toggle between linear and nonlinear history, choose History Options from the palette menu.

The ImageReady History Palette

ImageReady's History palette is a simplified version of Photoshop's. It acts as a retainer of performed commands, or History states, that can be accessed by clicking them by name. Otherwise, it has none of the features of Photoshop's History palette. But it does one thing that Photoshop does not: ImageReady's History states can be dragged to the Actions palette for use as steps in an action.

Jumping Between Applications

ImageReady and Photoshop were made to work together. You might find yourself jumping to Photoshop for its superior image-editing capabilities or to ImageReady for its expanded set of Web graphics tools. To jump between these applications, click the button on the bottom of the toolbox.

Typically, when you attempt to close a file that has had changes made to it since the last time it was saved, you are prompted to save the file before closing it. However, if the file is also open in Photoshop or ImageReady (whichever you are not in currently) then you will not be asked. Don't worry; the changes have not been lost. They've been transferred to the other application. Switch applications and save the file if necessary. Be aware, though, that when changes are updated in the background application, they are only undoable as a batch, not individually.

Keep in mind that any file that is to be opened in ImageReady must be an RGB file. So, if you're jumping to ImageReady from Photoshop, first ensure that the file is in RGB format (Image>Mode>RGB).

DIFFERENT HISTORIES

History states are not shared by Photoshop and ImageReady. When you jump to ImageReady from Photoshop, the current state of the image will be added to ImageReady's History palette as the most recent state.

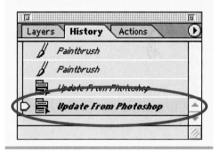

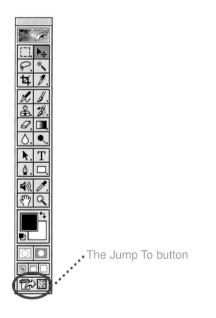

The Jump To button

Making Selections

Making selections is more of a skill than you might at first think. Photoshop has great tools, but they won't mean a thing if you can't select exactly what you want. Master these tools to improve your Photoshop work. There isn't room in this book to go over the full range of selection operations, but here are the basics:

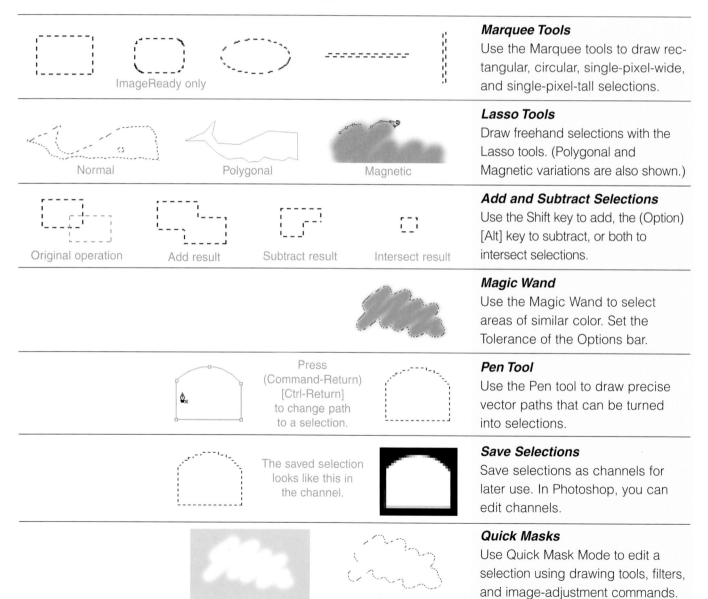

Marquee Tools
Use the Marquee tools to draw rectangular, circular, single-pixel-wide, and single-pixel-tall selections.

Lasso Tools
Draw freehand selections with the Lasso tools. (Polygonal and Magnetic variations are also shown.)

Add and Subtract Selections
Use the Shift key to add, the (Option) [Alt] key to subtract, or both to intersect selections.

Magic Wand
Use the Magic Wand to select areas of similar color. Set the Tolerance of the Options bar.

Pen Tool
Use the Pen tool to draw precise vector paths that can be turned into selections.

Save Selections
Save selections as channels for later use. In Photoshop, you can edit channels.

Quick Masks
Use Quick Mask Mode to edit a selection using drawing tools, filters, and image-adjustment commands.

Working with Layers

Layer work is the heart and soul of Photoshop and ImageReady operations. Keeping elements on separate layers means that they remain editable. This will save you a lot of time and work later. The following pages run through some layer basics.

To Create a New Layer

Click the New Layer icon on the bottom of the Layers palette. To rename the layer, double-click its name or the layer icon, depending on the type of layer.

To Delete a Layer

Drag it to the Layers trash can, or select the layer and click on the trash can. Click while holding the (Option) [Alt] key to delete the layer without confirming it.

To Move a Layer

Select and drag layers up and down in the list. Drag a layer onto a layer set folder to include it in the set.

To Change Layer Visibility

Turn the "eye" icon on and off. Layer sets can be turned on and off in whole or as individual layers. Layer effects also can be turned on and off.

To Link Layers

Select one layer, and then click the box next to any other layer to turn on the link icon. Linked layers are moved and transformed together.

To Merge Layers

Select a layer and choose a merge option from the Layers palette menu: Merge Down, Merge Visible, or Merge Set.

LOCKING LAYERS

Three aspects of a layer's contents can be locked: transparency, pixels, and position. When the transparency is locked, pixels cannot be added to the layer, and they can be cut only by deleting them. Using the Eraser paints the current background color on the existing pixels. When layer transparency is locked, simply press (Option-Delete) [Alt-Delete] to fill the existing pixels of the layer with the foreground color. If you lock the position, the layer is editable but not movable. If you lock the pixels, you can move the layer but not edit, delete, or add to its contents.

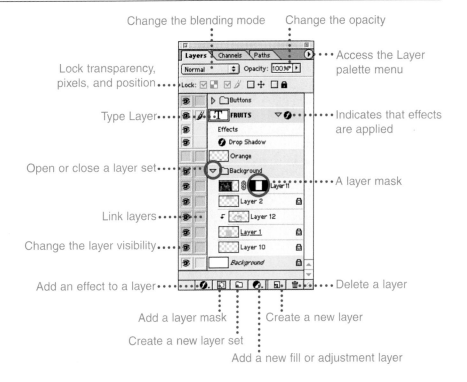

Layer Content Types

Layer types are distinguished by their content: normal layers, Type layers, Adjustment layers, Shape layers, and Fill layers. Normal layers are fully editable layers that you can use any of Photoshop's commands with. Note that styles and effects can be applied to all layer types.

Type Layers

These are indicated by a "T" and contain editable type, but have only limited editing features available to them.

Shape Layers

The content of a shape layer is bound by a clipping path. Use the

Shape tools to create a shape layer. In the Layers palette, the shape layer displays two icons side by side. The left determines the color for the clipping path, which is the icon on the right. Double-click the color to select a new one. Click the right icon to turn on the clipping path for editing by the Pen and Path Selection tools.

Fill Layers

These are also bound by clipping paths. To create a Fill layer, make a

selection or draw a path; then choose either Solid Color, Gradient, or Pattern from the Fill or Adjustment layer icon on the bottom of the Layers palette. In the dialog box, choose or edit a pattern, fill, or gradient (Photoshop only).

Adjustment Layers

Adjustment layers use image-adjustment commands such as

Brightness/Contrast and Hue/Saturation, to affect all layers beneath them without permanently changing the content of any of the layers. To create one, click the Fill or Adjustment layer icon on the bottom of the Layers palette and choose an option from the menu (Photoshop only).

> **Rendering Layers:** If you want to open Photoshop's full range of features for Type, Shape, Fill, or Adjustment layers, they must be rendered. To render a layer, choose Layer>Rasterize and select an option from the submenu. Afterward, these layers behave as normal layers, and lose the special functions they had in their original states.

Layer Sets

Layer sets are new to Photoshop 6 and ImageReady 3. A *set* is a folder of layers. This is a terrific way to organize layers. Often when building an element of a design, a button for example, you will use several layers. All of these layers can be kept in a layer set called "Button." A set, in turn, can be adjusted as a whole, as if it were a single layer. Drag layers in and out of sets just as you would files and folders on the desktop.

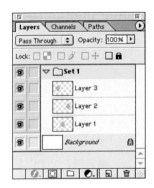

Layer Alterations: Opacity, Blending Modes, and Effects

Keeping elements in their own layers enables each element to be edited separately from all the other parts of the image. In addition, there are number of ways that layers can be altered without changing the actual pixel content of the layer. For example, you can change the Opacity of a layer such that the layers beneath show through it. You also can change the Blending Mode, which determines how the pixels of a layer are mixed with the pixels of the layers beneath it. Both of these settings always remain adjustable, and are at the top of the Layers palette.

Layer effects are special effects built into Photoshop and ImageReady that can be applied to the content of the layer. They are accessed by a menu at the bottom of the Layers palette and are discussed in more detail in Chapter 16, "Styles." These effects, also, affect only the appearance of the layer and not the actual pixels.

Layer Opacity effects

Blending Mode effects

Understanding these layer alterations can be important when working with rollover effects and animations. All these settings that simply alter the display of the layer contents without actually changing the pixels can be set independently for each rollover state or animation frame. So, the first frame of an animation might set the Opacity of a layer to 25%, and the second frame might set it to 50%. ImageReady will remember these Opacity changes and dynamically change the Opacity level as you switch between the frames.

COPYING LAYER CONTENT

When you use the Copy command in a multilayered document, the content of only the currently selected layer is copied. If you want to copy everything that you see in the image window, choose Edit>Copy Merged (Command-Shift-C) [Ctrl-Shift-C]. Keep in mind that when you paste this into another document, the contents are pasted as a single, merged layer.

DELETING LAYERS

Need to delete a lot of layers quickly? First, link all the layers you want to delete. If they're all in a row, click the link box for one and drag up or down to link the others. Then, choose Merge Linked from the palette menu. Finally, delete the merged layer.

CENTERING LAYERS

Need to center a layer? In ImageReady, select the layer and choose Layer>Set Layer Position. Set both values to 0 and press Return. In Photoshop, select the layer in the Layers palette, choose Select>All (or make any selection in which you want the layer to be centered), select the Move tool, and then click the Align horizontal centers and Align vertical centers buttons on the Options bar.

Aligning Layers

On this page are a few quick ways to align, distribute, and arrange layers. Aligning elements is very useful when setting up a design. Two commands in the Layers menu are particularly helpful: Align Linked and Distribute Linked.

Snapping Layers

Layers (and selections) also can be aligned to guides and the boundaries of the image. To use these features, turn on snapping to Guides or Document Bounds by choosing View>Snap To and selecting options from the submenu. Make sure snapping is turned on. Choose View>Snap to toggle snapping on and off.

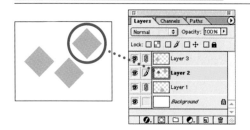

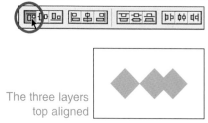

The three layers top aligned

To Align a Group of Layers

Select one of the layers and link the others to it by turning on their link icons. Then, select the Move tool and click one of the Alignment options on the Options bar. The selected layer holds priority, and the other layers move to align to it. In Photoshop, when a selection is active, these commands align layers to the selection (see below).

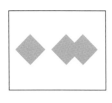

The three layers evenly distributed

To Distribute a Group of Layers

Select one of the layers and link the others (there must be at least three layers linked) to it by turning on their link icons. Then, select the Move tool and click one of the Distribute options on the Options bar.

The layer aligned to the selection

To Align a Layer to a Selection

Create the selection and select a layer in the Layers palette. Select the Move tool and click one of the Alignment options on the Options bar (Photoshop only).

Transparency Masks for Layers

A transparency mask limits the visibility of a layer's contents. After placing an image in a layer, you can add a layer mask to it that effectively crops the image without deleting any of it from the document. Then, if you unlink the mask from layer, you can shift the image within the bounds defined by the mask, or shift the mask without moving the layer's contents. While linked, however, the mask and layer move together.

add a layer mask

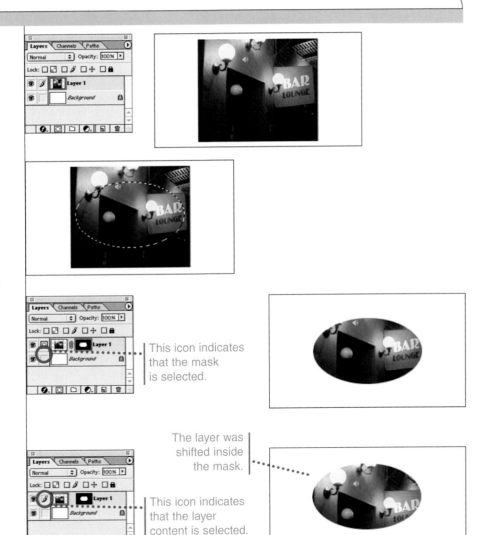

1. Place an image in a layer.

2. Use any selection tool (page 40) to create a selection. I created a simple oval.

3. Then, choose Layer>Add Layer Mask>Reveal Selection.

   In the Layers palette, a second icon is placed to the right of the layer icon. It previews the mask channel. When working with a layer and its mask, it is important that you have selected the appropriate icon. The selected icon is indicated by a border around it as well as change in the icon in the box to the left of the layer icon (see figure).

   To move either the image or the mask independently of the other, unlink them by clicking the link icon between them. Then, use the Move tool to reposition the element.

This icon indicates that the mask is selected.

The layer was shifted inside the mask.

This icon indicates that the layer content is selected.

The Notes Tools

These two new tools are too cool to pass up mentioning. With the Notes tool, you can place sticky notes on an image. The note, which can be moved around on the image, is displayed with an icon. When the icon is double-clicked, it is opened to reveal the text of the note. Notes do not show up in ImageReady, although they are not deleted, either. If your computer has a microphone, you can record voice messages (or any other audio, for that matter) with the Audio Annotation tool.

create a note   *Photoshop only*

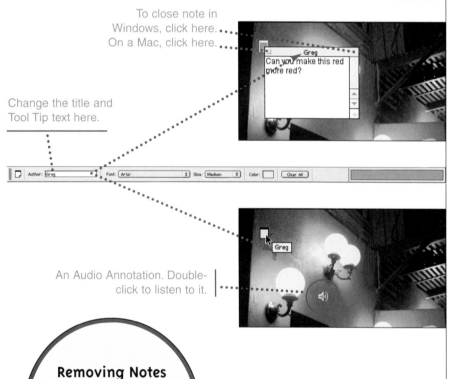

To close note in Windows, click here. On a Mac, click here.

Change the title and Tool Tip text here.

An Audio Annotation. Double-click to listen to it.

Removing Notes

To remove notes (or audio notes) from an image, simply drag them outside the image.

1. Select the Notes tool from the toolbox and click in the image area where you want to place the note.

2. Make changes to the color of the note, the font, or the size of the type in the Options bar.

3. Change the text in the title bar by changing the Author field on the Options bar. Hit Enter or Return to register this change.

   This text also appears in the Tool Tip box when the mouse is hovered over a note.

4. Click the Close Window box when finished or press (Command-W) [Ctrl-W]. Make sure the note is active when using this keystroke. Otherwise, you will close the entire document.

The Audio Annotation tool (also in the toolbox) works the same way. Make sure that you have a microphone connected and that it is chosen as the computer's sound input source. Also, make sure the volume is turned up when playing back these messages.

The Measure Tool

Frustration often sets in when you attempt to perform precision operations in Photoshop. Several tools help, including Rulers, Guides, and the Info palette. But sometimes it is difficult to be as precise as you want to be. The Measure tool, besides its usefulness in taking measurements, can be a great aid for precise operations. This example uses the Measure tool to create three evenly spaced guides, which can then be used to align elements.

use the measure tool   *Photoshop only*

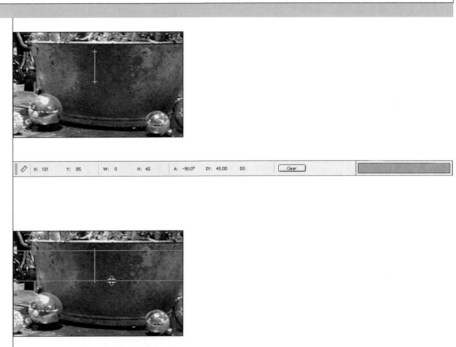

1. Select the Measure tool from the Tool palette (it's grouped with the Eyedropper). Then, click and drag in the image area to draw a measurement line. Hold the Shift key to constrain the measurement to 45° and 90° directions.

    This is all it takes to make a measurement. The Options bar displays measurement information.

2. Drag a guide to one of the points. If snapping is turned on, the guide will snap to the points. Drag a second guide to the second point.

3. Then, drag the actual measurement line down so the initial point touches the second guide. You can then make a third guide whose distance from the second guide is the same as the second's distance from the first guide.

    The Measure tool retains its shape, but disappears when you choose another tool.

Taking Advantage of Context-Sensitive Menus

Context-sensitive menus are menus you access right on top of an image or a palette. They save you the time of going to find things in the menus or on palettes. To access any of these menus, hold the mouse over a part of the image or an item in a palette, such as a layer effect and hold the Control key (Mac) or right-click (Windows). These menus adjust themselves to what's going on in the image—to the context. The menu can change, for instance, depending on whether or not a selection is active. Here is a sample selection of useful menus.

One of Photoshop's context-sensitive layer menus enables you to access general layer operations.

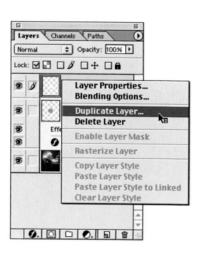

When the Move tool is selected, Photoshop's context-sensitive layer selection menu enables you to choose any of the layers beneath the pointer.

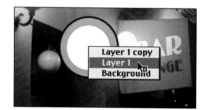

When one of the Marquee tools is selected, and a selection is active, Photoshop's context-sensitive menu lists some often-used commands.

ImageReady's general context-sensitive menu contains a range of features.

Keyboard Shortcuts

Here are some useful keyboard shortcuts.

Command	Windows Shortcut	Mac OS Shortcut
Preview Rollovers (IR)	Y	Y
Show Slices (IR)	Q	Q
Show Image Maps (IR)	A	A
Change Screen Mode	F	F
Hide All Palettes	Tab	Tab
Hide/Show Rulers	Ctrl - R	Command - R
Hide/Show Extras	Ctrl - H	Command - H
Snap/Unsnap	Ctrl - ;	Command - ;
Show/Hide Grid (PS)	Ctrl - Alt - '	Command - Option - '
Show Actual Pixels	Ctrl - Alt - 0 (zero)	Command - Option - 0 (zero)
Fit in Screen	Ctrl - 0 (zero)	Command - 0 (zero)
Zoom In/Out	Ctrl - +/-	Command - +/-
Switch Foreground/Background Colors	X	X
Set Colors to Defaults	D	D
Save for Web (PS)	Ctrl - Shift - Alt - S	Command - Shift - Option - S
Show Optimized (IR)	Ctrl - Y	Command - Y
Save Optimized (IR)	Ctrl - Alt - S	Command - Option - S
Transform	Ctrl - T	Command - T
New Layer via Cut	Ctrl - Shift - J	Command - Shift - J
New Layer via Copy	Ctrl - J	Command - J
Invert Selection	Ctrl - Shift - I	Command - Shift - I
Help	Ctrl - ?	Command - ?

4

Guides
✓ Grid
Slices
✓ **Document**
All

Name: NewDesign

Image Size: 616K

Width: 600

Height: 350

Resolution: 72

Laying Out Web Pages

From blank white document to operational HTML Web page, Photoshop and ImageReady can put together entire Web pages from scratch. This chapter offers advice on how to work smartly and shows you some useful tools for setting up designs and keeping everything organized.

So, You're Designing a Web Page

There are many tasks that Photoshop and ImageReady can help accomplish, and they are discussed individually in the various chapters of this book. Another thing they can be used for is creating an entire Web page. This chapter covers general issues that involve fewer step-by-step procedures than they do broader considerations of bringing a page to fruition.

The Design Process

Commonly, Web design is a two-stage process. A designer creates the visual layout and graphics and then hands off the files to an HTML coder, who turns the designer's vision into a reality suitable for display in a browser. There is no doubt that this division has its advantages because the designer can concentrate on his specialty and the coder on his. With adequate communication between the two, the system works. Photoshop and ImageReady, though, are designed such that these two parts of the process can become one. They make it easy to lay out an entire design within a single document and then generate HTML files and Web-ready graphics files from the design. The process is flexible and allows the user a reasonable degree of control over the graphics files and the HTML, although Photoshop and ImageReady offer much more to the creation of graphics.

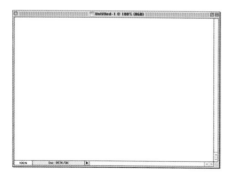

From blank white document to operational HTML Web page, with Photoshop and ImageReady you can put together entire Web pages from scratch.

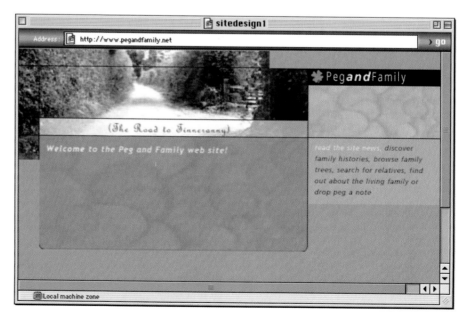

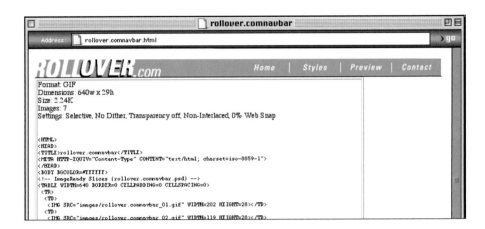

The Preview in Browser command shows both the optimized images and the code used to display them.

Preview in Browser

The Preview in Browser command (in both Photoshop and ImageReady) gives you an idea of what goes into creating an entire page. Not only do you see the graphics according to the optimization settings, but below the graphics a box reveals the code that Photoshop or ImageReady has generated to display the graphics in the browser.

Photoshop *Then* ImageReady

Photoshop and ImageReady both have tools to help put together Web pages, but they each have strengths and weaknesses that suggest the best way to work with them. Because of its superior graphics creation and image adjustment features, Photoshop is the better application with which to start the design process. Create the initial document there, create and lay out the basic graphic elements, work out the basic color scheme, and add the type. Generally speaking, it's time to switch to ImageReady when it's time to slice the design into individual graphics. Photoshop now has a Slice tool, so initial slicing can be done in Photoshop, but ImageReady still has a better set of slicing features. Once in ImageReady, add the Web-specific elements, such as rollovers, animations, and image maps. As you continue, jump back and forth as needed—neither application will strip elements added by the other even if it doesn't support or display them. Finally, use ImageReady to optimize the graphics and output the final HTML and image files. Although this can be done in Photoshop, it's much easier to do it in ImageReady. Photoshop's Save for Web command is best reserved for extracting single graphics from files and for their optimization.

Design Tips

Photoshop and ImageReady are only technical tools that facilitate graphics creation. All the design work is still up to you. If you're not a designer, here are some guidelines to get you by:

Organize. Know ahead of time everything that will be part of the design. Last-minute additions can louse up what was originally a clean, solid page. Draw a flowchart of all pages included in the site, so you'll know what content and links are needed on each page.

Hierarchy. Determine which elements are the most important and treat them as such. Establishing the hierarchy in design visually can be accomplished through color, relative size, position on the page, order of appearance, or simply the amount of space an item is surrounded by. These factors can fight with each other if care is not taken.

Work on a Grid. Set up a structure for the design. And stick to it for all pages. Even sites that appear wild are often built on top of a basic grid that organizes elements. Setting up a grid will help you organize the information on the page.

Limit the Number of Colors. Choose two to five colors to build all elements of the site. Forcing this limitation on yourself makes you create a better design. Also, steal color palettes—not only from other designs, but from everywhere you look. Take note of color combinations that catch your eye.

Let Type Do the Work. Spend adequate time choosing typefaces. Fonts go a long way in establishing the look of a page, and they will do this whether you pay attention to them or not. Keep the number of fonts limited. Two typefaces—one for heads, buttons, and other highlight elements and another for body text —are usually all that are necessary. Additionally, with Web pages you have to work with the limitations of fonts available to browsers. In practice, there are only a few available. Make sure the fonts you're using coordinate well with the typeface that will be used to fill in the HTML-generated text.

Consistency. You have to fight the urge to dump every new technique you learn into one design. Designs generally benefit from limiting the types of treatment that appear within it. Also, optimize images to a consistent quality, and be consistent with type point sizes.

Simplify. Fight the urge to overcomplicate a page. Any design can easily become too busy. Avoid obnoxious background tiles and other competing elements. Pare the design down to only the necessary elements.

Setting Up the Design

Get things set up right from the beginning and you'll avoid nagging problems later. Although the following steps are discussed separately, each part of the process affects the others.

Web Page Dimensions

The first step in creating a design is opening the New dialog box (File>New) and deciding on a size for the design. Web pages are designed for browser windows, and browser windows come in all different sizes. Monitor size limits the maximum browser window, but users also generally resize windows to suit their own personal dows to suit their own personal

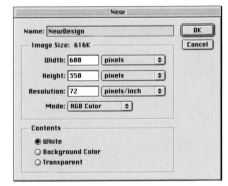

needs. This is a major challenge for Web designers. Ideally, the same design will look good and work well in a variety of window sizes. Some designers design for the lowest common denominator when it comes to screen size, which means designing layouts that will work on monitors with 640x480 pixel resolution. This ensures a usable and friendly site for a wide audience. Because some of the actual screen space is taken up by the borders and menu bars of the browser, the available Web page size is further reduced to approximately 600 pixels wide by 350 pixels deep. But, don't feel absolutely restricted to this size; larger monitors are commonplace and those with smaller monitors can always scroll through a design. Use these numbers as general guidelines.

Creating a long page that requires the user to scroll down is a common method of including a lot of information on a single page.

There are other factors to consider when choosing the size of the design. The audience is one. Sometimes you will know exactly who your audience is. If so, design specifically for the typical monitor size of that audience. Second, if the design of the page is part of its content, you may not want to sacrifice important elements for the sake of mass public usability. Third is the scrolling page. Because browsers allow pages to scroll, you can design for this. Commonly, pages scroll down. A depth of 1,000 pixels is reasonable. Pages also can scroll horizontally. Just keep two factors in mind. First, make sure you keep the most crucial elements of the design, such as the site's navigation menu, in an area visible to all displays—which means within the 600x350 pixel area mentioned above. Second, be sure to clearly indicate, through the design, to the user how the page is organized and where everything is.

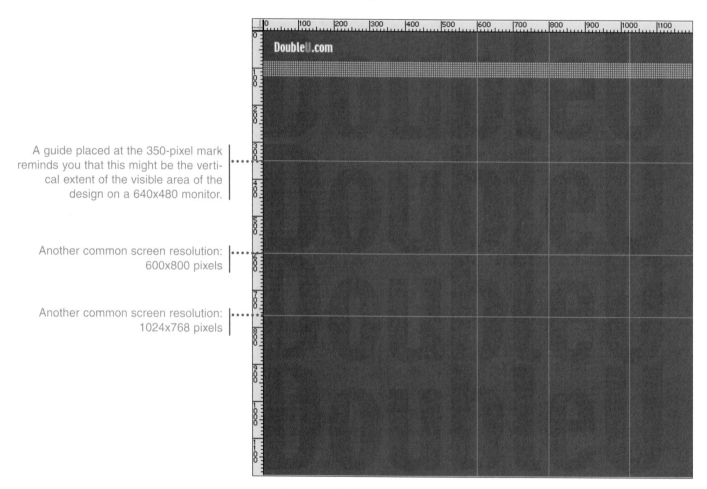

A guide placed at the 350-pixel mark reminds you that this might be the vertical extent of the visible area of the design on a 640x480 monitor.

Another common screen resolution: 600x800 pixels

Another common screen resolution: 1024x768 pixels

Use Rulers and Guides as reminders of which part of the page various-size browser windows will reveal.

Perfect Matches

With JavaScript, it is possible to force a browser to open a new window to an exact size. This makes it possible to create a design for particular dimensions. Why not make the browser fit the design instead of the other way around? Well, one reason is that it is considered a less fluid form of creating a page. Popping open a new window disrupts the "browsing" of the browser. A new window has no history, so the user cannot jump back to a previous page— a normal part of the Web experience. Also, users often want to control the size of the browser window themselves and will either resent its being changed or just change it again after it has been resized. User friendliness is greatest when you let the user control the size of the window. However, designs made for specific-size windows can have a more complete look because the layout can be perfectly framed by the browser window. Small pop-up windows can be useful and attractive for suitable content, such as important messages, illustrations, or videos.

Small pop-up windows for content, such as videos, are a common use of windows which have their size controlled by the designer.

Creating a design for a particular window size lets you incorporate the use of edges and framing into the design.

Steal Stuff

The Web is perfect for stealing, er . . . um, "borrowing" design ideas. There is no better way to learn what you can do with an HTML document and a bunch of GIFs and JPEGs than to surf the Web. When you find a site you're interested in, pick it apart. If you know, or are learning, HTML, look at the HTML source for the page (in Explorer, choose View>Source; in Netscape, choose View>Page Source). To find out how the file was sliced, click and drag on top of images. As you do this, "ghosted" versions of images are pulled across the browser. This gives you a chance to see the actual dimensions of the image. You can also download individual images by Control-clicking (Mac) or right-clicking (Windows) and choosing Download Image to Disk (Explorer) or Save Image As (Netscape). After downloading the images, open them in ImageReady. If they are GIFs, take a look at their Color Tables. If they're JPEGs, the Optimize palette displays the Quality setting they were saved at. You won't be able to discover all the techniques of Web designers by doing this, but you'll learn a few. Background images cannot be grabbed in the same manner as other images. To access them, you must view the source to find out where the image is; then manually type in its URL to load it. Afterward, you can use the standard method of downloading it.

Design for Flexibility

As someone once said, and many have since said, the only constant is change. And this is very apt to both design and the Web. Pages change constantly—they get new links, new images, and new logos for the company that just bought out the other. Taste and fashion are variable, too. What looked good yesterday won't necessarily look good today. For these reasons, it is a good idea to design for flexibility. The best way to stave off the kinds of changes that will completely upset a design is to build a well-organized, well-structured page. This means making big decisions first. Will the navigation be at the top? At the left? Both? How much area will it cover? Try to avoid squeezing things in. Build a structure and let it determine the placement of elements. It will only make your life easier.

The most flexible design is often the most rigidly constructed. The regularity of the slices in this Web page enables easy replacement.

A well-structured page divided into discrete areas. Notice that the navigation buttons are of equal sizes.

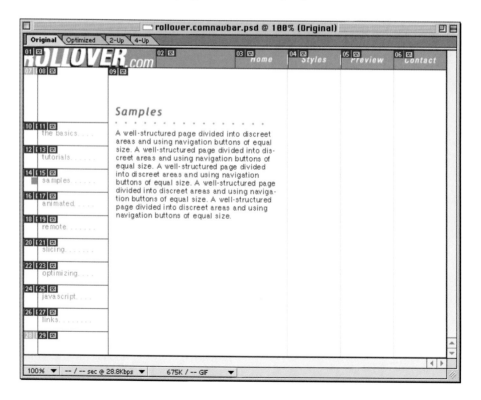

Using Color Palettes

Color is very important to design. It sets an overall tone, can be used to
highlight key elements, and works wonders through associative powers.
After creating a color scheme, you can save it for reuse as a Color Table or
Swatch palette. There are a number of ways to build a color swatch palette,
but I find the following one the most convenient.

build a swatch palette

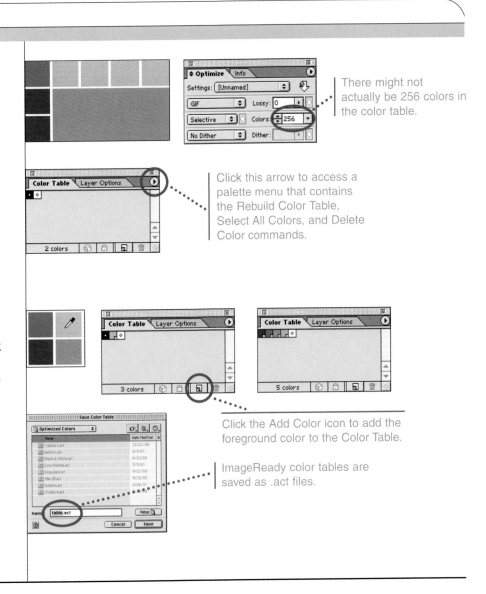

1. Open an image in ImageReady,
   and work in the Original window. On the Optimize palette,
   change the file format to GIF,
   the Color Reduction Algorithm
   to Selective, and the number of
   colors to 256.

   There might not
   actually be 256 colors in
   the color table.

2. Open the Color Table from the
   Window menu. If there are no
   colors in the table, choose
   Rebuild Color Table from the
   palette menu. Select all the colors in the Color Table and delete
   them. Black and white remain in
   the table.

   Click this arrow to access a
   palette menu that contains
   the Rebuild Color Table,
   Select All Colors, and Delete
   Color commands.

3. Use the Eyedropper to select a
   color from the image; then click
   the Add Color icon on the
   Color Table palette. Repeat this
   step to add colors to the table.

   Click the Add Color icon to add the
   foreground color to the Color Table.

4. When the table is complete,
   choose Save Color Table from
   the Color Table palette menu.

   ImageReady color tables are
   saved as .act files.

   *Color Tables saved in the
   default location (Adobe
   Photoshop>Presets>Optimized
   Colors) are listed in the Color
   Reduction Algorithm menu on
   the Optimize palette.*

load a swatch palette

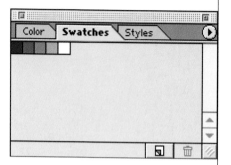

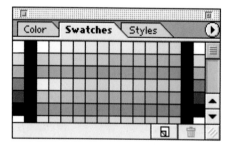

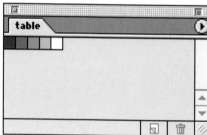

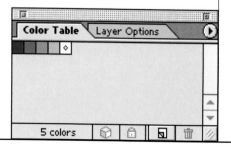

Photoshop:

1. To add colors to the current Swatches, choose Load Swatches from the Swatches palette menu.

   To replace the current Swatches colors, choose Replace Swatches from the Swatches palette menu.

   Then, go and find the .act file that was saved previously. The default folder for .act files is Adobe Photoshop>Presets> Optimized Colors.

ImageReady:

1. Choose Load Swatches from the Swatches palette menu.

   Go and find the .act file that was saved previously. The default folder for .act files is Adobe Photoshop>Presets> Optimized Colors.

   It will open in its own window without affecting the current Color Table.

or

1. Choose Load Color Table from the Color Table palette menu.

   Go and find the .act file that was saved previously. The default folder for .act files is Adobe Photoshop>Presets> Optimize Colors.

Color Palette Files

Another way to create color palettes is simply to build a small image file that contains the colors in blocks. The colors can be selected with the Eyedropper tool. In Photoshop, the file doesn't even need to be in the foreground to select colors from it—the Eyedropper grabs colors from any open file. The advantage of this method is that you can make the swatches large enough so that you can see them interacting with each other. You get a sense of how they work together before using them.

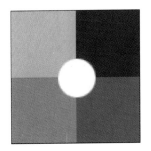 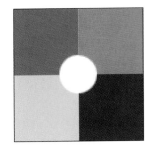 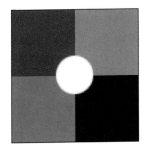 

Keeping Things in Line

To reiterate, structure and organization are keys to creating a solid design. Here are a few Photoshop and ImageReady features to help keep things aligned and organized as you work.

Rulers, Guides, and Grids

Rulers help keep you oriented in the image, especially when zooming in. Guides and grids help break down the image area before laying in images and other elements. Guides are useful during the design stage to align elements precisely and uniformly. Other good uses for guides include defining areas of the page by use. For example, a vertical guide might be used to indicate the right edge of a menu bar that runs down the left side of the page. A horizontal guide might run under the header at the top. Guides are also used well for dividing the page into columns. Grids are helpful in providing orientation for the general spacing of elements on the page. Think of them as extensions of the rulers.

Rulers

- To turn rulers on or off, choose View>Show Rulers or View>Hide Rulers (Command-R) [Ctrl-R].

- To change the ruler measurement units, hold the Control key (Mac) or right-click (Windows) anywhere in the horizontal ruler to access a menu of options. (ImageReady rulers are always in pixels.)

- To move the origination point, click and drag from the intersection of the horizontal and vertical rulers and drag the pointer to a new location. The rulers adjust accordingly.

- To reset the origination point to the upper-left corner of the image window, double-click the intersection of the horizontal and vertical rulers.

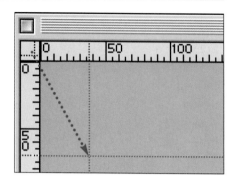

Grid   *(Photoshop only)*

- To turn the grid on or off, choose View>Show>Grid. This also selects the grid as an option in the Extras menu. Showing or Hiding Extras (Command-H) [Ctrl-H] turns the grid on or off.

- To set grid spacing and color options, choose Edit> Preferences>Guides & Grid.

Guides

- To turn guides on or off, choose View>Show>Guides. This also selects Guides as an option in the Extras menu. Showing or Hiding Extras (Command -H) [Ctrl-H] turns the guides on or off.

- To place a guide, click in the rulers and drag into the image window.

- To place a guide precisely in Photoshop, choose View>New Guide. Enter a value and choose an orientation in the New Guide dialog box.

- To remove a guide, select the Move tool, and click and drag the guide back to the rulers.

- When snapping is turned on (see next page), guides are snapped to grids, selections, and the bounds of the currently selected layer's contents or active selection.

- To create a set of evenly spaced guides or a grid of guides (ImageReady only), choose View>Create Guides and select options in the Create Guides dialog box.

- To clear all guides, choose View>Clear Guides.

- To lock all guides, choose View>Lock Guides.

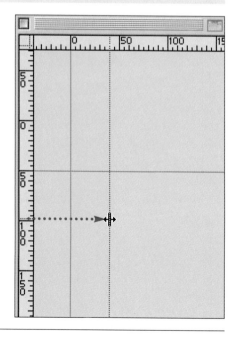

Snapping

Snapping, a convenient method for aligning elements, works by drawing the pointer or a layer's contents to, among other things, guides and grids. It activates a sort of magnetic field that draws in the element. For example, assuming that snapping to guides is turned on, when dragging a marquee selection, the pointer "snaps to" any guide that it comes within 8 screen pixels of. In Photoshop, the snap feature is available for guides, grids, slices, and document bounds, and it can be turned on or off in any combination. In ImageReady, snap options are limited to guides and slices.

The Snap command and the Snap To menu in Photoshop's View menu. ImageReady's Snap To menu contains a shorter list of options.

Snap features are handled like Extras. Snap options are chosen from a list (View>Snap To), and then all chosen options are turned on or off together by turning snapping on or off (View>Snap, or Command-; [Mac} Ctrl-; [Windows]). In addition to the options listed in the Snap menu, guides are snapped to the bounds of the currently selected layer's contents, unless a selection is active. In that case, the guide snaps to the selection.

Here is a less-than-obvious method of aligning the contents of layers that demonstrates the usefulness of guides and snapping used in tandem.

snapping layers to guides

1. Open a file and create two or more layers with objects in them.

2. Turn on the Rulers and Snapping. Then, drag a vertical guide to meet the left edge of the currently selected layer. The guide snaps to the edge of the layer's contents.

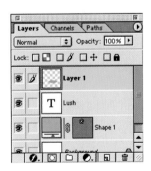

3. Then, select the Move tool and turn on Auto Select Layer in the Options bar. Click and drag one of the other elements and drag it just to the right of the guide. It snaps in place and is left-aligned with the ellipse. Repeat this step for other layers.

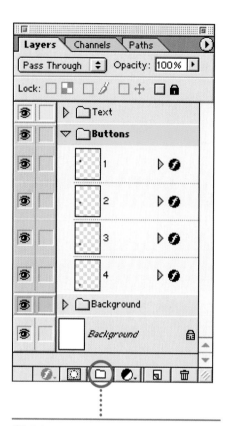

Click here to create a new set. To change a layer's color, select it and choose Layer Options (ImageReady) or Layer Properties (Photoshop) from the Layers palette menu.

This text, which will be added to the HTML document later by an HTML editor, was placed on a layer in Photoshop and can be turned off before optimizing the graphics and saving the final files.

Organizing the Layers Palette

Besides keeping the design organized, keeping the Layers palette organized is also important. Navigating through a mess of unnamed and unorganized layers is difficult. When you start layering images and adding animations and rollover states, layers quickly accumulate. You now can put layers into folders, called *sets*. All states of a rollover button, or all the layers that make up the background image, could be kept in a set. In this manner, the Layers palette can be organized as a list of sets titled according to the parts of the design: Home Button, Link Buttons, Images, Logo, Header, and so on.

Grouping Layers in a Set

To make a set of a group of layers, link them and then choose New Layer Set from Linked from the Layers palette menu.

Temporary Layers

When laying out a page in Photoshop, it is useful to include elements that will appear on the page but will be generated by the HTML document and not Photoshop itself—paragraphs of text, for example. It is a good idea to include these elements as layers in Photoshop while designing so that you don't forget they have to be there and because they affect the final look of the page. You should have some idea of how much text needs to fit in each area of the page. When you are finished designing and ready to optimize and save the final images and HTML file, just turn off these layers in the Layers palette.

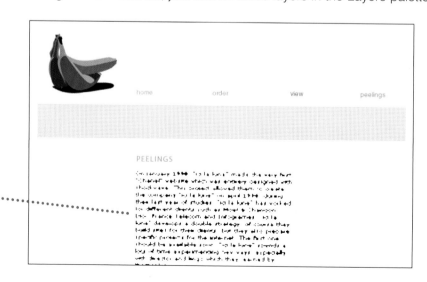

Finishing It Right

The final steps of creating a design include slicing, optimizing, and saving the final graphics and HTML files. These topics are covered individually in Chapter 7, "Optimizing Graphics," page 110, Chapter 6, "Saving Files for the Web," page 96, and Chapter 11, "Slices," page 192. Following are some general considerations and tips on dividing a design into slices, as well as a few notes about the HTML file.

Slicing a Design

Proper slicing is key to using Photoshop as a layout tool. Without the ability to slice a design into smaller components that will be optimized and saved as individual graphics, using Photoshop for layout would be impractical. Slices are discussed where necessary in this book (including Chapter 11, "Slices"); however, there are noteworthy considerations to make when it comes to slicing a design.

Function: Slice the design according to function. Menu items and any other elements that will have links attached must be contained within individual slices (unless you plan to create image maps). Sometimes slicing also involves thinking ahead to additional elements that are added in the HTML editor later. The area to contain body text of a page might be contained in a slice and deleted in the HTML editor later.

File Formats: Slice the design so you can separate elements into those best saved as GIFs and those best saved as JPEGs.

Rollover States: Make sure slices that have rollover effects attached are large enough to contain all states of the rollovers.

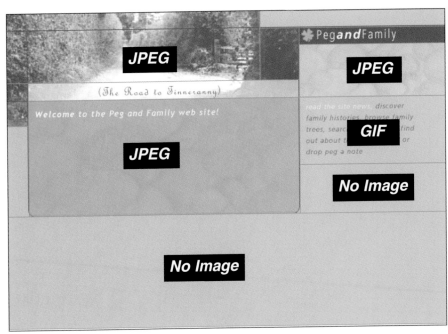

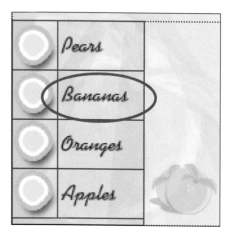

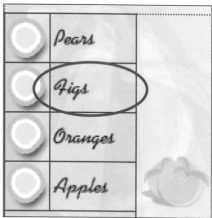

Uniformity: Creating uniformly sized slices for like elements makes a design more flexible. What happens if you must replace a menu item that is part of a navigation bar? Or switch the order of menu items? If the slices are uniform then this task is made easier. You can substitute or move graphics without upsetting other parts of the design. The entire navigation bar can first be wrapped by a single slice, then divided into separate slices for each item by using ImageReady's Divide Slices command in the Slices menu. This creates slices that are exactly the same size, and menus that consist of uniform slices are the most flexible.

Neatness: The totality of all slices in a design always creates a rectangle. This rectangle will become, in the HTML document, the size of the table. If you draw a slice in the middle of the image, other slices (called auto-slices) are automatically drawn around it. This is necessary for maintaining the correct positioning of slices in the table. However, these applications don't always create the auto-slices in the manner best for your design. And sometimes small slivers are created because of awkward positioning of elements. Stay away from this messiness whenever possible. Avoiding these situations really starts with the initial design process. A better structured page will have fewer of these types of issues.

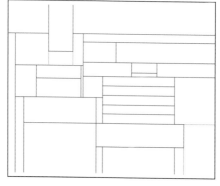
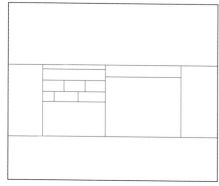

The slices in the image on the right create a much more manageable set.

No Image Slices: Whenever possible, convert slices that contain only a solid color into No Image slices. A No Image slice has no graphic file associated with it, and the color is added by the HTML code. No Image slices reduce download and processing time because there is one less image on the page. They are discussed in Chapter 11, "Slices" (page 192).

Snapping and Slicing: Photoshop and ImageReady slices can be snapped to each other while drawing them. It is almost always best to turn on this option (View>Snap To>Slices). It ensures that the slices abut each other perfectly and reduces the chances of extra auto-slices being drawn between two slices. With this option turned on, slicing is a quick operation. It doesn't completely eliminate the need to zoom in on the image, though. That is still necessary in some cases. It also might be best to turn off all other snapping options while slicing so the slices snap only to slices, not guides or other elements.

Naming Slices: Photoshop and ImageReady's automatic naming of slices is very nifty and at times convenient. Names match slice numbers so matching a slice in the image window with the file associated with it is easy. However, naming files by the number of the slice is less than informative about the content of the graphic file, to say the least. This name also is used as the beginning of the filename for all states of any of that slice's associated rollover states.

The HTML File

While creating a Web page design in Photoshop and ImageReady, an HTML file is also being built. The code is written for you, but you control the content and its parameters. Creating slices adds lines to the code, and reshaping them causes alterations. Some elements are entered directly, such as the ALT text that can be typed into the Slice palette.

You can view the HTML code by using the Preview in Browser command— it appears in a box below the graphics. But, although these applications write HTML files, you cannot access the actual HTML code until it has been exported and the resulting HTML file is opened in an HTML editor.

An HTML file almost always needs some type of alterations made to it in an HTML editor. Photoshop and ImageReady are graphics programs and as such have only basic coding capabilities. Photoshop cannot open HTML files, only the PSD file that was used to generate the HTML. So be careful when working with an HTML editor. It can open any HTML file produced by Photoshop, but it is not a two-way street. If you change a table cell size in the HTML editor, it will not be reflected in the Photoshop file. After you've reached the stage in the design process that the HTML file is being worked with in an editor, you will probably begin to deal with the graphics as individual files instead of saving the entire design again.

Updating HTML

If you do use Photoshop or ImageReady as the creator of the final HTML documents, some tools are available for reediting a page for which you have already generated graphics files and an HTML document. The HTML can be updated, and you can select specific slices to replace. Even if you copied and pasted the ImageReady HTML into another HTML document, ImageReady can update that isolated section of HTML within the document (as long as the ImageReady comment lines are left intact in the code). See page 107 of Chapter 6, "Saving Files for the Web," for more on how to update HTML.

Replacing Individual Graphics

If you make a change to one slice of a design that has previously been optimized and saved, you can choose to replace only that slice when resaving the file. After clicking Save in the Save Optimized or Save Optimized As dialog box, the application recognizes that the file already exists and displays a list of files (assuming that you have returned to the folder in which the original files were saved). By checking or unchecking them, you can decide which are replaced. Click Replace when you're finished to replace all checked files.

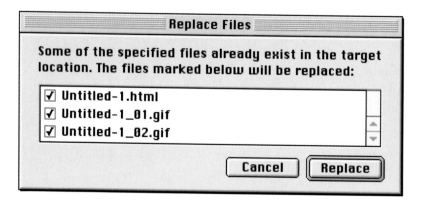

Photoshop Sketches

Even if you're not going to use Photoshop to assemble and create the final HTML documents, you can still use it as a layout program. Its editable flexibility makes it very suitable for the design process, which is by nature ever-changing and evolving. You can use it just to make quick mock-ups to e-mail off to clients or others as JPEGs, or save the page as a single graphic and place it in a visual HTML editor as a temporary background image as a backdrop on which to build the page.

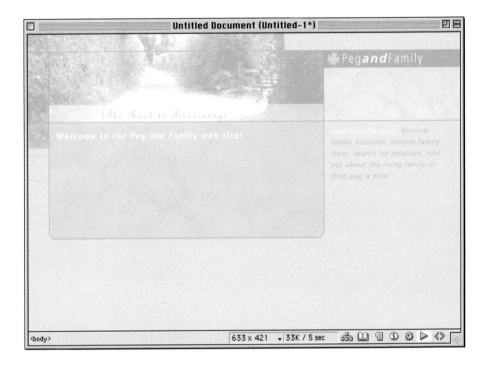

A dimmed version of a design was chosen as a temporary background image in a Macromedia Dreamweaver file for use as a guide and reminder while building a page.

The End

The following chapters discuss individual elements and issues of Web graphics in isolation. However, the final chapter of the book, Chapter 18, "Making a Web Page" (page 338), once again takes a broader perspective of the process. That chapter pulls together the isolated lessons and the general guidelines of this chapter to build and output a design.

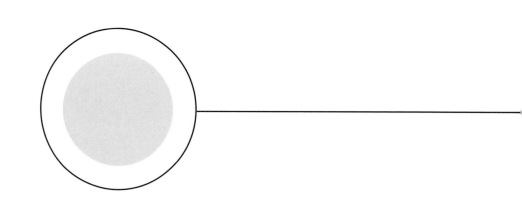

Part II

Web Essentials

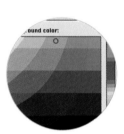

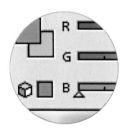

Web Color

RGB. Bit depth. Web-safe. Dither. Gamma. If these terms were part of your last dinner conversation then, God help you, you probably don't need this book. They are the concepts that form the basis of color issues for Web graphics. Becoming familiar with them enables you to anticipate and correct potential color problems. Photoshop and ImageReady have all the tools you need to control color, and in this chapter you learn how to use them.

Web Color Issues

Before moving on to practical matters, read through the next few pages to get a handle on basic color issues. Then, move on to the exercises that show you how to use Photoshop and ImageReady to control them.

RGB: The Web Color Mode

All graphics files operate in a *color mode*. The color mode is very important because it determines the way the image file stores color data, as well as which colors it can contain. The correct choice of color mode is determined by the intended use of the image. For images destined for the Web, RGB is the right choice. Why, you ask?

RGB (red, green, blue) is the color system monitors use to display images (or anything else, for that matter). Your monitor is an RGB display. Thus, because we're all looking at Web sites on our monitors, all Web graphics must be RGB files. In fact, it's the only kind of file that ImageReady can work with.

Photoshop supports a variety of color modes. So, you must be certain to set the color mode of your Web graphics files to RGB (Image>Mode> RGB). If you are creating a file from scratch, it's best to create it as an RGB file initially because changing the color mode later causes the colors to shift as they adjust to a new set of color possibilities available in that mode.

An important difference exists between Photoshop and ImageReady. ImageReady can operate only in the RGB mode. In fact, it doesn't have a Mode submenu of the Image menu and it doesn't even indicate what color mode the file is in. So, before jumping to ImageReady, you must convert your Photoshop images to RGB mode. Because we're all (almost all of us) viewing RGB images on RGB displays, there's a really good chance we're all seeing the same colors, right? Well . . .

WHAT COLOR MODE IS MY FILE IN?

ImageReady: All ImageReady files are in RGB mode. You cannot change the color mode of a file while in ImageReady.

Photoshop: The color mode is initially set in the New dialog box when the file is created.

Afterward, the mode can be changed by selecting Image>Mode and choosing an option. The color mode is also displayed in the title bar.

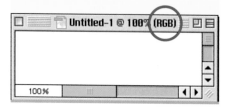

When you are working in Photoshop and use the Jump To icon to switch to ImageReady, you must first convert the image to RGB mode. If you don't, Photoshop politely requests you to do this.

Bit Depth: Available Color

Bit depth has meaning for both image files and displays. If it's easier, you could refer to bit depth as color depth because it describes the depth, or amount, of color available to a display or contained in a file. For the monitor, the bit depth describes how many colors are available for display on screen. An 8-bit display has 256 colors available to it (see chart below). A 24-bit display has millions. The greater the bit depth, the greater the range of color that can be displayed. For images, bit depth refers to the capacity of color information in the file. An 8-bit image contains enough color information to include 256 different colors in the image.

Common Bit Depths	
8-bit	**256 colors**
16-bit	**65,536 colors**
24-bit	**16.7 million colors**
32-bit	**16.7 million colors (plus an alpha channel for additional effects)**
(X-bit	**2^X colors)**

Try an experiment. Switch your monitor to 8-bit (256 colors) mode and surf the Web to see what difference it makes. See who is paying attention to the limited palette and who isn't. The biggest difference you will see is a lot of *dithered* images.

So, why does bit depth matter? When an image has more colors in it than the monitor is capable of reproducing, it must somehow compensate. It does so by *dithering* the image. Keep reading to learn about dithering.

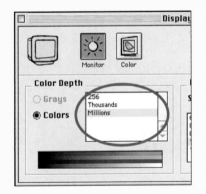

Web-Safe: 216 Universal Colors

The difficulties of dealing with color on Web pages stem from the fact that we're all using a variety of display systems that support various bit depths. The most common are listed in the previous page. The chances are that your system is capable of 16-bit color or higher, but not all are. Although 8-bit systems are quickly vanishing from the desktop scene, there used to be many more around. In order to make Web browsers as compatible as possible with the greatest number of machines, a color palette was developed that theoretically could be viewed on all systems. The Web-safe set of colors is drawn from the common colors shared by the Mac OS and Windows default color palettes. These system color palettes each contain 256 colors, but they are not the same 256 colors. The Web-safe set contains 216 colors that are included in both sets. This set has many names including the Web-safe palette, the browser-safe palette, and the 6x6x6 cube.

The 216 Web-safe colors as organized by Photoshop's Web Safe Colors swatches.

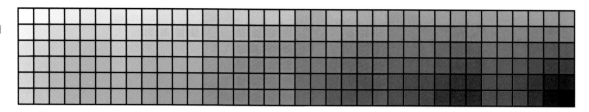

So, Web-safe graphics are 8-bit images that contain a set of colors common to all 8-bit displays. An important note about these 216 colors is that they cover the entire range of the RGB gamut. This is good because you wouldn't want the Web-safe palette to never have any greens just so it could have a lot of oranges. It is bad, and this is the weakest image reproduction factor for Web images, because you don't really have a lot of any color. To cover such a great range, the gaps between colors are great, essentially destroying any chance you have of creating gradations. Browsers have a way of compensating for this problem, and it's called "dithering." (Later in this chapter, you learn how to use dithering to create the optical illusion of colors outside the Web-safe palette.)

Dither: The Colors Between

So, what happens if a browser tries to display an image that contains colors not available to the system? It mixes pixels of the colors it can display in an attempt to approximate the missing color. This is called dithering. The browser is trying to create the optical illusion of the original color. Is dithering bad? That depends. For photographs, images you will save as JPEGs, it is an inevitable part of displaying photo-quality images on a display limited to 256 colors, and often the browser does an adequate job. But, if you have an icon composed of flat areas of color (something you would save as a GIF), dithering could absolutely upset the intentional stark color juxtapositions you have created, not only changing the color, but imposing an irritating pattern over the areas of color. As noted previously, you can use dithering to your advantage. It can help keep files small, and you also can use Photoshop's DitherBox filter to generate dithered colors based on a non–Web-safe color.

It's Supposed to Look That Way

Depending on how you look at it, dithering is either a way to make up for lost color or a useful and attractive effect.

LIMITED COLOR

Dithering and color shifting are most obvious in gradations. Below, the original gradient (left) was limited to only Web-safe color, without dithering (center) and with dithering (right).

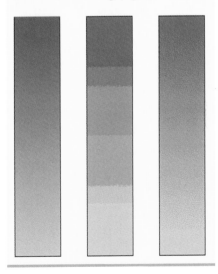

The image seen in 24-bit color.

The image seen in 8-bit color as it would dither on an 8-bit monitor.

The image limited to 16 Web-safe colors with no dithering.

The image limited to 16 Web-safe colors with Diffusion dithering.

Hexadecimal Color: The Triple-Double

Web-safe colors are written in an unconventional (to most of us, anyway) notation method using hexadecimal (base 16) values. Each color value contains six digits that are grouped into three pairs—one for each of the RGB color channels. The first pair indicates the amount of red in the image, the second the amount of green, and the third, the amount of blue.

The only hex digits used in Web-safe color values are 0, 3, 6, 9, C. and F. The only hex values used are: 00, 33, 66, 99, CC, or FF. This means that the amount of red in any Web-safe color is limited to six possibilities. The same is true for the amounts of green and blue.

If all 16 hexadecimal values were available to all six numbers, there would be more than 16 million possible colors. But because Web-safe color values are limited to these six values, Web-safe color is limited to 216 colors (6x6x6=216). To shift the red value only one notch, from 33 to 66, for example, you are actually skipping 50 color values. This is a numeric way of showing the limitations of the Web-safe palette—the lack of fine gradations between colors. But it's the only way that 256 values can cover a range of more than 16 million colors.

A typical Web-safe color value, this one, a Caucasian skin-tone, looks like this: FFCC99. The "triple-double" pattern of this color value is common to all Web-safe colors (not just to Caucasian ones). In this example, the FF is the amount of red in the color, the CC is the green, and the 99 is the blue.

The Real World: A Rainbow of Colors

Must you stick to these 216 colors? Having invoked the magic number 216, the set hereafter and in many circles known as the Web-safe palette, let it be known that you are not really limited to 216. Because the vast majority of people surfing the Web have monitors that display many more than 216 colors, you could just as well ignore this limitation and your images would be fine in most cases.

8-bit displays? Are we already talking about the past? Will this problem soon be obsolete? On one hand, desktop computers certainly will all soon display many colors, but the Web is moving into so many areas of business and leisure that people are surfing it on a greater variety of devices—most of them portable, and therefore with limited color capacities. Just as you need to design HTML that works on many platforms, your images need as much thought and TLC. Learning to control color is a valuable image preparation skill.

INFO PALETTE

#FFCC99:

Photoshop:
Info Palette showing the hexadecimal value

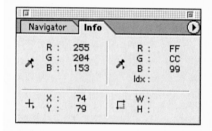

ImageReady:
Info Palette showing the hexadecimal value and a slightly different configuration

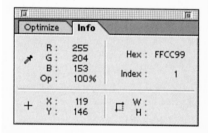

The Index (ImageReady) and Idx (Photoshop) tell you where the selected color is located in the Color Table for that image. Color #FFCC99 is in the first position. Color Tables and index numbers are relevant only to GIF images.

Gamma: Platform Values

So, all your graphics are Web-safe. That means they'll look the same on all computers, right? Well . . .. it is true that 216 identifiable shared colors exist on both the Mac and Windows platforms, however (you knew it was coming), these two systems use different default *gamma* settings. Gamma controls the lightness and darkness of the middle, or gray, values on your monitor. On a Mac, the default is 1.8; in Windows it is 2.2. What does this mean? The same Web-safe image looks darker on a Windows-based machine than it does on a Mac. You might have set the gamma for your display once when you set up your computer for the first time, but most likely you are using the system default. (It is not often altered.)

If you're creating images on a Mac, and you realize that most users have PCs, you might want to compensate when preparing your images for the Web. Otherwise, all the PC users will see your images a little darker than how you see them. Photoshop and ImageReady enable you to preview the effects of gamma differences, and ImageReady offers a built-in feature for quickly altering the values of an image to appropriately accommodate gamma differences. Also, see Chapter 2, "Preparing Photoshop and ImageReady for Web Work," for more information about gamma settings.

Just the Facts

Web-safe color *is a set of 216 colors that are available to virtually all computer displays (Mac or PC).*

Bit depth *is the measure of the amount of color available to either an image or a monitor.*

Gamma *is a setting that determines the relative lightness and darkness of the middle (or gray) values of an image.*

Dithering *is a method of mixing pixels of various colors to produce the optical effect of another color.*

Hexadecimal color *is the notation system used to specify the 216 Web-safe colors. It appears as a six-digit code.*

GAMMA DIFFERENCES

An image in Mac OS:

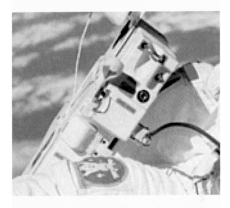

The same image in Windows:

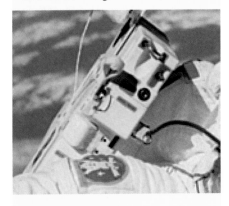

See page 93 for a quick method of adjusting Gamma for cross-platform images.

Choosing Web-Safe Colors

How do you make sure that you are using Web-safe colors? Follow me. As with all things Photoshop, there's more than one way to get a Web-safe color, or any color, for that matter. Essentially, you can select a color and then have Photoshop find the nearest Web-safe color, or you can have Photoshop allow you to choose only colors that are Web-safe.

---

choose a Web-safe color: the color picker

ImageReady and Photoshop

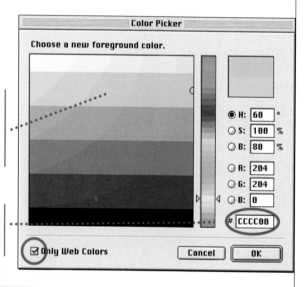

Each of these areas is a Web-safe color. Here, it is impossible to pick a color out of the Web-safe range.

Notice the hexadecimal value has snapped to a Web-safe value.

Method 1

1. Click the foreground or background color swatch on the toolbox.

2. Check the Only Web Colors check box in the bottom left of the Color Picker.

   The large color picker area is divided into discreetly sectioned areas—each of which is a Web-safe color.

3. Choose a color and click OK.

WEB GAMUT CUBE

The Web Gamut Cube can appear in the Color Picker and on the Color palette. Click it to force the current color to the nearest Web-safe color. Do not confuse this with the printing gamut warning that indicates that the color is out of the CMYK gamut and is therefore not reproducible in 4-color process printing.

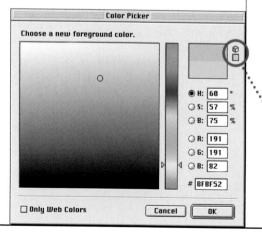

Method 2

Alternatively, after doing step 1, you can select any color from the contiguous color area, and then click the cube (the Web Gamut Warning) next to the color swatch. Doing this snaps the color you selected to the nearest Web-safe color. Using this method gives you an idea of how drastic the changes can be.

choose a Web-safe color: the color palette

1. Choose Web Color Sliders from the Color palette menu. Now, If you drag the RGB sliders, they snap to the Web-safe hexadecimal values.

    Note the hash marks that appear inside the color bars to indicate the six possible color values for each color channel.

    The Web gamut warning cube displays here if a color is out of the Web-safe gamut.

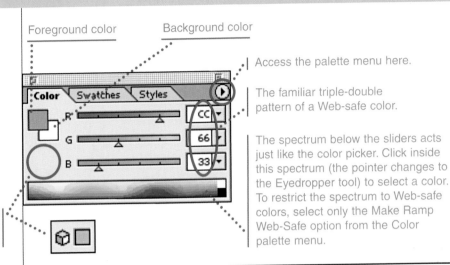

Foreground color

Background color

Access the palette menu here.

The familiar triple-double pattern of a Web-safe color.

The spectrum below the sliders acts just like the color picker. Click inside this spectrum (the pointer changes to the Eyedropper tool) to select a color. To restrict the spectrum to Web-safe colors, select only the Make Ramp Web-Safe option from the Color palette menu.

Choosing a Web-Safe Color: Using Swatches

Using the Swatches palette is a great way to keep your colors in line. You can set the swatches so that all the Web-safe colors, and more importantly no others, are available. Sticking to the palette's limited options when selecting colors ensures Web-safe choices.

choose a Web-safe color: color swatches

1. Open the Swatches palette (Window>Show Swatches). Open the palette menu and select any of the Web-safe options (indicated in this figure). I chose Web Spectrum.

    When asked whether you want to append or replace the current set, click Replace to make sure that only Web-safe colors exist on the palette, or choose Append to add the new colors to the bottom of the palette.

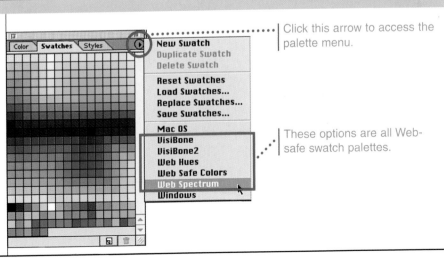

Click this arrow to access the palette menu.

These options are all Web-safe swatch palettes.

Mixing Colors

If you've just got to find that perfect blue of your grandmother's hair, as mentioned previously, you can "mix" two Web-safe colors to give the illusion of a color that falls between the proper Web colors. The two colors are intentionally "dithered" to create the third color. Here's how to do it:

mix a Web-safe color: the DitherBox filter

ImageReady and Photoshop

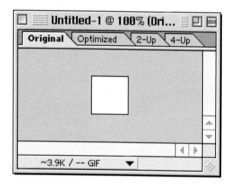

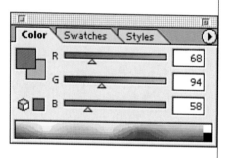

1. Select the non–Web-safe color you want to emulate.

   To do this, you may have to turn off Web Color Sliders or Make Ramp Web Safe in the palette menu.

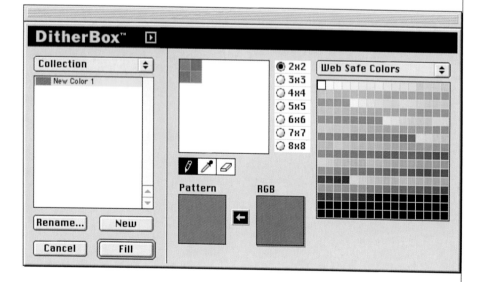

2. Choose Filter>Other>DitherBox. This dialog box automates the process of creating the new color.

   The box in the center shows you a close-up of the checkerboard pattern that is creating the color in the Pattern box below it.

   The current pattern was mixed to approximate the color selected in step 1. If you click Fill now, the image will be filled with what you see in the Pattern box.

mix a Web-safe color: the DitherBox filter   *ImageReady and Photoshop*

3. If you want to try a different color, click the RGB swatch to open the Color Picker. Choose a color and click OK to return to the DitherBox.

4. Click the left-pointing arrow next to the RGB swatch. The Pattern box shows the new color that has been mixed. It won't perfectly match the color you chose, but it will be close. Click OK to fill the image with what you see in the pattern.

    You also can edit the pattern by selecting colors from the palette to the right and using the tools (located below the window). You also can create, name, and delete colors.

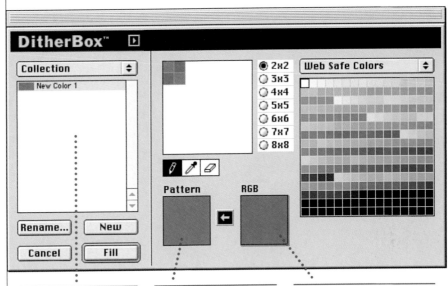

Organize colors here.

The new color as it will be seen at 100%.

Click the RGB swatch in the bottom middle of the DitherBox dialog box to open the Color Picker.

Web-Safe Color Ramps

The color ramp on top consists of only Web-safe colors. As you can see, the jumps between colors are not very subtle.

The color ramp below it contains dithered colors between the Web colors. These colors also are Web-safe because they are "mixed" from Web-safe colors. The pixels are small enough that you can't see that more than one color is actually there.

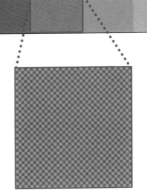

This close-up shows the dithered pattern that was used to make the second color in the second color ramp.

Custom Dithered Patterns

Sometimes the DitherBox doesn't do a very good job of finding the color you want. And sometimes it is painful to work with. In those cases, you can make your own dithered colors without much difficulty. Follow these steps:

---

mix a Web-safe color: custom pattern   *ImageReady and Photoshop*

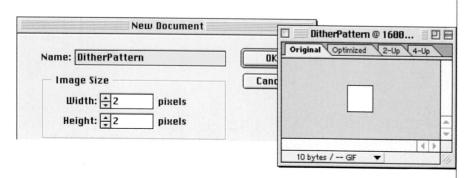

1. Open a new file. Set the image size to 2 pixels by 2 pixels. You will create a tiny 2-by-2 pattern. Zoom in to magnify the image to 1600%.

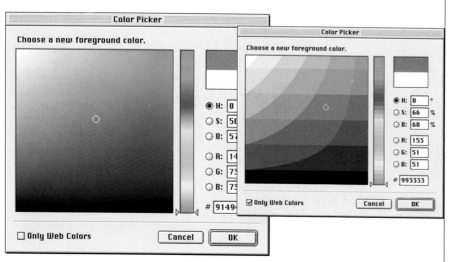

2. Click the foreground color swatch on the toolbox to open the Color Picker. Then turn off the Only Web Colors option and select the color you want to emulate.

    Then turn on the Only Web Colors option. The cursor moves to the center of one of the Web color areas. Take note of the direction that the cursor moved. Click OK to select this color.

3. Get the Pencil tool and select the smallest square brush from the Options bar (the very first brush—it is a 1-pixel brush). Use the Pencil to click once in the upper left and once in the lower right.

mix a Web-safe color: custom pattern

4. Go back to the Color Picker. The cursor will be in the same spot. Choose an adjacent color in the direction from which the cursor moved in step 2.

   Sometimes determining which color to choose is difficult. You can return to this step if the next step produces unsatisfactory results.

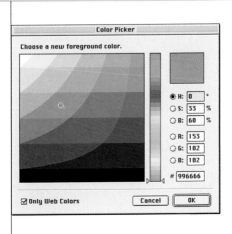

colormix.com

Check out this Web site for an easy-to-use interface that mixes Web-safe colors to emulate a non–Web-safe color of your choice.

5. Click OK to select the color and get the Pencil tool again. This time fill in the other two corners of the 2-by-2 pattern.

6. ***ImageReady:***
   Choose Edit>Define Pattern. The entire image, all 4 pixels, has been defined as a pattern. To fill any selection with it, use the Edit>Fill command, and choose Pattern from the Contents menu in the Fill dialog box. Click OK.

   Photoshop:
   Choose Edit>Define Pattern. Name the pattern, and click OK in the Name Pattern dialog box. The entire image, all 4 pixels, has been defined as a pattern. To fill a selection with it, use the Edit>Fill command. In the Fill dialog box, choose Pattern from the Contents menu, and then choose the new pattern from the menu of patterns. Click OK.

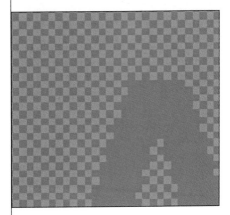

The pattern was used to fill the background of the image above. It helped to make a subtle two-tone effect when the type was made with one of the Web-safe colors that was used to make the pattern.

In the close-up (left), you can see the dither pattern fill and that only two colors are in the image.

Copy Color As HTML

This simple feature can come in handy when you want to match colors in an HTML document with a specific color in an image. It copies the hexa-decimal value of the color, the familiar triple-double, to the Clipboard so you can switch to an HTML editor and paste it into the code. It actually copies to the Clipboard more than just the value. After using this command in Photoshop, pasting in the editor produces the following: `COLOR="#AA0033"`. In ImageReady, it produces: `COLOR=#AA0033`.Be forewarned that it does not automatically snap the color to a Web-safe value. If you want a Web-safe color, you must make sure the color you are sampling is Web-safe first.

---

copy color as HTML: the eyedropper tool   *Photoshop*

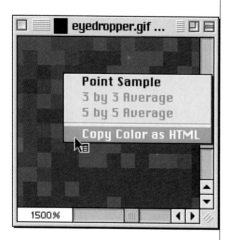

You can see what color will be copied by viewing the Info palette before executing the Copy command.

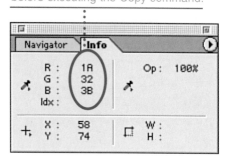

Set Eyedropper preferences on the Options bar. For this exercise, you would normally set it to Point Sample.

1. After selecting the Eyedropper tool, Control-click (Mac) or right-click (Windows) on the color in the image that you want to copy. This forces the contextual menu to appear. Scroll down and select Copy Color As HTML.

    When using the Eyedropper tool, the color selected depends on the tool's current setting. It can select a color from a single pixel, or "point," or average a 3x3 or 5x5 pixel area. The setting is changed in the Options bar. It is important to know because if you've zoomed in on the image and are trying to select the color from a single pixel and the Eyedropper is set to 5 by 5 Average, the selected color could be way off the mark. See page 29 of Chapter 2, "Preparing Photoshop and ImageReady for Web Work," for more information.

copy color as HTML: the eyedropper tool

1. Use the Eyedropper to select a color as the foreground color.

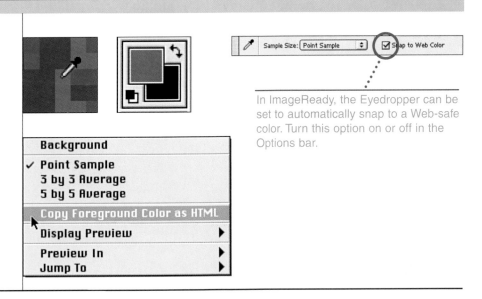

In ImageReady, the Eyedropper can be set to automatically snap to a Web-safe color. Turn this option on or off in the Options bar.

2. Then, Control-click (Mac) or right-click (Windows) the image to access the Eyedropper's contextual menu. Choose Copy Foreground Color As HTML.

copy color as HTML: the color palette

1. Choose Copy Color As HTML from the Color palette menu.

   This method copies the hexadecimal value of the color listed in the Color palette's sliders whether it is the foreground or background color.

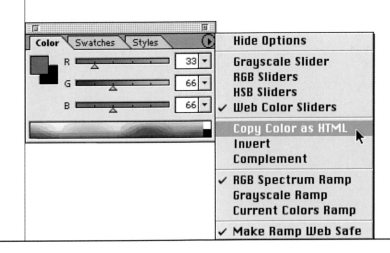

Color Correcting a Non–Web-Safe Image

Often, when creating graphics for Web pages, you will use a variety of applications to create them. Sometimes you'll use several applications to create one image. Photoshop might be used to just prepare the graphics for the Web. Unfortunately, as you bring graphics in and out of various programs, the colors can shift. But you can do a few things to correct this problem.

If the file in question is a photographic image to be saved as a JPEG, you generally do not need to worry about making it Web-safe. The user's browser will take care of presenting the image the best that it can. Let it do the work, and get on with making that spinning logo. But, if the image is a GIF, you're at the right place. In this exercise, I use ImageReady to transform a non-Web-safe image into a Web-safe image. This exercise uses the Color Table. Make sure that the Optimize, Color, and Color Table palettes are visible. You can open them via the Window menu.

color correct a non–Web-safe image

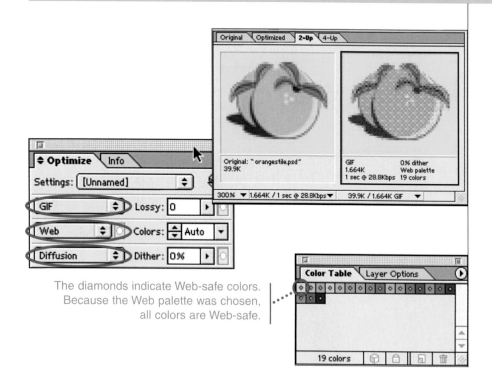

The diamonds indicate Web-safe colors. Because the Web palette was chosen, all colors are Web-safe.

1. Open the file in ImageReady.

2. Click the 2-Up tab above the image. Then, choose GIF, Web as the color palette, and Diffusion as the Dither method on the Optimize palette.

   What you see on the right is what this image looks like on an 8-bit system. Technically speaking, the image would now be Web-safe if you saved it with the current Optimize settings, but it has unwanted dither. To get rid of the dithering, the original colors must be shifted to Web-safe colors. Note: ImageReady chose 19 selected for this image's Color Table.

color correct a non–Web-safe image

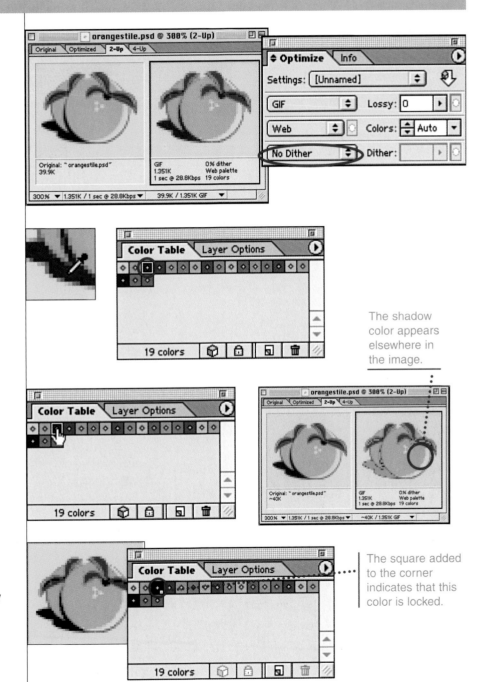

3. If you want ImageReady to select the Web-safe colors nearest to the original colors then simply select No Dither in the Optimize palette. If you like the results, skip to step 10 to save the Optimized image.

   Compare the two images to judge how the color changes.

4. If you want to change a particular color in the image, use the Eyedropper to select the color from the image. I'm going to turn the shadow color to black.

   When you do this, that color is highlighted in the Color Table.

   The shadow color appears elsewhere in the image.

5. Before changing this color, you should check to see where else it appears in the image. Click and hold that color in the Color Table. It will invert the color in the image preview.

6. To replace the color, double-click the highlighted color in the Color Table palette to open the Color Picker. Choose a new Web-safe color, and click OK. The new color replaces the old throughout the image.

   Notice there are still only 19 colors in the Color Table.

   The square added to the corner indicates that this color is locked.

color correct a non–Web-safe image

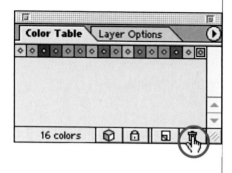

7. Some of the colors in the Color Table are present only in a few pixels. Choose Sort by Popularity from the Color Table menu to move these colors to the end of the list.

8. To delete these colors, select them and click the Trash icon.

Selective and Permanent Changes

Changing a color in the Color Table changes it everywhere it appears in the image. But, sometimes, it is necessary to change a color in only a specific area. For example, reducing the colors in the Color Table might have caused two similar color areas to use the same color from the Table. To differentiate them, you can edit the original image, and then make sure that the Color Table contains all the colors it needs. In the example below, a color in the original image was changed to get rid of the dithering in the optimized version.

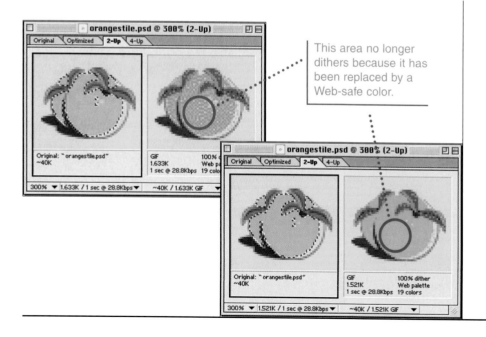

This area no longer dithers because it has been replaced by a Web-safe color.

9. To change colors in the original image, click in the Original image tab and select the color area to change (I used the Magic Wand), choose a Web-safe color to replace it, and then fill the selection. You could even choose the new Web-safe color from the existing Color Table.

   The Optimize preview changes automatically. Note that Dithering was set to 100% Diffusion in this example.

10. Choose Save Optimized to save the corrected image.

More About Working with Color

The Color Picker

The Color Picker provides the largest preview of color and can display color choices in many ways. Color is displayed according to the option chosen from the radio buttons. In the example to the right, the G is chosen and the vertical slide controls the amount of green in the color. The larger area displays all the available colors that contain as much green.

The Color Table

This is a register for all the colors present in a GIF or PNG-8 image.

Web-Safe Color
indicated by the diamond in the center of the swatch.

Current Color
indicated by the white highlight box.

Locked Color
indicated by the small square in the lower-right corner.

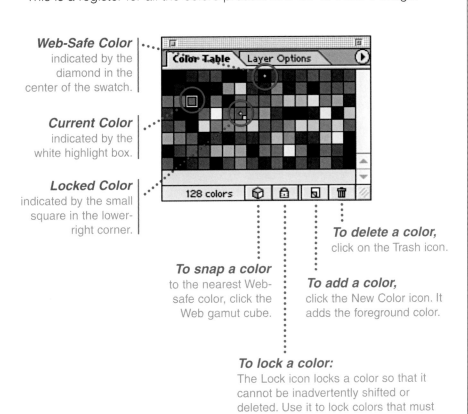

To delete a color,
click on the Trash icon.

To snap a color
to the nearest Web-safe color, click the Web gamut cube.

To add a color,
click the New Color icon. It adds the foreground color.

To lock a color:
The Lock icon locks a color so that it cannot be inadvertently shifted or deleted. Use it to lock colors that must be kept in the image.

ImageReady's Color Picker

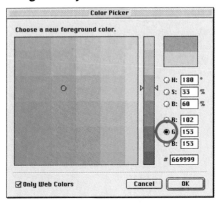

Photoshop's Color Picker
has all the same options as ImageReady's, plus more for choosing non–Web-safe colors.

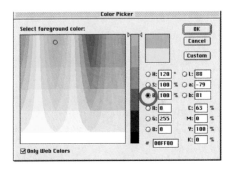

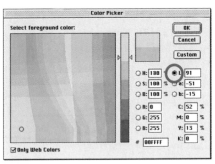

Previewing Browser Color Effects

While working on images and adjusting color, sometimes it's convenient to check how the images will look after they're on the Web and on someone else's computer. Two features give you valuable foresight.

preview browser dither

The same image with and without ImageReady's Browser Dither preview turned on. This option emulates how the image will appear on a display limited to 256 colors.

Original: "DSCN0547-crop.psd" ~230K

JPEG 60 quality
10.01K
4 sec @ 28.8Kbps

ImageReady

While in one of the Optimized views, choose View>Preview>Browser Dither.

Photoshop

While in the Save for Web dialog box, choose Browser Dither from the arrow menu at the top of the dialog box.

preview Windows/Mac OS color differences

While working on a Mac, the image on the right is viewed as it will appear on a standard Windows machine. The main difference is its relative darkness.

Original: "DSCN0547-crop.psd" ~230K

JPEG 60 quality
10.01K
4 sec @ 28.8Kbps

ImageReady

While in one of the Optimized views, choose View>Preview> Standard Macintosh Color or Standard Windows Color.

Photoshop

Choose View>Proof Setup> Macintosh RGB or Windows RGB, or . . .

While in the Save for Web dialog box, choose options from the arrow menu at the top of the dialog box.

Previewing and Correcting Gamma

As discussed on page 79 of this chapter, gamma refers to the relative lightness or darkness of the middle, or gray values, of an image or monitor. Because Mac OS and Windows use different gamma defaults, ImageReady has a built in feature that automatically adjusts the image's gray values. This is especially useful if you're working on a Mac and know that your audience will mostly consist of Windows users. It's quick and easy to use and can be a useful part of an action to adjust a batch of images. Here's how to use it.

---

adjust the gamma of an image   *ImageReady only*

With any image open, choose Image>Adjust>Gamma. In the Gamma dialog box, use the slider to select an image or choose one of the preset options: Windows to Macintosh or Macintosh to Windows.

The original image as it looked on a Mac (and as it will look on a Windows machine if the gamma is adjusted [lightened] by the Macintosh to Windows command).

The image after it was lightened by the Gamma feature.

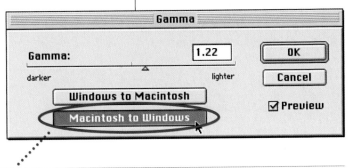

Choosing Macintosh to Windows lightens an image so that when it is viewed on a Windows machine, which displays images darker by default, it will look like it did on a Mac before this adjustment was made.

Using Color Tables

Sometimes when building a design for a Web page, you will develop a color scheme you want to maintain throughout a set of graphics—navigation buttons, for example. In these cases, you can build a Color Table and force all the images to use only colors from this table. The Color Table can be the Color Table from a single image or one built from colors selected from several images. Colors can be deleted, added, and changed. Jump back to page 91 for a quick reference on working with the Color Table palette. This exercise was done in ImageReady, but can also be accomplished in Photoshop's Save for Web dialog box.

---

build a color table   *ImageReady*

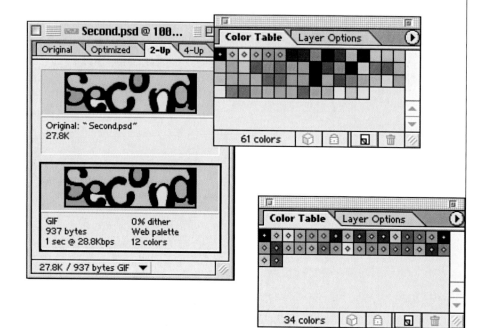

1. Let's say these three images represent a set of images. You can open one, generate a Color Table, refine it, save it, and force it on the others. Open one of the images in ImageReady.

2. Click the 2-Up tab so you can keep track of what's changing from the original image. Here is the original Color Table.

3. On the Optimize palette, change the palette setting to Web. This reduces the image to 34 Web-safe colors.

build a color table

4. On the Optimize palette, set the number of Colors to 12—a good number for this image that has 6 bold colors (plus 6 more in-between colors to keep the jagged edges away).

5. The image can now be saved as a GIF with this Color Table.

6. The Color Table can be saved separately for use with another image. To do this, choose Save Color Table from the Palette menu. The Color Table is saved as an ACT file (Adobe Color Table).

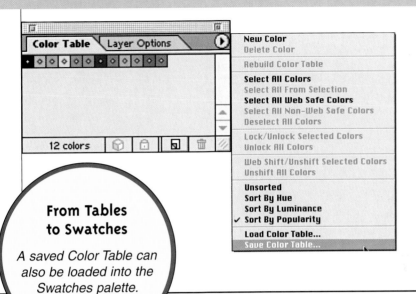

From Tables to Swatches

A saved Color Table can also be loaded into the Swatches palette.

apply a color table

1. After the Color Table has been saved, open another image. Click the 2-Up tab to view the optimized version alongside the original. Here it is with its original Color Table.

2. From the Color Table palette menu, choose Load Color Table and find the Color Table you saved. As soon as it opens, the 12 colors from the saved table appear in the Color Table and the optimized version of the image is adjusted to use only these 12 colors. Save the optimized image to accept the changes and save the Color Table with the image.

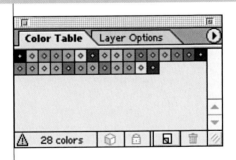

Any Color Table saved in the Optimized Colors folder in Photoshop's Presets folder shows up in the Optimize palette Color Reduction Algorithm menu.

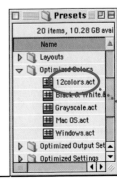

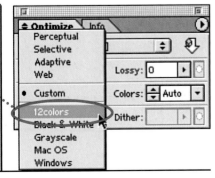

6

Name
Cetology.html
images
Cetology.
Cetolo
Export Origin
Revert
Save Optimized
Save Optimized
Output Settings
Update HTML.

Settings: Include GoLiv
HTML
Formatting
Tags Case: BODY
Indent: Tabs

Saving Files for the Web

Saving files for the Web can be more complicated than just saving images. If you've sliced the image, or included rollover effects, image maps, or background images, you'll also need an HTML file that contains the code to ensure that these features work in a Web browser. ImageReady and Photoshop can create this HTML file, and this chapter shows you how to work with it. The following chapter shows you how to deal with the images.

What's Different About Saving Files for the Web?

There are two things special about saving files for the Web with Photoshop and ImageReady. The first is that graphic files must be saved in formats that are supported by common Web browsers. The second is the HTML file that can be saved along with the images.

Is the HTML File Necessary?

When you slice an image in Photoshop or ImageReady (see the "Slice" chapter, page 192), a common part of working with Web graphics, the image is literally cut into several graphic files. In order to reassemble the images so they look the same in a browser as they do in Photoshop, an HTML table must be produced. ImageReady and Photoshop can do this. So, any time you use the Slice tool to segment an image, the HTML code will be very useful and saves you the painstaking effort of manually reconstructing the individual images into a table. The HTML file can also contain the necessary code for other browser effects, such as rollovers, image maps, and background images.

ImageReady HTML

```
        <IMG SRC="images/spacer.gif" WIDTH=1 HEIGHT=67></TD>
    </TR>
    <TR>
        <TD COLSPAN=5 ROWSPAN=2>
            <A HREF="#"
                ONMOUSEOVER="changeImages('Cetology_02', 'images/Cetology_02-Cetology_06_ove.g
'Cetology_12', 'images/Cetology_12.gif', 'Cetology_13', 'images/Cetology_13.gif'); return true;
                ONMOUSEOUT="changeImages('Cetology_02', 'images/Cetology_02.gif', 'Cetology_04
                ONCLICK="changeImages('Cetology_04', 'images/Cetology_04-Cetology_06_cli.gif',
                    <IMG NAME="Cetology_06" SRC="images/Cetology_06.gif" WIDTH=115 HEIGHT=20 BORDER
        <TD>
            <IMG SRC="images/spacer.gif" WIDTH=1 HEIGHT=13></TD>
    </TR>
    <TR>
        <TD ROWSPAN=4>
            <IMG NAME="Cetology_07" SRC="images/Cetology_07.gif" WIDTH=139 HEIGHT=107></TD>
        <TD>
            <IMG SRC="images/spacer.gif" WIDTH=1 HEIGHT=7></TD>
    </TR>
    <TR>
        <TD COLSPAN=2>
            <IMG SRC="images/Cetology_08.gif" WIDTH=39 HEIGHT=20></TD>
        <TD COLSPAN=2>
            <A HREF="#"
                ONMOUSEOVER="changeImages('Cetology_02', 'images/Cetology_02.gif', 'Cetology_04
'Cetology_12', 'images/Cetology_12.gif', 'Cetology_13', 'images/Cetology_13.gif'); return true;
                ONMOUSEOUT="changeImages('Cetology_04', 'images/Cetology_04.gif', 'Cetology_07
                ONCLICK="changeImages('Cetology_07', 'images/Cetology_07-Cetology_09_cli.gif');
                    <IMG NAME="Cetology_09" SRC="images/Cetology_09.gif" WIDTH=39 HEIGHT=20 BORDER=
        <TD>
            <IMG NAME="Cetology_10" SRC="images/Cetology_10.gif" WIDTH=37 HEIGHT=20></TD>
        <TD>
            <IMG SRC="images/spacer.gif" WIDTH=1 HEIGHT=20></TD>
    </TR>
    <TR>
        <TD>
            <IMG SRC="images/Cetology_11.gif" WIDTH=21 HEIGHT=18></TD>
        <TD COLSPAN=2>
            <A HREF="#"
```

Although Photoshop and ImageReady can generate an HTML file for any image, it is not always necessary to produce the file. If you're simply saving a single image that has not been sliced and has no other effects attached to it, the BODY section of the HTML file is only going to contain a command to insert that image on a page. It would be easier to just import the image into the HTML editor, or code the image tag yourself, than to use the Photoshop HTML file.

What's in the HTML File?

The HTML files that these applications produce are complete and ready for use in any standard Web browser, and include both the HEAD and BODY sections. This means they contain more than just pointers to images. The HEAD section includes the title (this appears in the title bar of the browser window), which is taken from the name of the ImageReady or Photoshop file, and the necessary JavaScript for any rollover effects. The BODY section includes a table for arranging sliced images; image map information; information about the page's background (a color or a tiled image); and more commands for handling rollover effects. Additional HTML tags and attributes that you can specify, as discussed in the "Slices" chapter (page 192), can also be included in the code.

Comment lines, indicated by an exclamation mark, are embedded in the HTML file to indicate that it was produced by ImageReady.

```
</HEAD>
<BODY BGCOLOR=#FFFFFF ONLOAD="preloadImages();">
<p> <!-- ImageReady Slices (Cetology.psd - Slices: 06, 09, 12) -->
<TABLE WIDTH=115 BORDER=0 CELLPADDING=0 CELLSPACING=0>
<TR>
```

ImageReady and Photoshop create a single HTML file for each complete Photoshop file, and they are capable of including only one HTML table per HTML file. Because Web pages are often composed of more than one table, and pages that use frames are composed of two or more HTML documents, ImageReady and Photoshop can't compose all types of Web page designs. Those designs must be composed in an HTML editor. You can, however, use an HTML editor to paste together the code from several Photoshop or ImageReady HTML files.

Finally, comment lines are inserted in the HTML code to indicate exactly where the ImageReady table coding begins and ends (see the figure above). They are helpful when cutting and pasting the HTML into another HTML file— and necessary for using the Update HTML command (page 107).

The Saved Files

When saving both the HTML file and the images, the HTML file is saved in the folder you select, and the image files are saved in a folder named, surprise, images (you can change this name). If you name slices in the Slice palette, ImageReady uses those names for the slice filenames. Otherwise, it uses an adjustable automatic naming system. This is discussed on pages 102 and 103.

The HTML file and the images saved in the images folder.

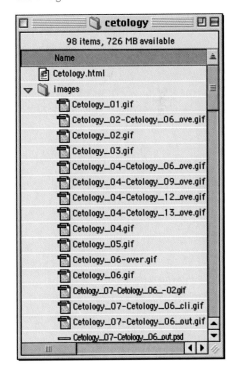

Save and Save Optimized

There are two save options in Photoshop and ImageReady. They reflect the two stages of creating images for the Web: image creation and image optimization. In the first stage, use the standard Save command to save PSD (Photoshop Document) files of all your original graphics files. This format preserves all the document information, including layers and any special Web effects. (In ImageReady, PSD is the only non–Web file format choice.)

For the second stage, producing the actual files that will be uploaded to the server and downloaded into browsers, use Photoshop's Save for Web command, or ImageReady's Save Optimized (As) command. These commands save the images according to selected optimize settings, and create an HTML file (if you choose to) according to selected Output Settings.

> **Saving a Background?**
>
> *Saving a Background image is discussed in Chapter 10, "Backgrounds," page 170.*

Photoshop or ImageReady?

Both applications have the capability to save images in Web formats and produce HTML files that can control tables. However, when saving anything other than a single image, ImageReady has much better saving and optimizing features. ImageReady is built for integrating optimization into the general interface—it's all taken care of on floating palettes.

In Photoshop, Web issues, other than defining slices, are not dealt with until saving the file. To save optimized files, you can simply use the standard Save command and choose a Web format, but this is not generally recommended because you could save over the original. Use the File>Save for Web command, which compresses most of ImageReady's optimizing features into one dialog box.

> **A LITTLE HTML**
>
> *Both ImageReady and Photoshop have a Copy Color As HTML command that saves the HTML code for indicating color to the Clipboard. It could be useful to grab a color, and then jump over to an HTML editor and paste it in. In ImageReady, for the color black, this feature would produce the following code:*
>
> ```
> COLOR=#000000
> ```
>
> *See page 86 of the "Web Color" chapter for information on how to use this feature.*

Save Preferences: Output Settings

The Optimize palette in ImageReady and the Save for Web dialog box in Photoshop are where you set compression settings for images. The Output Settings dialog box, accessible in Photoshop and ImageReady is where you control the HTML file. In ImageReady, access it from the File menu or in the Save Optimized (As) dialog box. In Photoshop, access it from the Save for Web dialog box. This is where you can control what the generated HTML file contains, as well as set its formatting options. There are four subdivisions of the Output Settings set: HTML, Background, Saving Files, and Slices.

HTML

These options control the formatting of the HTML document.

Formatting:

Tags Case, Attribs Case, and Indent format the style of the HTML text, but do not affect its function. Choose the appropriate Line Ending option for your platform: Mac, Win or Unix. If your files are destined for a Unix or Linux web server, as most are, it's best to choose Unix.

Choose one of the four subdivsions of the Output Settings dialog box here.

Coding:

Leave the Include Comments checked to place comments that indicate the beginning and end of the ImageReady code inside the HTML file. This is necessary if you're going to use the Update HTML command (page 107). Check the Include GoLive Code box if you intend to implement the HTML into GoLive. This ensures that all features are fully editable. Note: It is not necessary to save the HTML file when working with GoLive. A PSD is directly importable into GoLive.

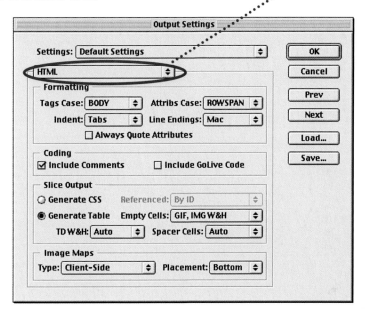

The default HTML Output Settings.

Slice Output:

Generate Table is the standard method of arranging and aligning slices. However, you can choose the Cascading Style Sheet alternative. The Empty Cells setting determines how No Image slices (page 201) are handled. The two GIF options produce a spacer.gif file—a one-pixel transparent GIF that is stretched by the HTML code to fill the empty table cell. It is placed in the same folder as the rest of the images. When Spacer Cells is set to Auto, the default and recommended setting, code is included that helps hold the table together.

Image Maps:

Client-Side image maps are those in which the area for the image map is defined within the HTML document. ImageReady includes the code in the HTML if you choose this option—the most typical and default method of producing image maps. The Placement option lets you set where in the HTML ImageReady will include the image map information. Bottom is the default.

Use these options to set how the current document is previewed.

Choose a background image here.

Click the arrow to access a menu of color options.

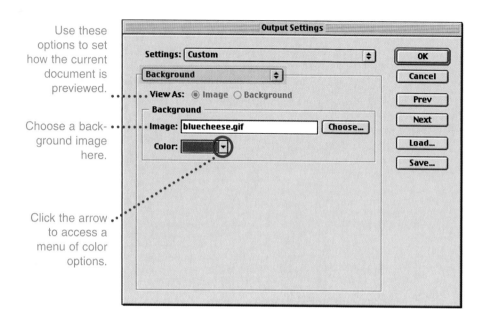

Background

Here you can designate a Web-ready image to be used as the tiled background image for the current HTML document Or, you can select a color to be used. It is a good idea to designate a color even if your design will be completely covered by images. The color will load more quickly, and, along with any text, set the tone for the coming images. See the "Backgrounds" chapter for more (page 170).

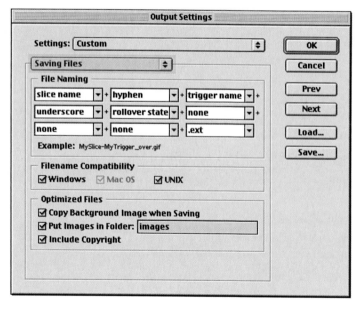

Saving Files

File Naming:
This is an automatic naming system for the images produced by slices and rollover effects.

Filename Compatibility:
Turn on all options for best compatibility.

Optimized Files:
The Copy Background Image When Saving includes a copy of the background image, selected in Background section, into the images folder, no matter where it is currently stored. The second option enables you to name the folder in which the images are saved. Keep in mind that the name of this folder becomes part of the pathname for the images in the resulting HTML file.

Slices

This is an automatic system for naming slices similar to the File Naming section in the Saving Files subdivision discussed on the previous page. The options here determine what goes in the "slice name" slot in that section. The Example displays a preview of a filename produced by the current settings.

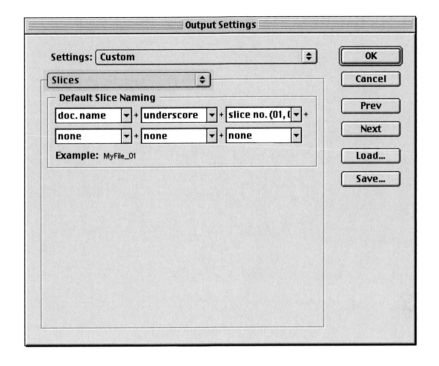

Saving the Images and Files

When the designing and optimizing are complete and you're ready to save files for Web use, what do you do? In Photoshop, you use the Save for Web dialog box. In ImageReady, you use Save Optimized (As) dialog box, where you have some saving options. Note that in Photoshop, the Save for Web dialog box is also where you optimize images. Optimizing is discussed in the next chapter, "Optimizing Graphics," page 110.

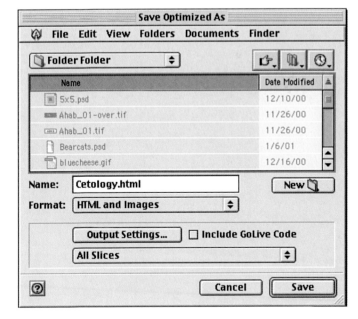

From the Format menu, you can choose to save images, an HTML file, or both. From the pop-up menu at the bottom, you also have the option of saving images and/or an HTML file for only the slices currently selected. If you do this, the HTML table produced will include all slices that are necessary to maintain the current spacing of the selected slices. This can mean that spacer.gifs (or Empty Cells) are used to fill in what would have been empty spaces between selected slices.

save a file

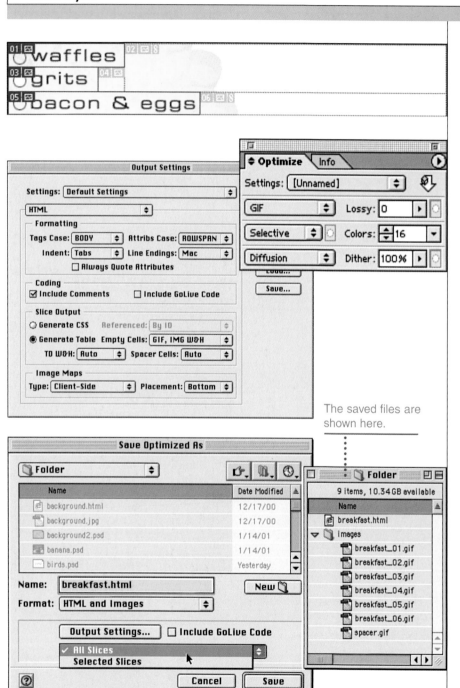

The saved files are shown here.

1. Open or create a file in ImageReady or Photoshop.

2. If you're working in ImageReady, set optimize options first. Then, you can either choose to set the Output Settings from the File menu, or choose File>Save Optimized As and access them there.

   In Photoshop, choose Save for Web, set optimize settings, and click OK. The Output Settings are available in both the Save for Web dialog box and the Save Optimized As box that opens when you click OK. It does not matter where you set these options. If you're going to save only selected slices then select them here with the Slice Select tool and the Shift key.

   Choose options as discussed in the previous pages.

3. In the Save Optimized As box, choose options for which files and which slices to save. Name the file, and click OK, and you're done. Remember that the name of the file shows up in the slice names. Do not include spaces in the filename. The only acceptable punctuation marks are the hyphen, underscore, and period.

Getting the HTML Code into an Editor

After you've designed the page, optimized all the images, and saved the files and HTML, what do you do with all of it? Typically, the HTML ImageReady writes will not take care of all your needs. Also, you might select only a portion of the code to use. Or, the code will be only a portion of the complete page design. This would be true if you, for example, designed a navigation bar for a page in ImageReady. Normally, the next step is to open the HTML file in an editor.

If you're working in an editor, you can just open the HTML file that ImageReady saved directly. There it will behave as any other file within that program and you can edit it as such.

You can either add the other elements to this document or copy the code and paste the desired portions into another file that contains the other page elements. If you do copy the code from one file to another, make sure you get everything you need. This means gettings all the table coding necessary to maintain its structure. ImageReady HTML tables begin with a comment line that looks like this:

Using GoLive?

If you use GoLive, or plan to, to build your Web pages, see page 109.

```
<!-- ImageReady Slices (Cetology.psd) -->
```

The filename in parentheses indicates the ImageReady/Photoshop file from which the HTML was created. The table ends with a similar line:

```
<!-- End ImageReady Slices -->
```

When copying code to paste into another document, keep these comment lines. They enable you to use the Update HTML command if needed, even in a document not initially created by ImageReady. Copy everything between these lines to get the entire table.

If you have rollover effects, you should also copy the JavaScript that is contained in the HEAD section. This code also begins and ends with comment lines that indicate it. Paste this code into the HEAD section of the final HTML document. You must also copy the ONLOAD statement from the BODY tag of the original document and place it in the BODY tag of the final document. The ONLOAD statement is typically: ONLOAD="preloadImages();". These steps are necessary for the rollovers to work properly.

Copying HTML

ImageReady enables you to quickly export HTML code without saving a file. This feature copies to the Clipboard the HTML either for the whole image or just for selected slices. This could come in handy if you're jumping back and forth between ImageReady and an HTML editor. The code that is copied (to the Clipboard) does not contain the HEAD code, it contains only the code that pertains to the images—it produces code for an HTML table. The HTML is formatted according to the Output Settings discussed previously.

copy HTML *ImageReady only*

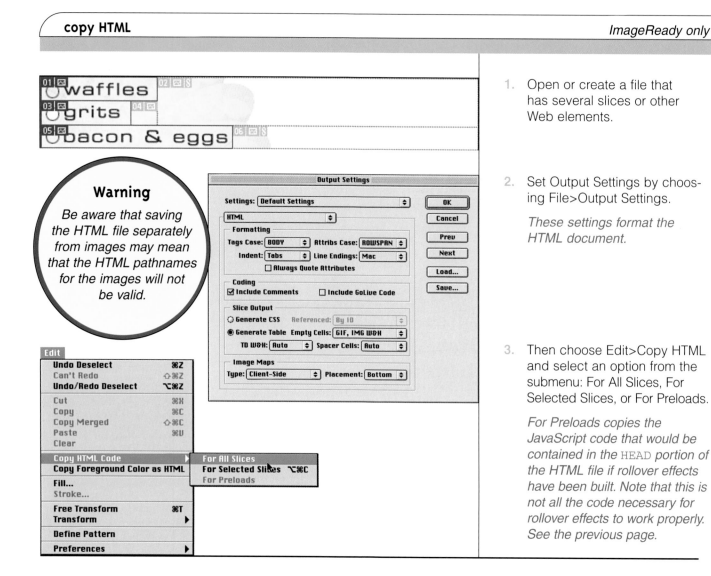

1. Open or create a file that has several slices or other Web elements.

2. Set Output Settings by choosing File>Output Settings.

   These settings format the HTML document.

3. Then choose Edit>Copy HTML and select an option from the submenu: For All Slices, For Selected Slices, or For Preloads.

   For Preloads copies the JavaScript code that would be contained in the HEAD portion of the HTML file if rollover effects have been built. Note that this is not all the code necessary for rollover effects to work properly. See the previous page.

Updating HTML

ImageReady offers a way to update its own HTML that has been pasted into another HTML file. If you've saved an HTML file with a set of graphics and pasted the HTML into another HTML document that you built in an editor and you want to update just the HTML section that handles the images that came from ImageReady to reflect changes that you made in the ImageReady document then use this feature as an automatic quick fix. In order for this feature to work, the comment lines inserted by ImageReady must be left in the HTML file (see page 105). Otherwise, ImageReady will not know what to replace and you will get an error message that says: No Tables Replaced.

---

update HTML   *ImageReady only*

---

1. Open an ImageReady file that has been optimized and saved as an HTML document.

2. Make adjustments to the slices and image as necessary and save the file.

   I turned these slices into Layer Based slices.

3. Choose File>Update HTML and find the HTML file in which the ImageReady HTML code was previously pasted. Click Open.

   If you chose to save images with the update (I recommend you do to ensure that all changes are reflected in the new document) then a prompt will ask you to confirm which images you want to replace. As a default, they are all selected. Click OK to update the files.

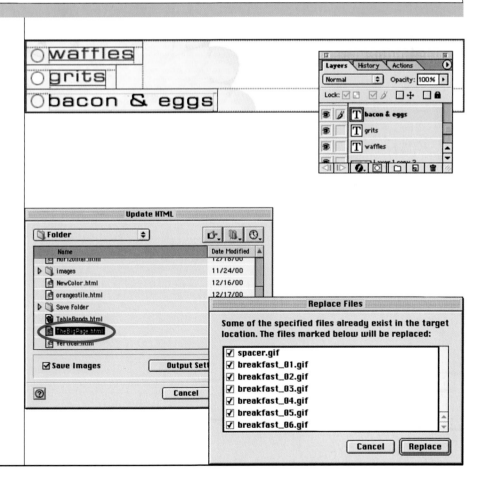

The Export Original Command

If you want to save a flattened copy of an image or page design, you can do this with ImageReady's Export Original command. Use this feature when you need to share the file with someone else, for viewing purposes only, or when you just want to save an image that could be placed in a document for printing. It is the only way for ImageReady to save a file in any format other than PSDs and Web-ready formats. Because the image is being flattened, all extra information, such as slices and rollovers, is removed.

export original

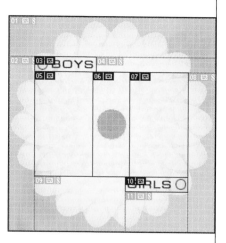

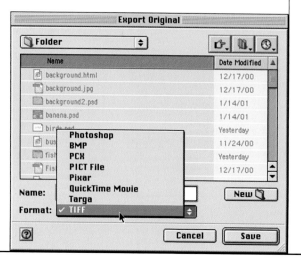

1. Open or create an ImageReady file.

2. Choose File>Export Original. From the Format menu, choose a file format.

    If this image will be printed, TIFF is generally your best option. If you choose TIFF, several compression methods are available. LZW is the standard lossless compression method for TIFFs.

    Click OK. It's now ready for importing or printing.

Saving Files for Adobe GoLive

Using Adobe GoLive to construct Web pages that include ImageReady and Photoshop files has its advantages. You can simply save a file from Photoshop or ImageReady as a PSD file, and import it directly into GoLive. All slices and rollover effects are editable from within GoLive. You don't even need to save an HTML file. But, if you do save an HTML file and you plan to use it in GoLive, you must choose the Include GoLive code option in the HTML section of the Output Settings dialog box to take advantage of full editability in GoLive. Including the GoLive code in a file that won't be used by GoLive does not bother other HTML editors, but it can produce a larger HTML file that includes unnecessary code. Check this option only if you plan to use its benefits.

After saving a PSD in Photoshop or ImageReady, open GoLive and choose File>Import>Photoshop As HTML. A Save for Web dialog box (almost identical to Photoshop's) opens for you to optimize each slice in the PSD. Afterward, the file is ready for use.

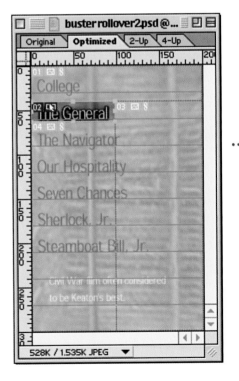

The ImageReady file (left) was opened in GoLive (right).

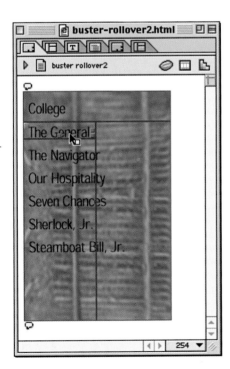

7

Optimizing Graphics

When images are saved for use on the Web, they must be saved in particular file formats. The choices are limited by support from the most popular browsers (Netscape Communicator and Microsoft Internet Explorer) and include GIFs, JPEGs, and PNGs, each of which has its advantages and disadvantages. This chapter gives you a basic understanding of these formats, helps you choose the correct one for the job, and shows you how to create them.

Optimizing Versus Saving

The only thing that makes an optimized image any different from any other image is the file format it is saved as. An *optimized* image is one that is saved in a Web format: GIF, JPEG or PNG. These formats, which have applications beyond their use as Web images, all utilize compression schemes to crunch images down to a minimum file size to speed its delivery over the Internet. When you create an image in Photoshop or ImageReady, you will save it in any of various formats—normally as a PSD (Photoshop's native format) because this format retains all parts of the file. When you prepare the file for the Web, you save a version of that file in a Web format. Think of optimizing a file as its last step on its way out to the Web. In conclusion, simply stated, an optimized image is a compressed version of the original.

Even though this chapter is about optimizing, I can't emphasize enough the need to save PSD versions of everything you create. If you need to alter the image after it has been optimized, open the PSD file, make necessary changes, and then optimize it again to create a new optimized version.

Color Ready?

To understand optimizing, you must understand color issues specific to the Web. Review Chapter 5, "Web Color," if necessary.

The Battle: Speed Versus Quality

So, what's the big fuss about optimizing? It's because good Web design should produce fast-loading pages that do not sacrifice visual appeal. Having said that, optimizing is all about sacrificing. The sacrifices vary depending on the format you use, but will either be in the clarity of the image or the number of colors it contains. But because the GIF, JPEG, and PNG compression schemes do such a good job, you can get a pretty good-looking image that is pretty small.

JPEG, quality: 100
13.89K, 6 sec.
download @ 28.8Kbps

JPEG, quality: 30
2.768K, 2 sec.
download @ 28.8Kbps

GIF, 16 colors
3.161K, 2 sec.
download @ 28.8Kbps

The battle between speed and quality is a never-ending concern because we seem to like to live on the edge of frustration—with information just fast enough to keep us interested without pulling out all our hair. How can you resist putting the latest gizmos on your site?

The Contenders

There are three standard Web formats: GIF, JPEG and PNG.

JPEG

JPEG is characterized mainly by its 24-bit color support (up to 16.7 million colors). The only way to reproduce the smooth continuous tones for which we love photographs is that the image contain many colors. Because JPEGs can contain such a wide range of colors, it is generally the best choice when optimizing photographs. And it can get these images very small.

When you save a JPEG, you set the degree to which it is compressed. The lower the setting (Quality), the smaller the file and the worse the image looks.

JPEG does not perform as well with very contrasty images. Often JPEGs look the worst at edges within the image, because these are the areas that contain the most contrast. The results of this effect are called artifacts. When you see them, you've probably compressed it with too low of a Quality setting.

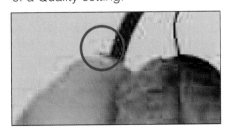

JPEG artifacts

GIF

A GIF image is characterized by its use of a Color Table. This table, which is an index of all the colors that exist in the image, is saved as part of the image data. Each pixel in the image is linked to one of the colors in the table. A GIF color table is limited to a maximum of 256 colors. Because one of the colors can be "transparent," GIF can support transparency. Finally, it is the only format that supports animation.

Generally, GIF is good at compressing graphics that contain solid areas of a single color. That is because that color can be stored once in the image's color table and called as many times as needed. The 256-color limit means there are not enough colors available to reproduce fine gradations, but is more than enough to contain all 216 Web-safe colors.

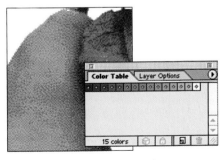

This GIF dithered because there are only 15 colors in its Color Table.

PNG

PNG is a relatively new file format, which means that it is not supported on older browsers and not yet in prominent use on the Web. Use this format only in situations in which you know that the browser used to view it supports PNGs.

There are actually two different types of PNGs. The PNG-8 format, which behaves similarly to a GIF (without animation support), and the PNG-24 format, which behaves similarly to a JPEG, but also supports multiple levels of transparency.

The PNG-24 format does not have varying degrees of compression as does the JPEG format, which means that it normally produces larger images.

 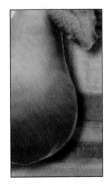

A PNG with a soft drop shadow and transparent areas can be placed on different backgrounds.

Choosing a Format

Which format do you use? The characteristics of the file formats make each suitable for particular types of images. In general, if the image has fine gradations and continuous tones, save it as a JPEG and if it has flat areas of color save it as a GIF. There are cases when the choice will become more difficult. Very small photographs, for example, generally compress better as GIFs. Also, although type is generally a good candidate for the GIF format, what if it has a soft drop shadow? How will you keep that smooth transition to the background? Make it a JPEG. Perhaps. Or, dither the shadow.

Images Suitable for GIF and PNG-8 File Formats

Vector graphics typical of illustration programs such as Adobe Illustrator and Macromedia FreeHand

Graphics that will have transparent areas

Type

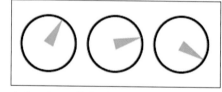

Animations (GIF only)

If You Want to Make a Smaller GIF:

- Use an image with large areas of flat color to best take advantage of GIF's compression method. This also will aid in creating a GIF with less dithering.

- Reduce the number of colors.

- Increase the lossy compression setting or eliminate it.

- Reduce the dithering amount.

- Make the image smaller.

Images Suitable for JPEG and PNG-24 File Formats

Photographic images

Type with a drop shadow (Also can work as a GIF. Try both.)

Graphics that contain multiple levels of transparency (PNG-24 only)

Graphics that contain smooth gradations

If You Want to Make a Smaller JPEG:

- Use an image, such as a photograph, in which the colors gradually grade from one to the other to best take advantage of JPEG's compression method. This also will create a better-looking JPEG with fewer artifacts—see page 122.

- Lower the Quality setting.

- Blur the image.

- Reduce the contrast in the image.

- Turn on the Optimize option.

- Make the image smaller.

WHO JPEG'D MY JPEG?

You shouldn't resave a JPEG as a JPEG. Always begin again from the original if possible. JPEGs resaved as JPEGs suffer further losses in image quality.

However, GIFs do not suffer any loss in quality when reoptimized. They are easy to work with in this manner. You can open a GIF, change a few colors in the Color Table, and resave it without worrying about image degradation. In Photoshop, GIFs are opened in Indexed color mode. If you want to make substantial changes to them, consider converting them to RGB mode (Image>Mode> RGB Color) first for better results. This conversion is also necessary to jump to, or open the file, in ImageReady.

Optimizing and Color

Any image is limited to displaying only the colors available on the monitor on which it is viewed no matter what color information is in the image. But, JPEGs and GIFs approach this color issue from very different perspectives.

A JPEG can contain color information for millions of colors, but if it's viewed on a monitor limited to 256 colors, the display system will compensate for the missing color by dithering colors to approximate the colors in the original image. With JPEGs, you take the chance that they dither on systems that can't display the color information they contain. However, you give the image the best chance of looking its best. It is true that the number of 8-bit monitors is decreasing, but thanks to the growing popularity of alternative Web-browsing–capable devices, such as PDAs, limited color displays will likely be a concern for some time to come.

A GIF, on the other hand, enables you to have precise control over its colors. Each color in the image is listed in its own Color Table which is viewable and editable. If it includes a color that is not in a display system's range, a GIF will dither as well. But, if you want to be certain of the colors in the image, you can include in the Color Table only Web-safe colors. These colors will not dither regardless of the browser or operating system. For more on dithering, Color Tables, and Web color, see Chapter 5, "Web Color," page 72.

Optimizing a Multiple Slice Image

When you save an image that has been divided into a number of slices, each slice must be optimized and saved as a separate graphic. Even if you don't select them and manually set the optimize settings, each slice still has its own optimize settings that it acquired when it was created. Often you will save a number of slices or all the slices of a document with the same settings. In these cases, you can select several slices at one time (using the Slice Select tool while pressing the Shift key) and optimize them at once. After selecting them, you also could link them (in ImageReady only: Slice>Link Slices). Thereafter, if you change the optimize settings for one slice in the set, the rest of the slices also will be changed. Even if you don't want the settings to be identical, you could still select them all, set general options such as file format, and then select each individually and fine-tune the settings—to vary the compression rates, for example.

Linking Saves Time

Linked slices share optimize settings. To link slices together, Shift-select several slices and choose Slices>Link. (ImageReady only)

Resizing an Image While Optimizing

Before getting to optimizing, here's a special feature in Photoshop that deals specifically with the size of optimized images. Getting things on the Web is not only about working with compression and color. Often, especially when dealing with a load of various-size photographs, you must fit an image into a space in a design—perhaps a particular table cell. If you use the Image>Image Size command then you change forever the image size of the original, but if you use the Image Size feature in the Photoshop Save for Web dialog box, only the optimized image is resized. To resize an original image in Photoshop to fit it inside particular dimensions, use the Fit Image command (File>Automate>Fit Image).

resize an image in Photoshop

1. Open an image and choose Save for Web. Click on the Image Size tab in the lower-right area of the dialog box.

2. Set the size.

   Turn on Constrain Proportions to make sure the image does not get distorted.

3. Click Apply to see the resized image and the new optimized sizes.

   Note: After you've made adjustments in this Image Size box, you cannot revert the optimized image to the original size without cancelling the Save for Web operation and returning to the normal image window. Jot down the original settings before making any changes.

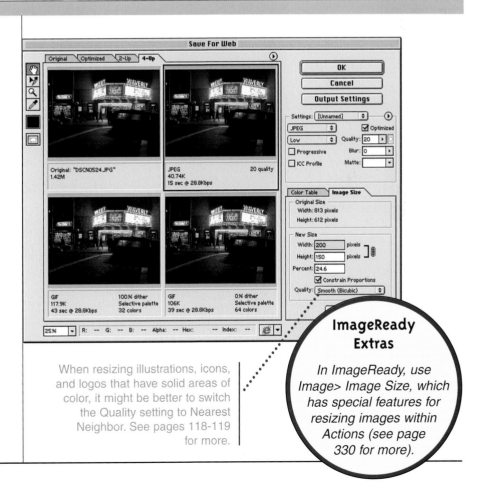

When resizing illustrations, icons, and logos that have solid areas of color, it might be better to switch the Quality setting to Nearest Neighbor. See pages 118-119 for more.

ImageReady Extras

In ImageReady, use Image> Image Size, which has special features for resizing images within Actions (see page 330 for more).

Optimizing Tools: ImageReady's Window and Palettes

The Image Window

changes depending on the display option chosen.

Original	The file without optimize settings applied
Optimized	The file with optimize settings applied
2-Up	Original and Optimized views side by side
4-Up	Original image plus three optimized views

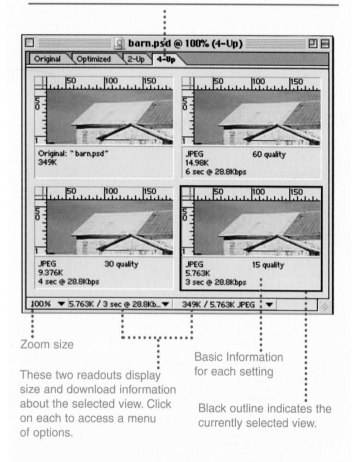

Zoom size

These two readouts display size and download information about the selected view. Click on each to access a menu of options.

Basic Information for each setting

Black outline indicates the currently selected view.

Browser Preview:

Don't forget to use ImageReady's browser preview features in the View>Preview submenu. These include browser dither and platform color gamuts.

The Optimize Palette

changes depending on the file format chosen. For the GIF format, it displays the options seen in Photoshop's Save for Web dialog box on the facing page.

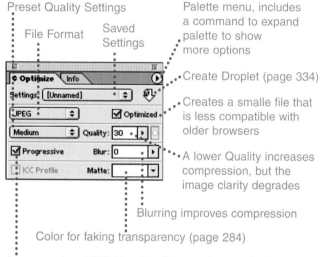

Preset Quality Settings

File Format

Saved Settings

Palette menu, includes a command to expand palette to show more options

Create Droplet (page 334)

Creates a smalle file that is less compatible with older browsers

A lower Quality increases compression, but the image clarity degrades

Blurring improves compression

Color for faking transparency (page 284)

A progressive JPEG "develops" from a low-resolution image to a high-resolution image in the browser.

The Color Table: GIF and PNG-8 only

displays all colors in a GIF or PNG-8 image. Open the palette menu to choose among several options for arranging the colors. Select a color to make the icons available.

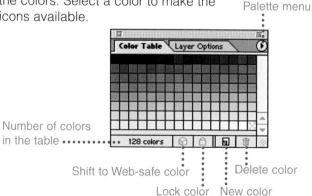

Palette menu

Number of colors in the table

Shift to Web-safe color

Delete color

Lock color   New color

Optimizing Tools: Photoshop's Save for Web Dialog Box

Slice Select tool and View Slices

See facing page about these options

Preview options, including browser dither, modem speed, and platform color gamut.

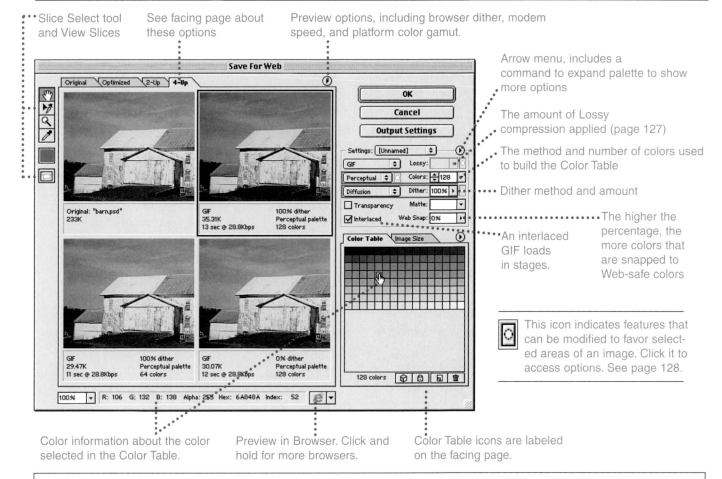

Arrow menu, includes a command to expand palette to show more options

The amount of Lossy compression applied (page 127)

The method and number of colors used to build the Color Table

Dither method and amount

An interlaced GIF loads in stages.

The higher the percentage, the more colors that are snapped to Web-safe colors

This icon indicates features that can be modified to favor selected areas of an image. Click it to access options. See page 128.

Color information about the color selected in the Color Table.

Preview in Browser. Click and hold for more browsers.

Color Table icons are labeled on the facing page.

Hidden in the Optimize Palette Menu:

Repopulate Views: In the 4-Up view, this command resets the optimize settings of the other two optimize views to variations of the currently selected view.

Optimize to File Size: Generates optimize settings based on a target file size (see page 130).

Hidden in the Color Table Palette Menu:

Regenerate Table: Regenerates the Color Table based on changed optimize settings.

Sort by Popularity: Lists colors in the Color Table in the order based on which are the most common in the image.

In Photoshop's Save for Web Dialog Box:

Remember/Reset: Hold the (Option) [Alt] key to access these buttons. **Remember** sets the current settings as the Remembered ones. **Reset** reverts optimize settings to the last Remembered setting.

optimize a photograph as a JPEG

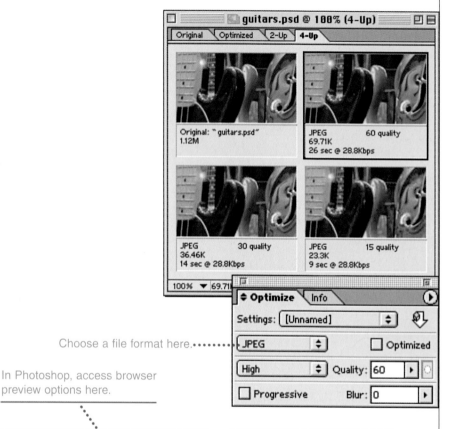

Choose a file format here.·········

In Photoshop, access browser preview options here.

On a Mac: The preview was changed to emulate browser dither and Windows gamma.

1. Open an image.

   Photoshop: Choose File>Save for Web.

   ImageReady: Click the 4-Up tab and make sure that the Optimize palette is open.

2. Choose JPEG as the file format.

   Photoshop: To the right of the image previews.

   ImageReady: Do this on the Optimize palette.

3. Before continuing, take a moment to adjust the display to emulate browser effects such as dither or varying color gamuts.

   Photoshop: Choose options from the pop-up menu at the top of the Save for Web box.

   ImageReady: Choose options from the View>Preview submenu.

   See page 92 for more on pre-viewing browser effects.

optimize a photograph as a JPEG

4. Set the Quality level.

Quality refers to the quality of the image. This is the primary setting for adjusting the compression. The lower the number, the smaller the file and the more the degradation of the image.

Your best tool for choosing a Quality setting is your eyes. Keep dragging the slider down until the image quality becomes intolerable. Generally speaking, you should be able stay in the under-50 range—except in cases where detail is very important.

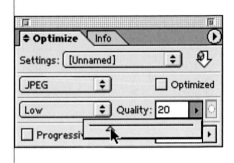

What Quality Setting Was Used?

After opening a JPEG in ImageReady, the Optimize palette shows the Quality setting that was used to save it.

REPOPULATE—NOW!

When using the 4-Up view and working with optimize settings in one of the quadrants, you can force the other quadrants to make variations of the settings you're working with. To do this, choose Repopulate Views from the Optimize palette menu (ImageReady) or the Optimize menu (Photoshop). For a JPEG, this means that the Quality is cut in half in one of the other views and cut in half again in the last view. This is a great way to get a quick look at your options.

5. Turn the Progressive option on or off.

A progressive JPEG is one that loads progressively in the browser. A low-resolution version loads that is successively replaced by higher-resolution versions until downloading and decompressing are complete. This can improve user experience because they get an idea of what's in an image before it decompresses completely.

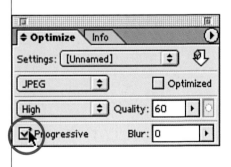

optimize a photograph as a JPEG

More Blurring

Instead of using the Blur slider to globally blur the image, consider selectively blurring areas of the image that are less important than others.

MACHINE-MADE ARTIFACTS

The nasty things about JPEG compression are artifacts. When you start to push the image quality too low, they become glaringly visible. They are most notable at the edges within the images.

That is where contrast is highest and because JPEG doesn"t handle contrast well, the artifacts really show up. Some subtle blurring could significantly reduce the artifacts. You also can see the blocks that are the result of the 8x8 JPEG compression scheme.

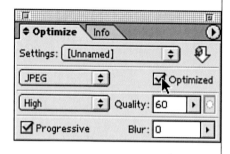

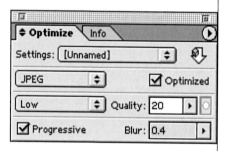

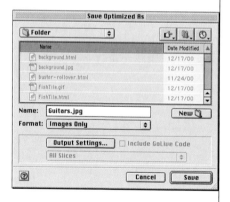

6. Check the Optimize box.

   Optimizing a JPEG takes advantage of better compression, but is not supported by older browsers. Unless you're concerned about old browsers, it's generally safe to use this option.

7. Set the Blur amount.

   Because JPEGs are good at compressing smooth tones, blurring an image reduces contrast and aids compression. You can usually get away with a little blur and still get a good image.

   Setting the blur to 0.4 reduces the file size of this image by more than 20%.

8. Click on one of the four images to select it and then save it.

   Make sure you select the correct one because only the selected view will be saved as an optimized version.

   Photoshop: Click OK.

   ImageReady: Choose File>Save Optimized.

   If in Photoshop, or ImageReady's Save Optimized As dialog box, name the file and click OK. To learn more about the options in this dialog box, see Chapter 6, "Saving Files for the Web," page 96.

Selective Compression Techniques: JPEG

Often an image contains areas that are more crucial than others. In these cases, you can influence which areas receive more compression than others. This is done by creating an alpha channel with areas of varying lightness and darkness that is used to modify the JPEG quality setting.

Photoshop Channels

For finer work, use Photoshop to create the channel. It has better tools for creating graded areas and for working with channels.

use selective JPEG compression

1. Make a selection around the most important areas in the image. This selection will become the alpha channel.

   Normally, there is a clear division in an image between the important and unimportant areas. If so, the Lasso tool provides an easy way to make this selection. See page 128 for another technique.

2. Choose Select>Save Selection, to name and save the channel.

3. Click the icon to the right of the Quality setting in Photoshop's Save for Web dialog box or on ImageReady's Optimize palette. In the dialog box, choose the channel just saved. Then, use the sliders to adjust the Maximum and Miinimum Quality settings.

   The white slider sets the Quality level for the areas within the completely white part of the alpha channel. The black slider works for the black areas. After you've made this adjustment, the Quality value on the Optimize palette operates as the Maximum setting. Adjust it to adjust the Maximum setting.

THE ALPHA CHANNEL

This channel acts as a map of the varying amounts of compression that will be applied to the image. The amount of compression depends on the values in the channel. Black areas represent the areas of the image that are compressed the most; white areas the least; and gray areas vary according to their relative lightness and darkness..

A representation of the white and black areas of the selected channel created in step 1.

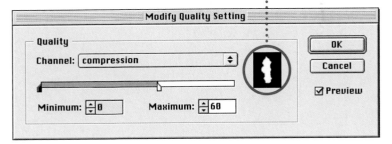

Notes:

This technique works best with larger images. With smaller images, this technique can even increase the file size. Blurring the unselected areas might be a better option.

To cancel the selective compression, open the Modify Quality Setting dialog box again and choose None from the Channel menu.

optimize a graphic as a GIF

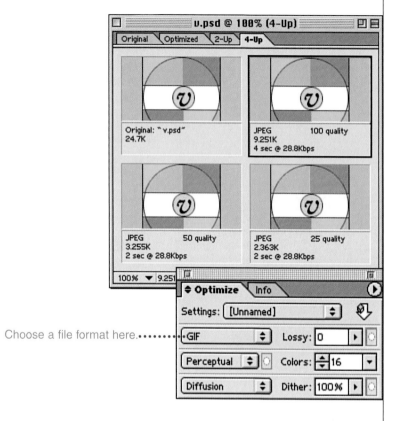

Choose a file format here.········

Turning on the preview Browser dither option reveals that this green is not a Web-safe color and will dither in a browser on an 8-bit display.

1. Open an image.

   Photoshop: Choose File>Save for Web.

   ImageReady: Click the 4-Up tab and make sure that the Optimize and Color Table palettes are open.

2. Choose GIF as the file format.

   Photoshop: To the right of the image previews.

   ImageReady: Do this on the Optimize palette.

3. Before continuing, take a moment to adjust the display to emulate browser effects such as dither or varying color gamuts.

   Photoshop: Choose options from the pop-up menu at the top of the Save for Web box.

   ImageReady: Choose options from the View> Preview submenu.

   See page 92 for more on pre-viewing browser effects.

optimize a graphic as a GIF

4. Choose a Color Reduction Algorithm.

   All GIFs are limited to a maximum of 256 colors. The algorithm is the method used to determine which colors will end up in the Color Table. The Color Table is editable, but these algorithms normally do a great job. The four standard choices are defined in the sidebar.

   Use the definitions in the sidebar as a guide. Try them all and use the one that looks best.

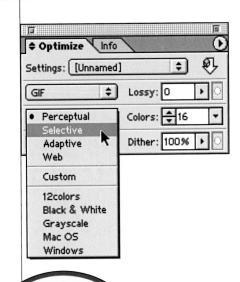

Color Table News

The steps on this page generate the GIF Color Table, but this table is completely editable. See page 91 for more about working with the Color Table.

5. Set the number of colors.

   Reducing the number of colors in a GIF reduces its size. Try to squeeze down the number of colors as far as you can. As you reduce the number, the selected color algorithm is used to generate a new color table.

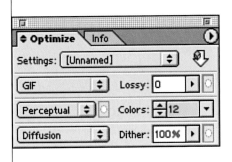

COLOR REDUCTION ALGORITHMS

This Photoshop manual defines the color algorithms as follows:

> **Perceptual:** Gives priority to colors for which the human eye has greatest sensitivity.

> **Selective:** Similar to the Perceptual, but favors broad areas of color and the preservation of Web colors.

> **Adaptive:** Samples colors from the spectrum appearing most commonly in the image.

> **Web:** Limits the colors to the 216 Web-safe colors.

The manual also states that the Selective method "usually produces images with the greatest color integrity."

optimize a graphic as a GIF

DITHER DATHER

Dither methods affect the look of the image. Here are the four options:

No Dither: *Colors can shift, sometimes drastically, but remain solid.*

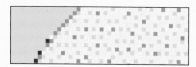

Diffusion: *The random spray of pixels pleasantly softens the image.*

Pattern: *The patterning seems to flatten the image because of its regularity.*

Noise: *Looks like noise has been applied to the image.*

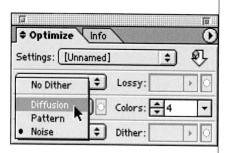

6.   Choose a Dither Algorithm.

If you limit the number of colors so that some colors in the image are not in the Color Table, these colors either will be shifted to the closest equivalent in the Color Table (if you choose No Dither) or will be dithered to approximate the color (if you choose Diffusion, Pattern, or Noise).

This setting is all about appearance. Choose the option that looks best with the particular image.

7.   Set the Dither amount.

If you use Diffusion dithering, you can set the amount of dithering. Colors not dithered will be shifted.

Dither methods and degrees are more noticeable in photographs. This image is for illustration only. The left image was set to 100% dither, and the right image was set to 50% dither.

optimize a graphic as a GIF

8. Choose a Lossy setting.

   This feature adds dither to the image and can drastically reduce its file size. The higher the setting, the smaller the file and the worse the image will look.

   A lossy GIF is still a GIF. No difference in file format exists between one that uses this lossy feature and one that doesn't.

9. Choose a Web Snap setting. In ImageReady, you might need to choose Show Options from the palette menu to see this setting.

   This feature sets a tolerance for snapping colors to the nearest Web-safe equivalents. The higher the settings, the more colors that are shifted to Web-safe colors.

10. Check the Interlaced box.

    An interlaced GIF loads a low-resolution image in the browser before the full image.

    Note: *Lossy compression is not available to interlaced GIFs.*

11. Click one of the four images to select it, and then save it.

    Photoshop: Click OK.

    ImageReady: Choose File>Save Optimized.

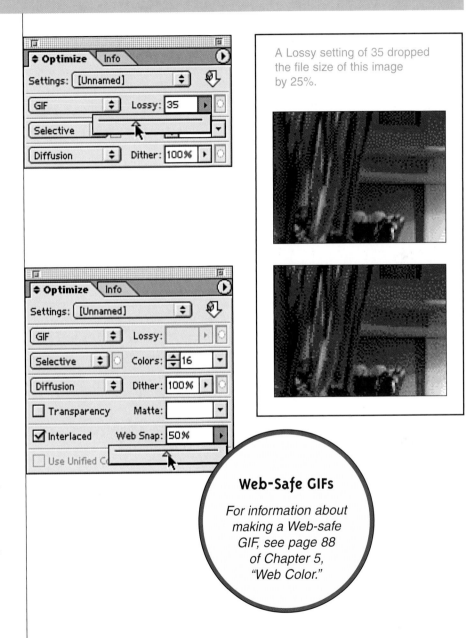

A Lossy setting of 35 dropped the file size of this image by 25%.

Web-Safe GIFs

For information about making a Web-safe GIF, see page 88 of Chapter 5, "Web Color."

Selective Compression Techniques: GIF

With GIF images, there are three ways to use channels to modify compression. You can modify the Color Reduction Algorithm, the Lossy compression amount, and the Dither amount. You can even use one channel to modify all these settings. Page 123 provides more information on alpha channels.

---

use selective GIF compression

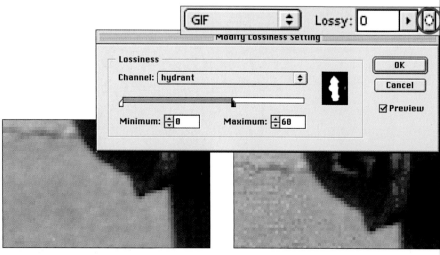

Areas outside the selection are dithered more after selective lossiness.

1. Make a selection around the most important areas in the image. This selection will become the alpha channel.

    On page 123, the Lasso tool was used to make the selection. You can use it here, as well. If you're using Photoshop then you could jump into Quick Mask mode (press Q), paint the selection with the Paintbrush tool, leave Quick Mask mode (press Q), and choose Select>Inverse.

2. Choose Select>Save Selection, to name and save the channel.

3. Click the icon to the right of the Lossy setting. In the dialog box, choose the channel just saved. Use the sliders to adjust the Maximum and Minimum settings.

    These settings determine how much the channel affects the compression of the image. The white slider sets the compression amount for the white areas of the alpha channel. The black slider works for the black areas. The higher the value, the more compression and the more dithering that occurs.

use selective GIF compression

4. You also can use a channel to to make ImageReady or Photoshop favor certain areas of the image when building the Color Table. Click the icon to the right of the Color Algorithm setting.

   The white areas of the channel will be favored. Here are the Color Tables before and after modifying the Color Reduction Algorithm.

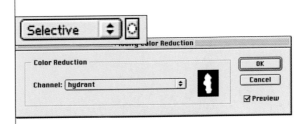

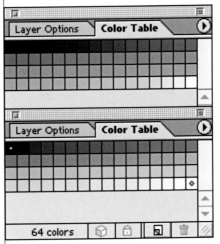

5. Finally, the dither amount can also be adjusted selectively. Click the icon to the right of the Dither setting. In the dialog box, choose a channel. Then, use the sliders to adjust the Dither amount for white and black areas.

   You can see the reduction in dithering in areas outside the fire hydrant after modifying Dither with the channel selected in the Modify Dither Setting dialog box.

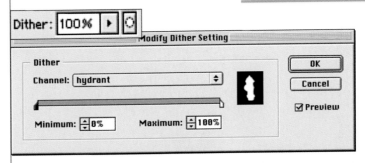

Compressing an Image to a File Size

Because file size is a major issue for Web graphics, often when optimizing images, it will be your primary concern. You can have ImageReady or Photoshop automatically choose optimize settings based on a target file size. If you want, it will run through both GIF and JPEG options to find the nearest size (not the smallest possible size) to the target size.

compress an image to a file size

The Big Squeeze

If you select all slices before choosing Optimize to File Size, you can squeeze an entire navigation bar or page design to a selected size.

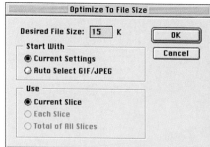

1. Open an image to optimize.

   ImageReady: Choose Optimize to File Size from the Optimize palette menu.

   Photoshop: Optimize to File Size from the Optimize menu in the Save for Web dialog box.

2. Set the target size.

3. Choose a Start With option to set the file format.

   Use Current Settings maintains the file format of the currently selected optimized view.

   Auto Select chooses a GIF or or JPEG.

4. Click OK.

   Notice the new Quality setting on the Optimize palette and the updated optimized file size.

Saving Settings

When working on a project, you might want to treat images with the same compression settings for quality control purposes, or after working with optimizing tools for a while, you might determine settings that you think generally work best for the work you do. Photoshop and ImageReady allow you to save optimize settings. Once saved and named, the settings show up as options in the Settings menu on the Optimize palette (ImageReady) or in the Save for Web dialog box (Photoshop).

save optimize settings

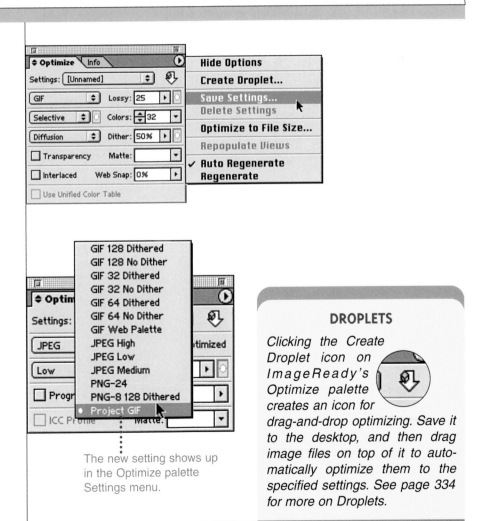

1. Open an image and set the optimize settings.

2. Choose Save Settings from the Optimize palette menu and name the file.

    I suggest naming settings according to a project name or something that includes the actual settings such as "NavBar GIFs."

3. In the Save dialog box, you also can choose where to save the settings.

    The default location is in the Optimize Settings folder inside Photoshop's Presets folder. If you save it there then it will show up in the Settings menu.

    Alternatively, you could save the settings as a file to copy and share with someone else.

The new setting shows up in the Optimize palette Settings menu.

DROPLETS

Clicking the Create Droplet icon on ImageReady's Optimize palette creates an icon for drag-and-drop optimizing. Save it to the desktop, and then drag image files on top of it to automatically optimize them to the specified settings. See page 334 for more on Droplets.

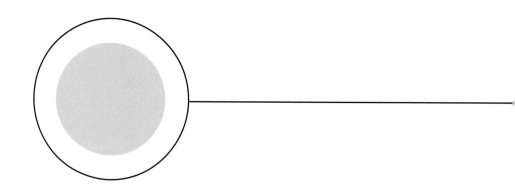

Part III

Web Graphics

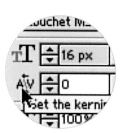

Type on the Web

You always have to deal with type in a design. When building Web pages, you can either use the limited options that HTML offers or use the Photoshop and ImageReady Type tools to do almost anything you want. This chapter goes over type basics, demonstrates special effects, and discusses Web type issues.

Type Types

Two methods are available to include text in a Web page. You can enter the text in the HTML document, or you can create graphics that contain type.

Type in HTML Code: Body Text

Text entered directly into an HTML file has the advantage of downloading quickly and being easily editable and replaceable. You never really have to worry about file size with HTML text. This is the best option for large amounts of text or text that will change often.

The problem is that browsers can only display fonts that a user has installed on his computer. Because everyone does not have the same fonts loaded on their system, you are limited to a handful of common fonts. However, if you're not concerned about backward compatibility, you can embed font information in an HTML file so you can use fonts not installed on the user's machine. If you're designing a page that makes extensive use of a font not available to most systems then this might be a good option.

But if you want to add some interesting heads to a page or create navigational elements that will not change often, Photoshop and ImageReady's type features are just the thing.

This type was made as a graphic because of the drop shadows and layered image.

This type was done directly in HTML. It is simple body text with style, color, and size attributes applied.

Type in Photoshop and ImageReady: Heads

In Photoshop and ImageReady, on the other hand, you can do just about anything with type. Type images are treated like all other graphic files—they're optimized, saved in a Web format, and embedded in the HTML code. But, because they are the same as any other graphic file, the only way to edit the type is to re-create the graphic. But, because you are using Photoshop or ImageReady to create the graphic files, the type can always remain editable in the original graphic file. When edits are needed, just open the original Photoshop file, make the necessary edits, and save it again in a Web-ready file format.

Type made this way is best suited for heads and navigation elements. You normally won't create whole paragraphs of type this way because the file would simply get too large. However, heads, normally optimized as GIFs, can be very small and will download quickly.

The Type Tool

Type operations are handled by the Type tool, the Type Options bar, the Character palette, and the Paragraph palette. You have great control over type. You can set the font and size, leading, color, anti-aliasing, justification, kerning, tracking, scaling, baseline shift, and paragraph indents. You also can create text that runs vertically, apply layer effects, and apply warp effects—and it all remains editable.

Even this type is editable.

Antialiasing and Readable Type

Ideally, type has smooth, crisp edges—the kind produced by laser printers and printing presses. But everything displayed by a computer monitor must be made of pixels, and pixels create jagged edges by nature. To solve this problem, Photoshop blurs the edges of a font at the pixel level to make it look smooth as you see it. This is called antialiasing, and generally speaking it works well and is a necessary part of creating graphic type for display on computer screens.

However, when type gets small, antialiasing can start to make the type too blurry and less readable. Therefore, you might get better-looking and more readable type by eliminating the antialiasing. Photoshop and ImageReady have four antialiasing options: None, Crisp, Strong, and Smooth.

ANTIALIASING ADDS EXTRA COLORS

Antialiasing also adds colors to the image. This can be bad for two reasons: Adding colors increases file size, and the colors that are added will almost certainly not be Web-safe even if the original type color was. Keep this in mind if your're saving the type as a GIF.

---

set antialiasing options

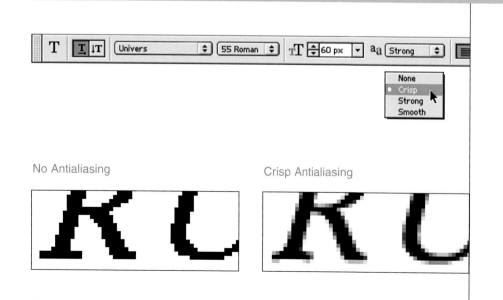

No Antialiasing

Crisp Antialiasing

With the text or the Type layer selected (and the Type tool selected), click the antialiasing menu on the Options bar. Choose an option.

Use your eyes to determine the best option. These definitions are general guidelines.

None: Turns off antialiasing.

Crisp: Creates the sharpest edges.

Strong: Makes the type look a little heavier.

Smooth: That's what it does.

Entering Text

ImageReady and Photoshop give you the option of entering Paragraph or Point type. Point type begins from a single point (that is movable) and runs in one direction until you press Return (or Shift Return). Paragraph type is set inside a bounding box. The text wraps as it runs to the edges of the box. The bounding box also can be distorted to uniformly distort all the text within the box but still keep it editable. The following exercises run through the basics of using the Type tool features.

entering text: point type

1. Open a new file (approx. 400 by 200 pixels). Get the Type tool and click in the new image to create an insertion point. Enter some text.

   A new Type layer is added to the Layers palette. It takes its name from the text.

2. The attributes for what you typed were taken from the Options bar. Take a look at it now.

   There you find the most basic, and most important, information about type you enter.

3. To change the font, highlight the text and select another from the Font menu.

   You also can change the point size and icons are available for left-, center-, and right-aligned text.

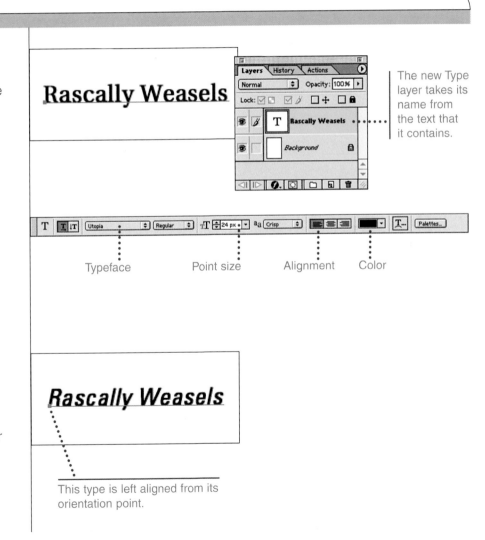

The new Type layer takes its name from the text that it contains.

Typeface   Point size   Alignment   Color

This type is left aligned from its orientation point.

entering text: point type

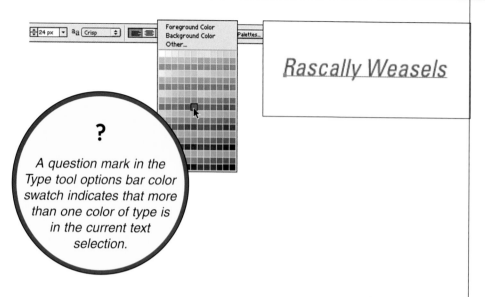

?

A question mark in the Type tool options bar color swatch indicates that more than one color of type is in the current text selection.

4. To change the color, click the swatch of color and choose a new one.

   Note that this color is not necessarily the same as the Foreground color on the Tool palette.

   In ImageReady, clicking the color swatch drop-down menu arrow brings up a Web-safe palette. To access the Color Picker, choose Other.

   In Photoshop, clicking the color swatch opens the Color Picker.

5. Click the Palettes button. The Character and Paragraph palettes open. On the Character palette are some of the same options as in the Options bar plus additional ones, including leading, tracking, scaling, and baseline shift.

   The scaling and tracking settings were changed to alter this text.

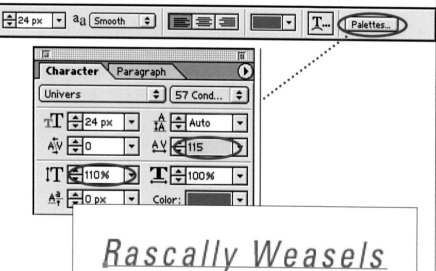

entering text: point type

6. In the Character palette menu are some options that used to be inside Photoshop's Type dialog box. There are more attributes here: Faux Bold and Italic, Strikethrough, Underline, Superscript, Small Caps, and more.

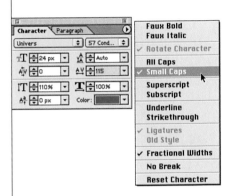

7. Click the Paragraph tab to bring the palette forward. These settings give you some limited control over paragraph formatting. You can set indents, spacing between paragraphs, hyphenation, and more justification options.

    The paragraph features are helpful in setting up a Photoshop-type file that will get changed from time to time. After the paragraph and character attributes are set, you can select all the type and replace it while its style remains intact.

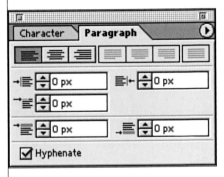

TYPE MISBEHAVIN'?

Type going in the wrong direction? Check the Orientation buttons on the left of the Options bar. If you used Vertical type the last time you used the Type tool then it will still be selected. Also check paragraph formatting. Photoshop remembers the last used settings. If the leading on 12-point type is set to 200, you might not see the rest of your text because so much space exists between lines that it won't fit in the image.

Entering Text: Paragraph Text

Paragraph text is contained by a bounding box that can contain any number of paragraphs. They aid layout by enabling you to set up type in blocks. By using the Paragraph palette, you can apply paragraph formatting to the text: indents and justification. Paragraph type also can be treated as a single element that can be stretched and skewed any way you like. This is useful for putting text on receding planes. However, paragraph text will remain editable. Paragraph text works a little differently in ImageReady and Photoshop. In Photoshop handles on the bounding box make it always editable. In ImageReady, you must use the Transform feature to distort the box.

entering text: paragraph type

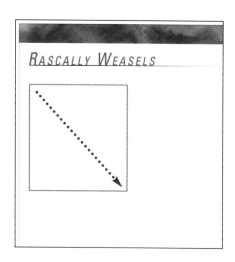

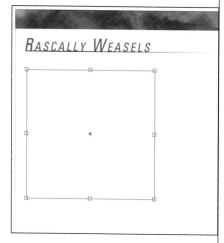

1. Select the Type tool and drag diagonally across the image area to draw the bounding box—just an approximation will do for now. You can fine-tune the dimensions later.

   Alternatively, to make a box of a precise size, hold the (Option) [Alt] key and click in the image area to open a dialog box that lets you set the size in pixels.

2. Enter some text.

   The initial attributes are taken from the current settings in the Options bar and Character and Paragraph palettes.

entering text: paragraph type

3. To resize the box in ImageReady, press Enter (not Return) and the handles appear. Drag them to resize the box.

   In Photoshop, the handles are always present.

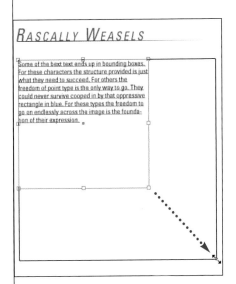

SKEWING PARAGRAPH TYPE

Photoshop: *Hold the (Command) [Control] key while dragging the handles. The handles work the same as they do for the Transform feature.*

ImageReady: *You can't skew the box while the cursor is active in the text. Press Enter or click outside the text box. Then, choose Edit>Transform and use the handles to skew the entire box of text.*

4. To set paragraph formatting, use the Character and Paragraph palettes by clicking the Palettes button on the Type tool options bar.

   Different paragraphs within the same bounding box can have different formatting. If you select all the text in a bounding box and start typing to replace it then the formatting for the last paragraph is used.

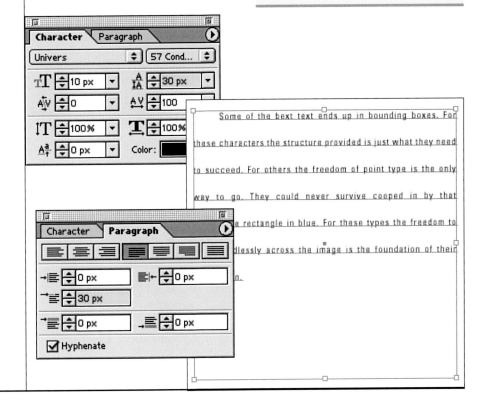

Working with Type

Type tool Options bar.

Antialiasing menu

Warp Text icon

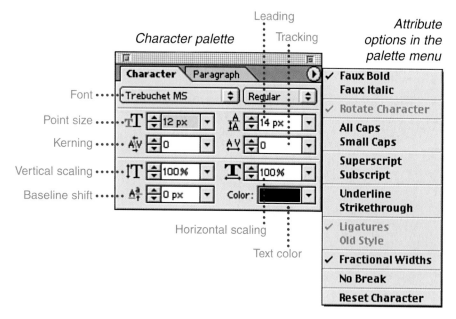

Leading

Character palette

Tracking

Attribute options in the palette menu

Font

Point size

Kerning

Vertical scaling

Baseline shift

Horizontal scaling

Text color

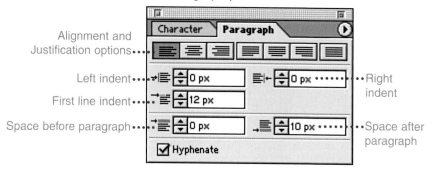

Paragraph palette

Alignment and Justification options

Left indent · · · · Right indent

First line indent

Space before paragraph · · · · Space after paragraph

TYPE TERMS

Leading: *The height of a line of text, including the space above. Increasing it spaces the text out vertically.*

Tracking: *How tight or loose the characters are to each other. Increasing it spaces the text out horizontally.*

Kerning: *The space between two characters. Adjust it to fine-tune the spacing within a word.*

Antialiasing: *A method of blending the edges of type into the background to make edges look smooth.*

Baseline Shift: *Raises or lowers the base of the text from the line of the other characters. Use it to create superscript and subscript characters such as footnote numbers.*

Fractional Widths: *When turned on, the spacing between characters is adjusted to account for varying widths of characters to maintain the best looks and readability.*

Working with Type

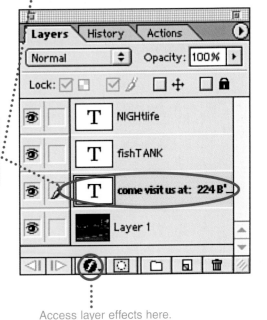

Use the Vertical type tool to create vertical lines of text. Vertical characters can be rotated by using the Rotate Character command in the Character palette menu.

Point type baseline. Photoshop does not display a baseline for type.

Paragraph type bounding box with handles

Type layers are indicated by a "T" and take the text they contain as their names. To change the name, double-click it.

Access layer effects here.

EDITING TEXT

Double-click the type's Type layer icon to select all type in the layer and the Type tool.

Press Enter (not Return) to set the type and accept any changes you've made.

While text is selected in Photoshop: Click the check mark on the Options bar to set the type and accept any edits. Click the "X" to cancel any edits.

In ImageReady, double-click the type's Type layer name to change it. In Photoshop, hold the (Option) [Alt] key while double-clicking.

SELECTING TEXT

Two clicks: *Selects a word.*

Three clicks: *Selects a line.*

Four clicks: *Selects a paragraph.*

Five clicks: *Selects all text in the current box.*

Editing Type Layers

You can change the attributes of the entire contents of a Type layer without selecting the text with the Type tool. Do this by selecting the layer in the Layers palette. This is often more convenient than using the Type tool. It is handy, for example, when changing the color of the type, or scaling more than one type layer at a time. The following exercise demonstrates this.

edit type layers

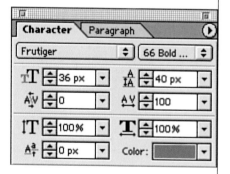

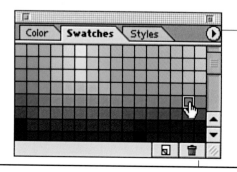

1. Open a file that contains a Type layer and select that layer in the Layers palette.

   Double-click the T icon to highlight the text. Start typing to replace it.

   Double-click the name of the layer to change it. In Photoshop, hold the (Option) [Alt] key and double-click.

2. Changes can be made globally to all the text in the layer by choosing the Type Tool and selecting options from the Type Tool Options bar or from the Type and Paragraph palettes.

3. To change the color of the type, choose a new color using the Color Picker, Swatches, or Color palette and press (Option-Delete) [Alt-Delete] to fill the type.

Rendering Type Layers

You can do a lot with Type layers and keep the text editable, but you can't do everything to them. To access features not available to Type layers such as the full list of filters and many color adjustment tools, a Type layer must be converted to a normal layer. After it is converted (rasterized, or rendered, which mean the same thing in this context), the content of the layer behaves like any other layer. The content is no longer recognized as text—just areas of color that happen to look like letters.

render a type layer

1. Select the Type layer in the Layers palette and choose Layer>Rasterize>Type. In Photoshop, you cannot rasterize a type layer that is being edited. Click the check on Options bar first.

   Or, hold the Control key (Mac) or right-click (Windows) and click the Type layer's name. Choose Render Layer (ImageReady) or Rasterize Layer (Photoshop) from the menu.

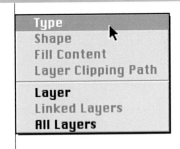

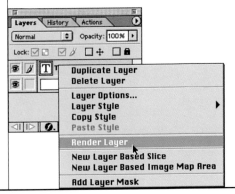

The layer icon loses its "T" after being rendered.

Warning

The text of a rendered Type layer is no longer editable. Save a copy of the document before rendering if you might need to change the text later.

Saving Type Images

Images that have type in them are treated no differently by browsers than any other type of image. So, generally, follow the same rules when optimizing and saving type images as you would with any other file. That means that most of the time, type should be saved in the GIF or PNG-8 format. But not always. If you want to maintain the fine gradation of a drop shadow beneath type, optimizing the type image as a JPEG is the best option.

Browserlike Text in Photoshop

Sometimes you need to create type in Photoshop or ImageReady that looks like text rendered by a browser. By this, I mean non antialiased body text in the Helvetica, Arial, or Times font. This is useful when you're designing a page and want to see (or want someone else to see) what the page will look like when it is filled with HTML text. You also can simply use it as part of the look of the design. That kind of text, after all, is part of the look and feel of the Web in general, and it creates very readable text at small sizes.

create browserlike text

Spend Your Money Here

Spend Your Money Here

Antiantialiasing

Only one antialiasing option can exist for a Type layer. You cannot change antialiasing for one word in a line.

1. Select the Type tool and draw a paragraph bounding box or click to start point type. Set the font to Arial or Helvetica for sans-serif type or Times or X for serif type.

2. These settings create the look: Set the Antialias option to None. Then, make sure that all the other attributes are turned off, especially the Fractional Widths feature. It ruins the effect. Use the Faux Bold attribute to emulate HTML text that has been bolded with the <b> tag.

   This look also works to create crisp, clear versions of fonts outside the conventional set of browser fonts, but some work better than others.

Setting Up an Editable Text File

If you're creating a design in which you want to include graphic type (non-HTML), but you know that it will change often, then there are ways to make the re-editing process run smoothly. First, don't ever render (or rasterize) the type or flatten the image in Photoshop or ImageReady. Second, choose type treatments that are created from font choice, color, and layer effects only. Third, if it's a paragraph of text set it up in a bounding box, and set paragraph attributes. Finally, if you must slice the document, do it in such a way that the area the type is in will be saved as one whole slice. That way, when it's time to re-edit the text, simply open the file, make the changes, select that slice only, choose Save Optimized As (or Save for Web), and choose Selected Slices Only from the drop-down list in the Save Optimized As dialog box. Only that one slice will be saved.

If the slice containing the text is part of a larger design, it might be best to isolate that slice in a new, editable PSD file. This is especially true if the text will be edited (in the image file) by a nonexpert. The possibility of affecting other parts of the document is eliminated. Here are steps for isolating the slice in ImageReady. Select it with the Slice Select tool and choose Select> Create Selection from Slice, and then choose Image>Crop. On the Layers palette, merge all the existing layers except for the type layer to create a 2-layer document. Choose File>Save As to save the new PSD file. Be sure to name it the same as it was named in the original, sliced design—paying attention to the slice number if applicable. All the text editor has to do is open the 2-layer PSD file in ImageReady, edit the text, and choose File>Save Optimized—the name and optimize settings are already set. Swap the new optimized file with the old version and you're done.

This file, created from the image below, was set up for convenient text-editing and replacement by isolating the slice containing the text and building a 2-layer PSD document.

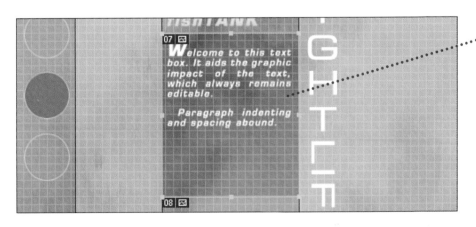

A slice with editable body text that uses a graphic type treatment.

Layer Effects and Type

Layer effects (or styles) and type layers were made for each other. Layer effects enable you to alter text in the most common ways: changing color, and adding drop shadows, glows, and bevels. And they leave the text editable. You can apply multiple effects to a single layer. The effects are in a menu at the bottom of the Layers palette and are discussed in the Styles chapter (page 296). This exercise demonstrates a typical use of a layer effect, adding a drop shadow.

create a drop shadow

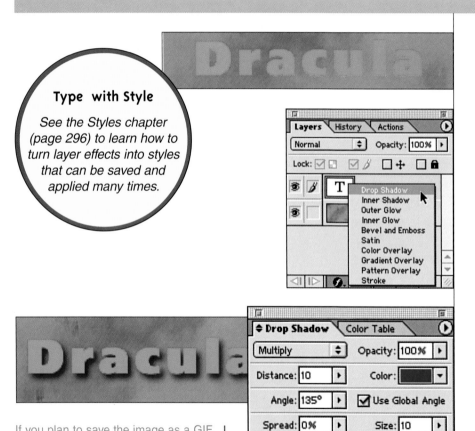

Type with Style

See the Styles chapter (page 296) to learn how to turn layer effects into styles that can be saved and applied many times.

If you plan to save the image as a GIF, adding some noise to the shadow will help you get a better-looking dithered shadow. Choose Show Options from the palette menu to reveal this option.

1. Use the Type tool to enter text or select a Type layer from the Layers palette.

2. Click the Effects (or Styles) icon on the bottom of the Layers palette and choose Drop Shadow from the list.

   In ImageReady, the Drop Shadow palette jumps forward. In Photoshop, the Layer Style dialog box opens.

3. The controls here are explained further in the Styles chapter (page 296). Use the settings seen here for a standard drop-shadow effect.

   It is always a good idea to use a color other than black for the shadow. Use something close to black that has a little coolness or a little warmth in it.

Layer Effects and Type

Effects: Inner Bevel, Stroke

Effects: Gradient Overlay, Stroke, Outer Glow, Drop Shadow

Effects: Pattern Overlay, Innner Bevel, Drop Shadow, Stroke

OSPREY

Effects: Satin, Stroke

SCALE EFFECTS

Effects do not scale when you scale the contents of a layer. But in Photoshop, you can choose Layer>Layer Style>Scale Effects to scale only the effects before or after scaling the contents of a layer.

Effects: Stroke, Drop Shadow (dithered), Inner Shadow

Crow

Effects: Pattern Overlay, Drop Shadow, Outer Glow

HERON

Effects: Gradient Overlay, Stroke

PIGEON

Effects: Inner Bevel, Stroke

Type and Special Effects

Type is a significant element of any design and is integral to its graphic look. Sometimes this requires treating type as a graphic and abandoning the options that typography and layer effects alone provide. Combining the Type tool with Photoshop's image manipulation features can produce great effects. The possibilities are as limitless as Photoshop's powers. Here's an effect that has a tech look that's appropriate for the Web. Many Web sites contain techniques for type effects, inlcuding some listed in the Web Resources appendix (page 360).

create block type

Photoshop

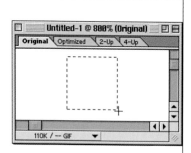

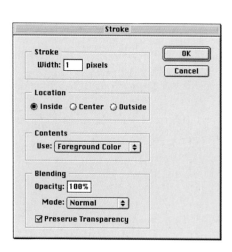

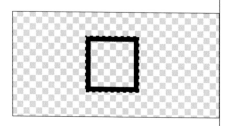

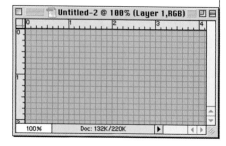

1. Open a new document and create a new layer. Select the Rectangular Marquee tool and drag a 10-by-10 pixel selection. Hold the Shift key and watch the Info palette to make a precise selection.

2. Set the Foreground color to black and choose Edit>Stroke. Use these settings: Stroke width: 1 pixel, Location: Inside, Contents: Foreground Color, Opacity: 100%, Mode: Normal. Preserve Transparency option should be turned off. Click OK.

3. Turn off the background layer and choose Edit>Define Brush. Name the brush and click OK.

4. Choose Edit>Preferences> Guides and Grid. Set Gridline every to 9 pixels and Subdivisions to 1. Then, choose View>Show>Grid. Turn on the Grid (Command-Option-') [Ctrl-Option-'].

create block type

5. Select the Paintbrush tool; then, click the Brush menu on the Options bar and find the brush you just made. Select it and click Enter to close the menu. Then, click the brush icon on the Options bar once to open the Brush dialog box. Turn off antialiasing and set the Spacing to 90%.

6. Turn on Snap to Grid (View>Snap to>Grid). Hide the layer on which the brush was created and deselect any active selections.

7. Create a new layer. Choose a color for the type, and then click the brush over a crossing point in the grid and drag to begin creating elements. The grid keeps the brush in line, but it's not perfect. The Spacing set in step 5 keeps the brush from overlapping itself if you click and drag either horizontally or vertically while holding the Shift key. You'll get the hang of the brush quickly.

Extra:

To create a grid to match this type, create a 9-x-9 pixel image that looks like the image to the right. Make sure the transparency checkerboard is visible. Choose Select>All, then Edit>Define Pattern. Create a new layer and use the pattern to fill it.

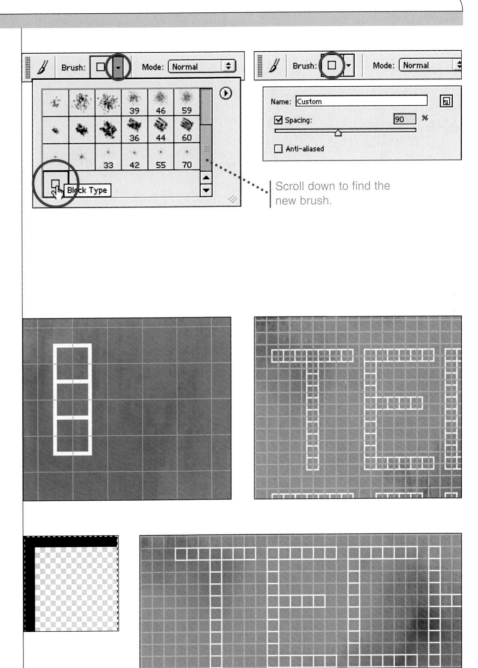

Scroll down to find the new brush.

Vertical Text

You might have noticed the Vertical type icon on the Type tool Options bar. Both Photoshop and ImageReady support this feature. When creating vertical text, you have the option of orienting it upright or rotated 90° clockwise. Of course, you can always rotate horizontal text into this position, but you might find this method easier to edit. More importantly, you can rotate only selected characters.

create vertical text

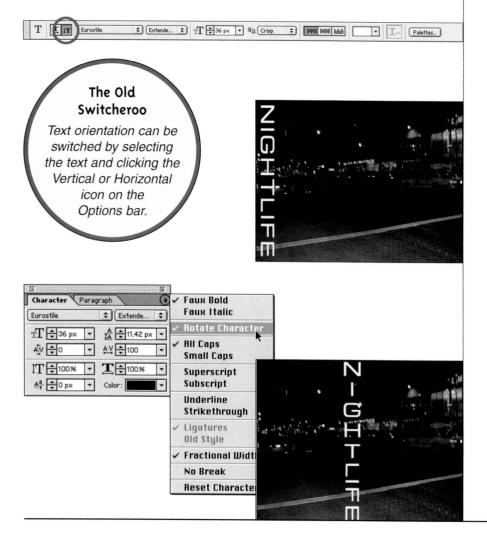

The Old Switcheroo

Text orientation can be switched by selecting the text and clicking the Vertical or Horizontal icon on the Options bar.

Change Orientation

1. Select the Type tool; make your font, size, and attribute choices and click the Vertical type icon on the Options bar.

2. Enter the text.

   While entering or editing text, the text orientation icons disappear from the Options bar. Press Enter to finish editing and get back the icons.

Rotate the Text

3. To rotate characters, select them with the Type tool, find the Character palette (if you don't see it, click Palettes on the Options bar), and choose Rotate Character from the Palette menu.

   Only the selected characters are rotated.

Warped Text

The type on page 137 of this chapter was created with the Warp text feature. The Warp text feature contains a list of styles to warp text in 12 different ways. Several parameters enable you to control the magnitude of the warping effects. This feature can be used to create animations of waving type.

create warped text

1. Enter some text with the Type tool. Use a big, bold typeface for effects like these.

2. Set color, size, and layer effects for the type.

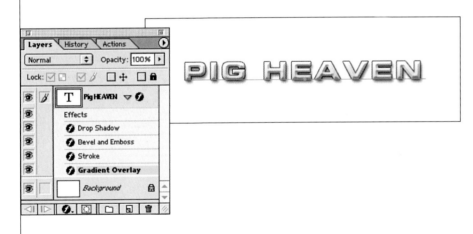

3. Then, select the Type tool, click the Warp text icon on the Options bar, and make a selection from the Style list.

   The names are not very helpful, but the effects preview in the image window as they are selected. Experiment to find the distortion you're looking for.

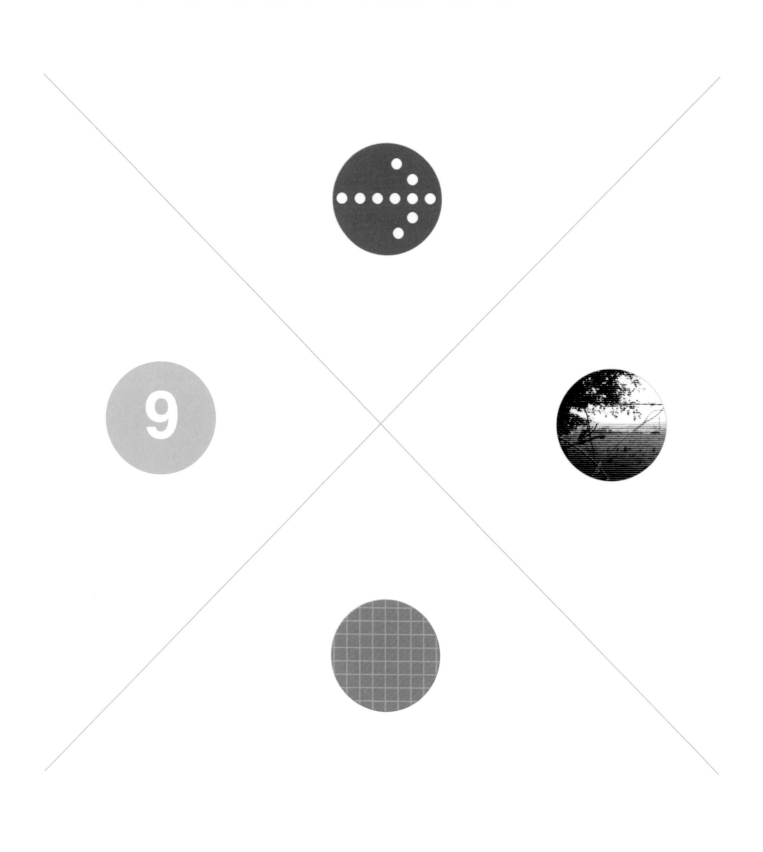

Graphic Effects

Surfing the Web these days, you come across a lot of similar graphic effects. I don't advocate toeing the line when it comes to designing and creating graphics for Web sites. However, as in any other field, conventions arise. This chapter is a collection of graphic effects that are common on Web pages—striped images, striped backgrounds, grids, 3D pushable buttons, and more.

Creating Depressed Buttons

Here are two methods for creating a depressed button effect. They both work by altering layer effect settings. Depressed buttons are used as rollover states to give feedback to the user. It gives the "impression" that the page is responding.

create depressed buttons

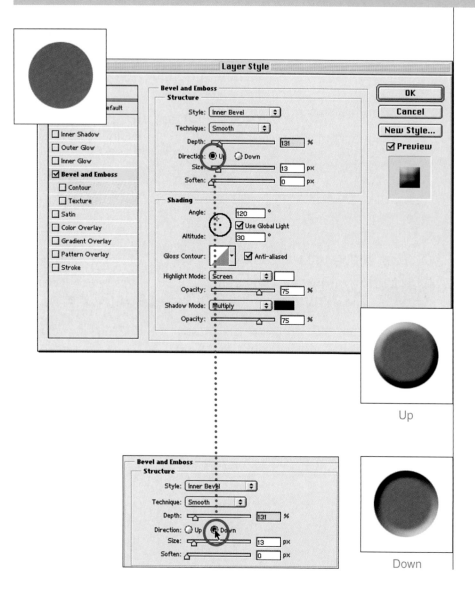

Up

Down

Creating the Raised Button

1. First, create a raised button using the Bevel and Emboss layer effect. Create a new layer, make a marquee selection for the button shape, choose a Foreground color, and fill the selection with the color. Deselect the selection. Then, choose Bevel and Emboss from the Layer Effects menu on the Layers palette. Watch the transformation in the image window and choose your preferred settings or match those shown here.

Method 1

This method works in both Photoshop and ImageReady, although it might be more suitable for ImageReady because that's where you build rollover states.

2. After creating a new rollover state, simply switch the Bevel and Emboss layer effect Direction from Up to Down in the Layer Style palette (Photoshop) or on the Bevel and Emboss palette (ImageReady).

create depressed buttons

Method 2

Because Photoshop has a more complete set of tools for manipulating contours, this effect must be built in Photoshop before switching to ImageReady to incorporate it into a rollover effect.

1. Do step 1 on page 158 to create the button.

> **MISSING THE CONTOUR?**
>
> *If the Cone-Asymetrical contour is not available, leave the Contour Editor and Styles windows and choose Edit>Preset Manager. From the Preset Type menu, select Contours, and then choose the contours.shc file from the bottom of the arrow menu. Click Append to add new contours to Photoshop.*

Set the Range to 50%.

2. Reopen the Layer Style dialog box by double-clicking Bevel and Emboss below the layer. Set the Size to about 25. In the Styles list at the left, click the word Contour that is indented below Bevel and Emboss. Then, click the contour icon once to open the Contour Editor. From the Preset menu, choose Cone-Asymetrical. Then, reduce the range to about 50%. You see the depression in the image window. Click Bevel and Emboss. Click OK.

    This is the depressed button. In ImageReady, you will readjust it to make the Normal state. You must make this state first because ImageReady has no option to select the Cone-Asymetrical contour.

Click here to open the Contour Editor.

3. Click the Jump to ImageReady icon on the toolbox.

create depressed buttons

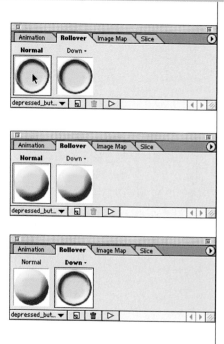

4. Find the Rollover palette and create a new state. Select Down from the the menu above the new state. Then, click the Normal state to select it.

5. Click the Bevel and Emboss effect below the button layer in the Layers palette. Find the Bevel and Emboss palette and, if it's not already open, choose Show Options from the palette menu to reveal a longer list of settings. Turn off the Contour at the bottom of the palette.

   Make sure that the contour is turned on for the Down state. To check, select the Down state on the Rollover palette and take a look at the Bevel and Emboss palette.

6. Select the Normal state again and set the Bevel Size to around 25.

   The image window should once again look like the original beveled button.

7. Click the Preview Rollovers button on the toolbox to test the effect.

Arrows

Arrows are often used on sites, both as graphic elements and as part of navigation menus. Here are some common arrow treatments.

create arrows

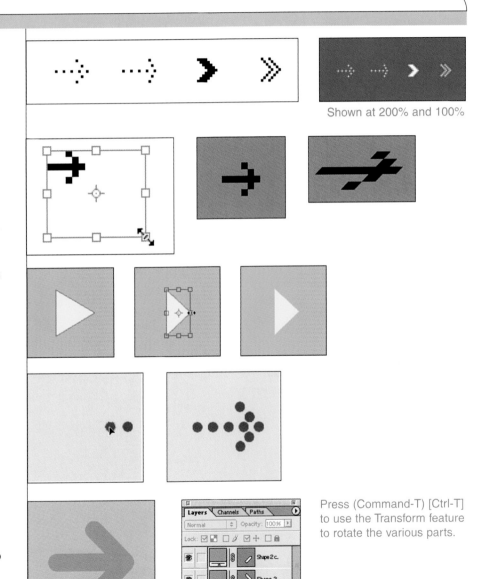

A. All these arrows were made by zooming in very close (1000%) and using the 1-pixel Pencil brush to draw them.

Shown at 200% and 100%

B. Use the Pencil tool as in A to create this arrangement of pixels. Then, set the Interpolation method to Nearest Neighbor, and use the Transform command to enlarge and/or skew it.

C. In Photoshop, select the Polygon tool and, on the Options bar, set the number of sides to 3. Afterward, press (Command-T) [Ctrl-T] to use the Transform feature to stretch or compact it.

D. Make one circle with the Circle tool; then select the Move tool and hold the (Option) [Alt] key while dragging it to make copies. Use the Shift key to constrain movement of the copy to 90° and 45° angles.

E. Select the Rounded Rectangle tool and set the Radius on the Options bar. As you draw the parts of the arrow, watch the Info box. The Height of the shape should be twice the Radius.

Press (Command-T) [Ctrl-T] to use the Transform feature to rotate the various parts.

Striped Images

Laying a striped pattern into photographic images seems to be a common graphic treatment on the Web right now. Maybe this is because they are so easy to make in Photoshop thanks to the Halftone Pattern filter. Here are the technique and a few variations.

add patterned stripes to a photo

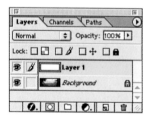

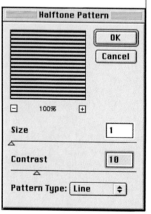

1. Open a photograph in Photoshop. This effect works with any image.

2. Press D to set the toolbox colors to their defaults—black for foreground and white for background.

3. Create a new layer (Command-Option-Shift-N) [Ctrl-Alt-Shift-N] and press (Command-Delete) [Ctrl-Delete] to fill the new layer with white.

4. Choose Filter>Sketch>Halftone Pattern. Choose Line from the Pattern Type menu.

    The Foreground and Background colors, set in step 2, are used by this filter to create the stripes.

add patterned stripes to a photo

The best Size and Contrast setting depends on the image size and desired effect. The highest contrast setting (50) produces stripes with no antialiasing—only black and white pixels (no grays). A 1 Size setting and 10 Contrast setting produce a good effect.

Click OK to apply the filter.

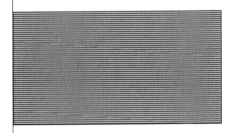

A close-up shows that the stripes are not solid black and white, but actually antialiased.

5. Change the striped layer's blending mode to Soft Light. Or, for a slightly harsher effect, choose Overlay.

   Lowering the layer Opacity softens the effect.

Variation: Checks

Instead of Line, select Dot for the Pattern Type (Size: 3, Contrast: 10).

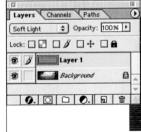

Variation: Color

Before choosing the Halftone Pattern filter, choose colors for the Foreground and Background colors.

>

Stripes

Stripes are used as background tiles for table cells and pages. Generally, the stripes are thin, one or two pixels wide, to keep the pattern subtle. Making stripes is made easy by defining a pattern.

create striped backgrounds

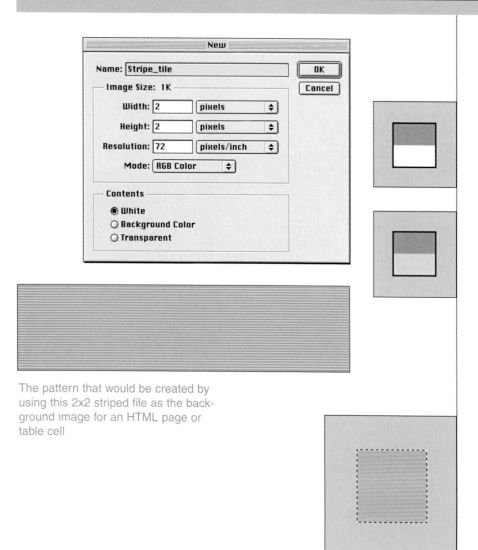

The pattern that would be created by using this 2x2 striped file as the background image for an HTML page or table cell

1. Create a new document in Photoshop or ImageReady. Make it 2 pixels by 2 pixels.

2. Choose a Foreground color, select the Pencil tool (1-pixel brush), and draw the top stripe.

3. Choose a second Foreground color, and with the Pencil tool draw the bottom stripe.

   This file can now be optimized (as a GIF with 2 colors) and saved for use as a background image.

Variation: Fill

If you want to fill a layer or selection with the stripes, choose Select>All, and then choose Edit>Define Pattern. Then, go to the area you want to fill and choose Edit>Fill. Select Pattern from the Use menu and select the pattern from the Custom Pattern menu. Click OK to fill.

Dotted Lines

Dotted lines are common on Web page designs to draw boundaries between elements. You can create these with the Pencil tool and use the brush Spacing setting to control the spacing of the dots and the Shift key to keep the lines straight.

create dotted lines

Photoshop only

1. Open any file to place a line in and create a new layer. Select a Foreground color for the dots.

2. Select the Pencil tool and choose the 1-pixel brush from the Options bar. It's the first and smallest brush in the default set. Close the menu.

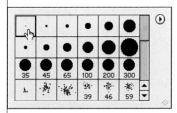

3. Then, click the brush icon once to open the Brush dialog box. The key setting here is the Spacing. This sets the spacing of the dots when dragging the brush. A setting of 400%, as used here, leaves three blank pixels between each colored pixel.

    To save the brush as a new preset (for later use), click the icon in the upper right. It shows up as the last brush in the Brush menu.

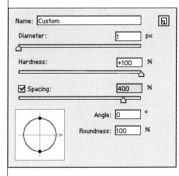

At 100%, dotted lines are a nice subtle effect.

4. Simply drag the brush while holding the Shift key to create straight dotted lines. Release the Shift key to draw freeform ones.

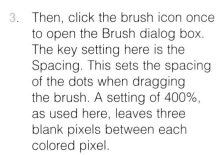

A dotted line close-up.

Pixelized Type

This type effect relies on changing the Interpolation—the method Photoshop uses to calculate how images are enlarged—to Nearest Neighbor. Be sure to change it back to Bicubic when finished.

create pixelized type

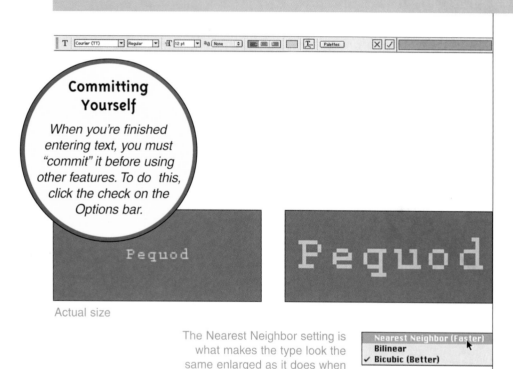

Committing Yourself

When you're finished entering text, you must "commit" it before using other features. To do this, click the check on the Options bar.

Actual size

The Nearest Neighbor setting is what makes the type look the same enlarged as it does when small.

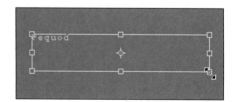

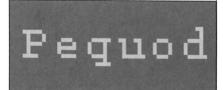

1. Select the Type tool. Choose None for the Antialiasing option on the Options bar. Then choose a font. Basic fonts work best for this effect. I chose Courier. Font size is very important. A size close to 10 works best, but it will vary depending on the typeface chosen. I chose 12.

2. Enter the text.

   Zoom in on the type. When the type is enlarged, it appears exactly as it does here. Adjust the size and typeface to get the effect you want. Click the check on the Type Options bar to commit the text.

3. Choose Edit>Preferences> General and set the Interpolation method to Nearest Neighbor.

4. On the Layers palette, select the type layer. Then, choose Layer>Rasterize>Type.

5. Press (Command-T) [Ctrl-T] to activate the transform tools. Use the handles to enlarge the text. Press Return when finished to confirm the transformation.

Grids

Grids are created by defining simple patterns. The pattern can be used as a tile in an HTML document or used to fill an area in a Photoshop document.

create a grid

Creating the Tile

1. Open a new document. The size varies with the actual pattern being created. It can be cropped later, so begin with a 10-by-10 pixel image. Zoom in to 1600% on the image.

   The size of the document determines the spacing in the grid. Adjust the size to fit your design.

2. Choose a color for the background and press (Command-Delete) [Ctrl-Delete] to fill the document. Then, select a second color for the grid lines and use the Pencil tool (with the smallest, 1-pixel, brush) to draw a vertical and a horizontal line as you see in the figure at right.

Saving It As a Background Image

1. Optimize the image as a two-color GIF, and save the optimized version.

   Placed as a background image in an HTML document, this single tile generates a black-on-white grid.

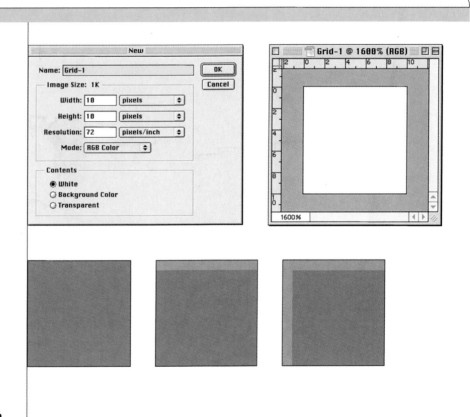

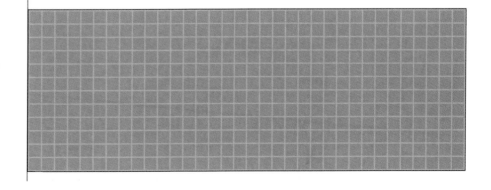

create a grid

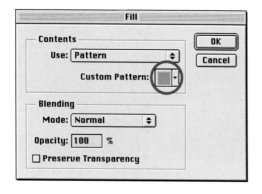

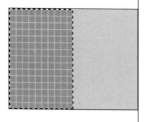

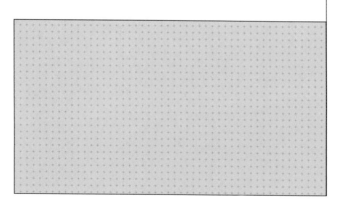

Filling with the Tile

1. Do steps 1 and 2 to create the tile.

2. Press (Command-A) [Ctrl-A] to select everything, and then choose Edit>Define Pattern. In Photoshop, you can name the pattern.

3. In a new, larger document, make a selection or select a layer, and choose Edit>Fill. In the dialog box, choose Pattern from the Use menu. In Photoshop, you must also select the pattern from the Custom Pattern list. If the pattern was just created, it will be the last one in the list. It also will be saved there until deleted.

Variation: Dots

With this technique, you can create a grid of any type. By placing a single dot in a tile, you can make a pattern that adds a nice subtle touch to the background.

create a grid

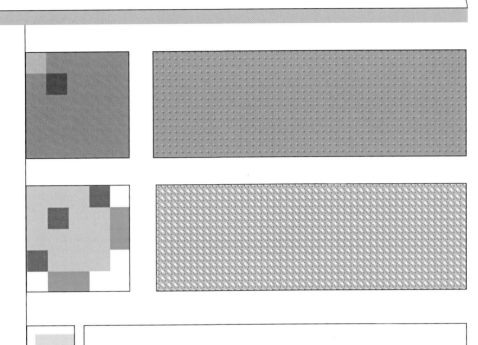

Variation: Shadow Dot

Using the Pencil tool to add just two pixels to the upper-left corner of this tile produces a nice effect.

Variation: Variation

Experiment with all kinds of tiles. The actual pattern, on the left, looks horrendous, but it creates a textured pattern that could add some interest as fill for a blank table cell.

Variation: Boxes

If the grid line color matches the background color on which the pattern is placed, the grid appears to be ordered boxes of color.

Variation: Gridded Image

By using layer blending modes, grids can be combined with photographic images.

10

Backgrounds

Dropped in behind Web page designs, background images are your chance to layer graphics in HTML. Learn the tricks to taking advantage of HTML's automatic tiling of backgrounds. Techniques for creating seamless tiles, uni-directional tiles, and full window images are all revealed in the following pages.

What Is a Background?

When speaking about background images for Web pages, we're referring to a specific HTML feature that enables you to lay an image under the other content of a page. It gives you a limited opportunity to layer images on a page—a great way to add some depth to the design. It also can be a great way to ruin one. Keep in mind what's going to be on top of the background. Don't let a wild background distract from the real content of the page. Subtlety goes a long way in backgrounds.

What's So Special About Backgrounds?

How is a background image different from other images? Answer: It's not. Any image file that is saved as a GIF, JPEG, or PNG can be used as a background image. A good way to think about backgrounds is that ImageReady can makes images; HTML can use images as background images. This happens when it is specified by the BACKGROUND attribute of the BODY tag.

So, if background images are just like every other image, why write an entire chapter on them? Because background images, and this is their special feature, are automatically tiled in the browser. No matter their size, they're repeated in both the horizontal and vertical directions.

Here is the BACKGROUND attribute of the BODY tag in an HTML file as created by ImageReady, the startile.gif file, and the tiled pattern it creates in the browser.

In an HTML document, Images designated as BACKGROUND images in the BODY tag automatically tile in the browser window.

```
<HTML>
<BODY BGCOLOR=#FFFFFF BACKGROUND="startile.gif">
</BODY>
</HTML>
```

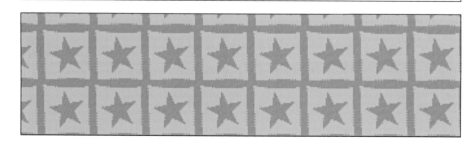

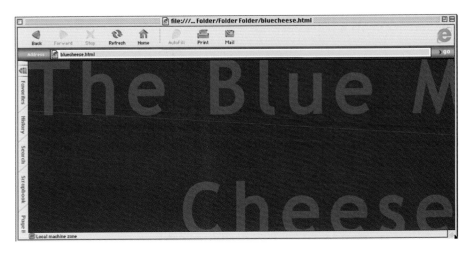

What you see of a background image depends on the size and shape of the browser window.

Background images cannot be resized in HTML, so you must get the size right in ImageReady. How much of the background image you see, or how many you see, depends on the size of the browser window relative to the size of the tile. Because windows are resizable, you have to allow for flexibility in your background image design. The example above shows how the same background image looks in two different-size windows.

Saving Backgrounds

Because any image can be a background image, you really don't have to do anything extra in ImageReady to make an image a background image. Just save the optimized image as you would save any other image for the Web, and use your Web page authoring application to select it as the background image. As with other ImageReady files, you have the choice of saving the image and an HTML file or just saving the file. As you can see in the HTML code on the previous page, the HTML is so simple that it is not really worth saving this extra file.

Previewing Backgrounds

After you've properly optimized this graphic for use on the Web, you can designate it in HTML as the background image. But you don't have to go through that if you just want to see what it will look like in a browser.

HTML BACKGROUND COLOR

The HTML BODY *tag also enables you to specify a background color. Although background images display over the top of the background color, you should specify a background color anyway. It will load more quickly than the image and can aid in making the page look good while the background image comes in. Choose a color that relates to the image.*

preview a background image

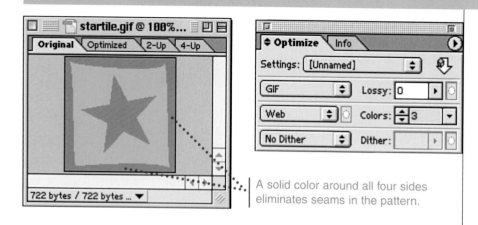

A solid color around all four sides eliminates seams in the pattern.

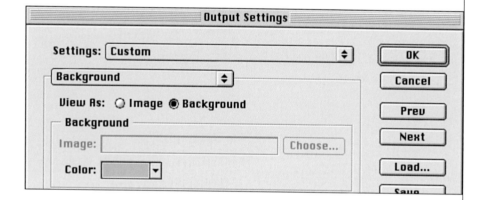

The HTML shows that the BACKGROUND attribute has been added to the BODY tag.

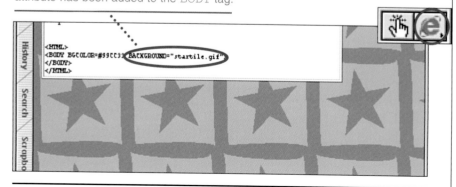

1. Open the tile candidate in ImageReady.

   It is important that the graphic is not touching the edges of the image. If all sides are the same, as in this image, you won't get seams in the pattern.

2. Use the Optimize palette to choose file compression settings. See Chapter 7, "Optimizing Graphics," about optimizing images.

3. Choose File>Output Settings> Background and click the Background radio button. Click OK to exit this dialog box.

   This tells ImageReady to create an HTML document along with the image that specifies it as the background image. After you have done this once for an image, you don't have to do it again. This makes re-editing and previewing easy. If you skip this step, you just see a single copy of the image sitting in the upper-left corner of the browser.

4. Click the Preview in Browser icon on the Tool palette. Or, click and hold to choose another browser other than the default browser.

   To view the background without the HTML box on top, save the HTML file with the optimized image and open the HTML file directly in a browser.

ImageReady Is Your Tile-Making Friend

There are several reasons for choosing ImageReady over Photoshop when creating repeating background tiles. The primary advantage is the ease of previewing the tiled effect in a browser (see facing page). You can do this in Photoshop, but you must leave the standard editing window and enter the Save for Web dialog box. ImageReady also has conveniently grouped its three tile-making aids into one submenu (Other) of the Filter menu. Of these three filters, only the Offset filter is available in Photoshop. And, for the purposes used in this chapter, as you will see, ImageReady's version of the Offset filter is easier to use. The other two tile-making aids are the Tile Maker filter and the DitherBox filter, which is also discussed in Chapter 5, "Web Color."

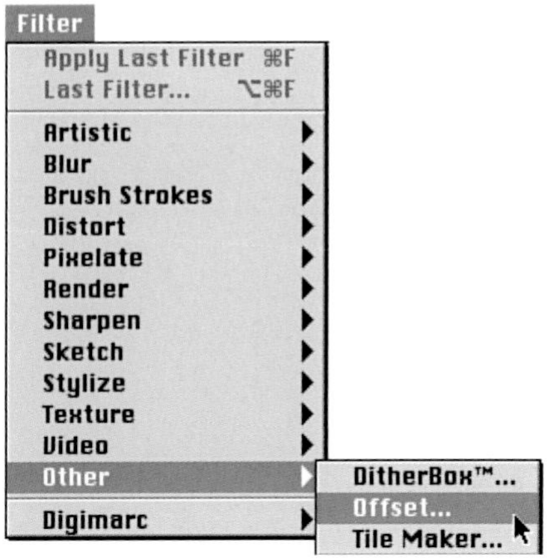

Your tile-making aids reside in the Other submenu of ImageReady's Filter menu.

What Kinds of Background Images Can ImageReady Help Make?

You have three options when considering the background images: a solid color, a repeating tile background, or inserting a single large image. ImageReady can help with each option, including the first.

Solid Color Backgrounds

Normally, when you use a solid color background for a Web page, you simply specify the color in the HTML document. This is easy to do, and you can choose both Web-safe and non–Web-safe colors. However, if you're going to stick to Web-safe only colors, you will be limited to only 216 choices. You can, with the help of ImageReady's DitherBox filter, create a graphic file that contains only Web-safe colors, but produces the illusion of a non–Web-safe color. This is done by using the DitherBox filter to mix pixels of different Web-safe colors into a checkerboard pattern. This graphic file is then designated in HTML as any other background tile image. When displayed in a browser, the pattern in the graphic is small enough that it appears to be a solid color. For greater control, you can build the pattern manually.

Emancipation Proclamation

I hereby declare all files tiles. Any image in a Web graphics format can be used as a background tile.

mix a new background color with the DitherBox filter

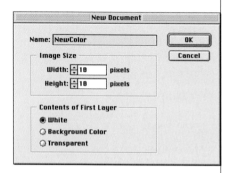

You know it's not a Web-safe color because the Web gamut warning icon is visible.

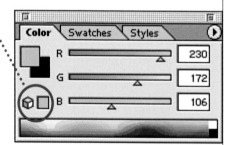

This checkered close-up will look like this in the browser.

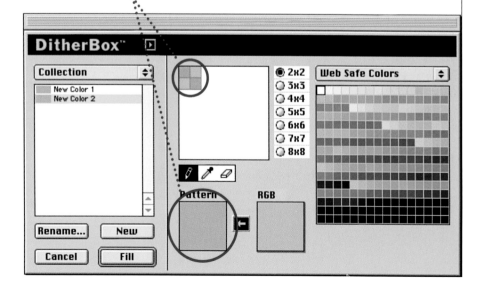

1. Open a new file.

   The size of the file is very important. It must be a multiple of the DitherBox tile size. You'll understand this better after you've been through all the steps once. For example, I made a 10x10 pixel file because I am going to create a 2x2 DitherBox pattern. Because 10 is divisible by 2, it works because the DitherBox filter can make tiles of 2x2, 3x3, 4x4, 5x5, 6x6, 7x7, and 8x8.

2. Choose a non–Web-safe foreground color you want to use.

3. Choose Filter>Other>DitherBox.

   In the center is the area in which you build the tile. It is an extreme close-up of a pixel pattern. On the right is the palette. By default, the colors are Web-safe, but you can load other colors if you want. Use the Eyedropper to select colors and the Pencil to draw. If you make a checker pattern similar to what you see here, the pattern it creates will be hardly noticeable when displayed in the browser.

mix a new background color with the DitherBox filter

4. Click Fill to fill the image with this pattern.

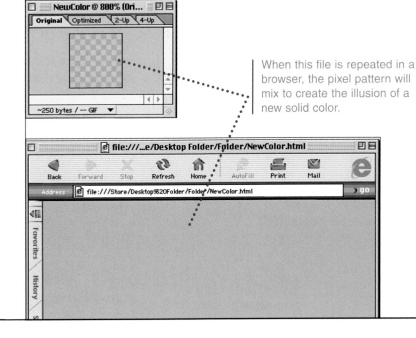

When this file is repeated in a browser, the pixel pattern will mix to create the illusion of a new solid color.

5. Preview the image or save it for use as a background image.

More DitherBox Tiles: Subtle Patterns

You can do even more with the DitherBox filter. With this filter you can produce "tiles" that do not look like tiles. This trick is a good way of adding some subtlety to a design. You could offset some Web-safe colored text by creating a background that is just a little different from the text color—something you can't do with Web-safe colors because of the large gaps between the closest Web-safe colors.

The DitherBox acts like an editing window for creating minute tiles. Instead of making a checkered pattern, you can create a tile of subtle stripes by laying two rows of colors on top of each other. Double up the rows in a 4-by-4 tile for stronger striping. Or you can build more varied textures in larger tiles.

Making Patterned Tile Backgrounds

Smile if you're making a tile.

ImageReady has several features to help make seamless tile backgrounds. The following tasks take you through several methods.

Choosing a Size for the Tile

The size of the file will be the size of the tile. So, what size do you make it? The best answer will depend on the effect you want: a tile so small that the repetition makes it look like a texture? Or a big, bold quilted pattern? As a guideline, think about the size of the browser window. If a window is open to 640x480 pixels—a common size—then a 40x40 pixel tile will repeat 16 times across and 12 times down, for a total of 192 individual tiles in the background. Various sizes are used in the following examples.

---

create a grid of repeated objects

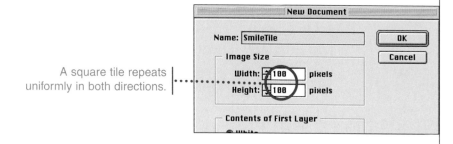

A square tile repeats uniformly in both directions.

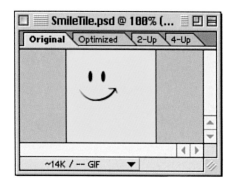

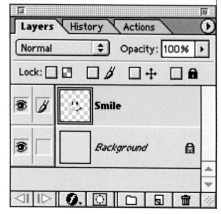

1. Choose File>New or Image>Canvas Size, and make the file a perfect square. This makes the pattern repeat evenly in both directions. This tile is 100x100 pixels. Fill the background with a solid color. This seamless effect depends on a flat color background.

   Background images do not have to be square. Altering the proportions of the file size alters the visual effect of the repeated pattern.

2. Place or draw an object, preferably on its own layer, above the background layer. Make sure that it is not touching the edges of the image.

create a grid of repeated objects

3. To center the object, make the layer containing the object the active layer and choose Layer>Set Layer Position. Choose Center, 0 pixels for both Horizontal and Vertical directions, and click OK. The file is now finished and ready for use.

4. Preview or save the background as instructed above.

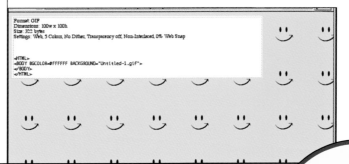

Overlapping Tiles

Repeating tiles don't have to be objects just floating in space. With some effort you can create a tile that repeats in a grid but appears to overlap itself. This tile was created by a combination of the Offset filter; some precise cutting, cropping, and pasting; and a few strokes of the Eraser.

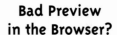

Bad Preview in the Browser?

Don't forget to set Optimize settings before previewing.

create a diamond grid of repeated objects

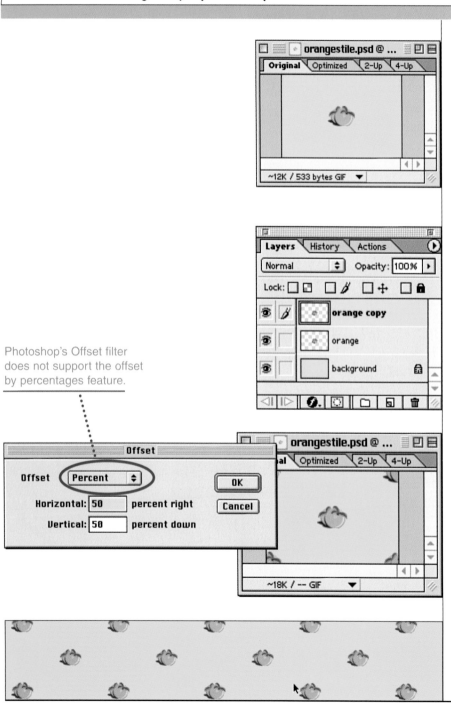

Photoshop's Offset filter
does not support the offset
by percentages feature.

1. Perform steps 1–3 in the previous example.

   If you create a nonsquare file size, the angles of the diamond pattern will compress in the direction that has the smaller dimension. This tile is 150 pixels wide by 100 pixels in height. You must perform step 3 to make this effect work correctly.

2. Deselect any active selections and make a copy of the layer containing the object. Make the new layer the active layer.

3. Choose Filter>Other>Offset. Choose Percent from the Offset menu and set both values to 50% and click OK.

   The tile will be sliced up and the pieces sent to the four corners of the image.

   The tile is now ready for use.

4. Preview or save the background as instructed above.

All-Over Patterns of Objects

Regular patterns like the last effects are the easiest tiles to make. If you want to use a repeating tile that does not look like one, you must do a little, but not a lot, more work and use some judgment along the way. Here are some helpful hints for irregular patterns: Use more than one graphic element; use different versions of the same element (change the size, shape, or color); make the tile large enough so that variation can exist within it; stay away from the edges; and make the elements as evenly spaced (but not gridded, Mr. Robot) as you can. If it doesn't look irregular as a single tile then it's not going to after it's repeated.

create an all-over pattern

1. Open a new file. This file is 180 by 180 pixels. Fill the first layer with the background color for the tile. Similar to the previous examples, this effect works only with a solid background.

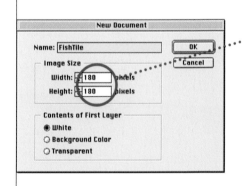

This tile does not need to be square, but it can help to conceal the repetition.

2. Create a new layer and add a graphic element to it.

   Keep adding elements to build the pattern. Try to create as much variation as you can. But most importantly, don't let anything touch the edges of the image. In fact, stay away from the edges because you might be placing the object too close to an object on the opposite side. This could ruin the irregular effect.

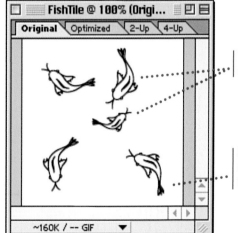

Vary the size and orientation of the elements.

Keep the elements away from the edges. Don't get them any closer than this.

create an all-over pattern

3. Merge all the layers except for the one containing the back-ground color.

   This is necessary because the Offset filter, used in the next step, offsets only one layer at a time.

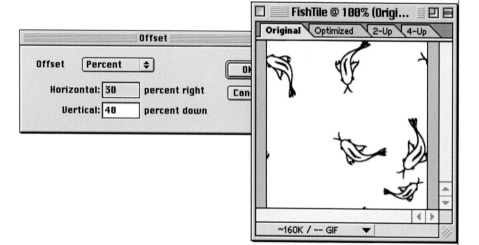

4. Choose Filter>Other>Offset. Choose Percent as the method and enter different values for each direction.

   Varying the values in this step helps to avoid regularity in the pattern.

   You could preview the effect now (page 174). You may have made the perfect tile in one pass. If not, continue.

Keep the spacing as even as you can.

5. Once again, add elements to the pattern, filling in empty areas and attempting to fill the image area as evenly as possi-ble. Fill empty areas and do not create a logjam by placing too many objects in one area.

create an all-over pattern

6. Merge the new layers with the previous one and repeat step 4. Choose new values for the Offset percentages.

Merge these layers before offsetting them.

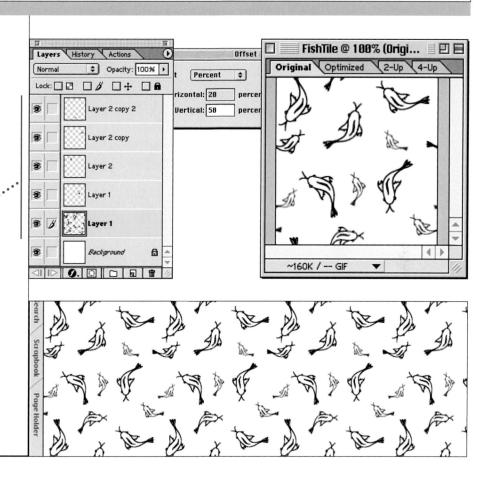

7. Preview the tile in a browser.

   If it looks okay, you're done. However, as a guideline normally you have to go through the Offset filter three times before getting good results. Here is the final tile and the pattern it creates.

An All-Over Hand-Drawn Tile

Creating an irregular pattern is somewhat easier if you hand draw each element. Bad drawing skills can even aid you in this case because they ensure that each element in the pattern is different. (Caffeine—don't fail me now.) I used the Paintbrush tool and ran this tile through the Offset filter only once to create a good effect.

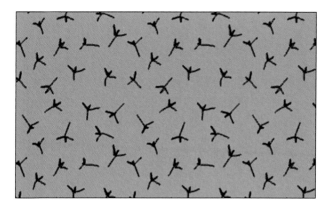

Repeating Photographic Textures

ImageReady's Tile Maker filter enables you to make tiling backgrounds from photographic images. You can use this effect to either create a textured background by selecting a relatively flat area of an image or create an Escher-like pattern of images that magically blend together.

create a photographic texture tile

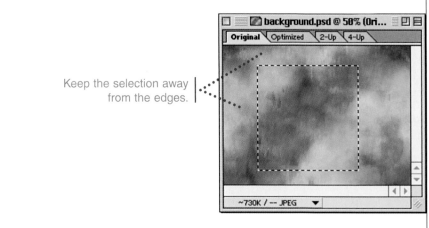

Keep the selection away from the edges.

1. Open a photographic image. Use the Marquee tool to select a rectangular area. You should make this selection at least 50 pixels in each direction. Keep the selection away from the edges of the image.

   You cannot select the entire image with this filter because it uses some information outside the selection area to blend opposite sides together.

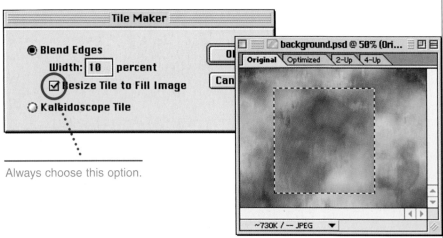

Always choose this option.

2. Choose Filter>Other>Tile Maker. Select Blend Edges, a Width of 10%, and Resize Tile to Fill Image. Click OK.

   Some blurring and shifting occurs inside the selection.

create a photographic texture tile

3. Choose Image>Crop to crop the image down to the tile. This image will repeat flawlessly.

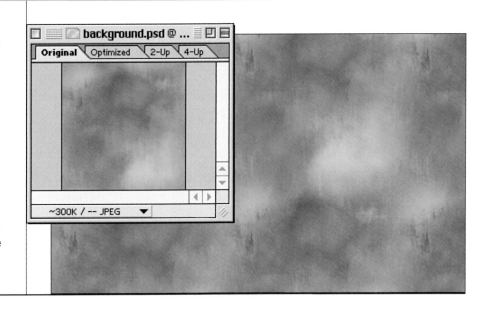

4. Follow the Preview Backgrounds steps (page 174) to view the background or save for use as a background image.

create a kaleidoscopic background tile

1. Open any file. Select a rectangular area.

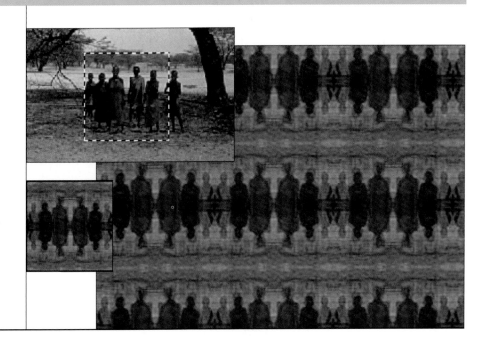

2. Choose Filter>Other>Tile Maker and select the Kaleidoscopic option. Click OK.

3. Choose Image>Crop, set the Optimize settings, and preview it as a background or save it for use as a background image.

Making Unidirectional Backgrounds

This effect is a great use of the automatic tiling of background images. You create an image that is very small in one dimension—maybe 20 pixels, but possibly as small as 1 pixel—and very big in the other dimension—big enough so that it won't repeat in the browser. When seen in a browser, it appears as a striped background you can use to visually organize the text and other elements that are placed on top. It is a great design trick that produces great looks and great file-size savings.

create a unidirectional horizontal tile

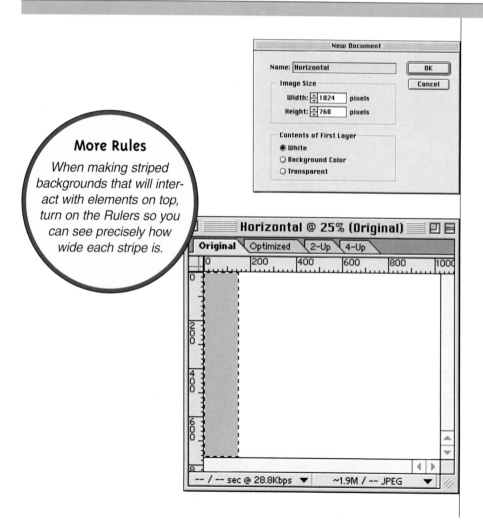

More Rules

When making striped backgrounds that will inter-act with elements on top, turn on the Rulers so you can see precisely how wide each stripe is.

1. Make a new file. I suggest making the image size the same as the dimensions of your design, including all areas which the users can scroll to. Working this way enables you to see what the stripes will look like after tiling in the browser. You can crop it down later.

2. Use the Marquee selection tool or the Rectangle tool to create the stripes.

create a unidirectional horizontal tile

3. When you are finished creating the stripes, use the Marquee tool to make a thin selection across the full width of the stripes. Then, choose Image>Crop. The tile is done.

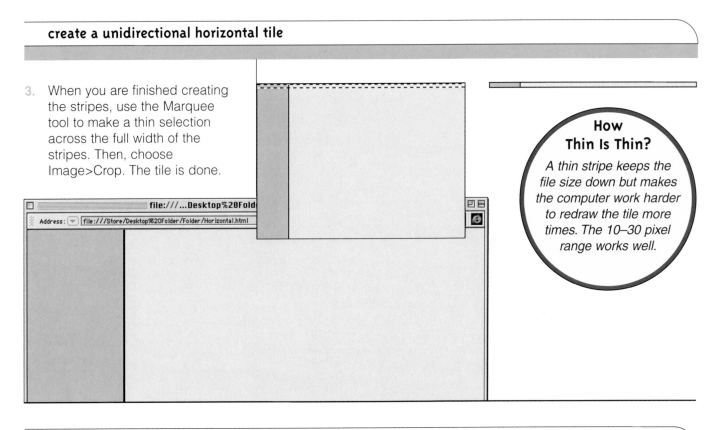

How Thin Is Thin?

A thin stripe keeps the file size down but makes the computer work harder to redraw the tile more times. The 10–30 pixel range works well.

create a unidirectional vertical tile

The same technique works in the other direction as well. This 1-pixel-wide vertical column created the background to the right. The black stripe on top would be a great place on which to build a navigation bar.

Make sure it's tall enough. This image will stretch to the right until it hits Rome, but will repeat down if the user scrolls down far enough.

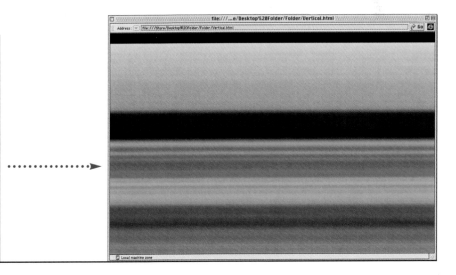

Making Full Window Background Images

I already mentioned that all backgrounds are tiled, but if you make the tile large enough to fill the entire browser window then, effectively, it will appear as a single image. If you want to do this, the question becomes what size to make it because browser windows can be all different sizes and also can be resized and reshaped by the user. A good general size is 1024x768 pixels, but beware that some monitors are large enough to allow larger browser windows.

create a full window graphic background

A browser window opened to 640x480 pixels shows only this portion of the image in the background.

1. The only key to creating a full window background is choosing the correct size for the image. And the correct size is a big size. This image is 1200x800 pixels—big enough that it will not repeat in any browser window.

   Of course, you also want to create an image that works within the design no matter how much of it is visible. Even though this image may not be seen in its entirety in smaller browser windows, it still functions to establish a color scheme for the page. And, if the text from the background appears elsewhere on the page, the user will understand what these chopped-off words are.

File Size Worry

Using a single image for a background is generally not advisable. This is because the size of an image that can cover the entire browser window must be so large that it will take too long to download and process. However, having a single bold image in the background can be a great effect. If you use a slightly blurred JPEG with broad areas of color and reduced contrast, you can create a file small enough to download quickly that will also tend not to distract from foreground elements. See page 115 for information on how to keep a file small.

Window Sizing

You can make a background image and then use JavaScript to open a browser window to the exact size of the image.

create a full window photographic background

blurrybackground.net

This design is all about the background image. The image works well because it has broad areas of color and low contrast and is very blurry. It is a dramatic, yet very small JPEG—the perfect combination for the Web.

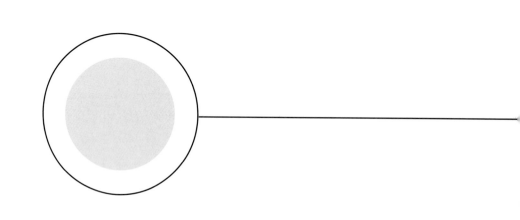

Part IV

Web Elements

Slices

Slices are one of the building blocks of web graphics operations. By slicing Photoshop images into smaller parts, you can begin to add other elements, such as rollovers and varying optimize settings. This chapter, a foundation for other chapters in this book, discusses how to create and edit the various types of slices you can create in Photoshop and ImageReady. The chapter ends with a long exercise that incorporates most of the aspects of slices discussed in the chapter.

What Is a Slice?

Creating slices is a way of dividing a single Photoshop or ImageReady image document into a number of graphic files. A slice is, simply, one section of the image. When the image document is saved as an optimized version, each slice is saved as a separate graphic file. Along with this set of files, an accompanying HTML document is saved. Included in the HTML code is a table that places the slices back together again when displayed in a Web browser. Reconstructed in the table, the set of images (or slices) will look the same as it did in Photoshop or ImageReady.

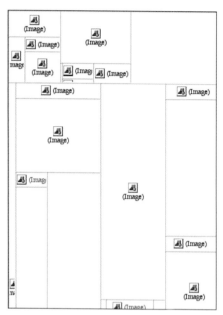

Does this look familiar? When you see this in a browser, you are viewing the bounds of table cells into which slices will be loaded. As they download, they are filled in and the image becomes complete again. By the way, to replace the text that reads "Image" with custom labels, see page 203.

When you draw a slice, you define the bounds of an image file. Every ImageReady file contains at least one slice. If no other slices have been defined, the entire image is a slice. The yellow border in the image to the right shows that this image consists of a single slice.

What You Do with Slices

Image files are sliced when you want to add links or rollover effects to one part of a Web page design, when you want to save one part of an image in a different file format from the others, or when you want to delete an area of the image and replace it with a solid color or HTML text.

Slices enable you to apply rollover effects to parts of an image. Rollover effects are triggered when the mouse is anywhere within the slice bounds.

Slicing an image enables you to save some slices as JPEGs and others as GIFs.

Slices Versus Image Maps

When you're viewing a Web page in a browser, image maps and slices that have links attached to them operate similarly. Both enable you to add interactivity to the graphics. However, they are fundamentally different in construction.

Rollovers are slice-based effects. As you roll over the default images, JavaScript causes new images to be substituted. A sliced menu built with rollover effects is composed of as many graphic files as there are choices in the menu multiplied by the number of rollover states.

An image map, on the other hand, is a single file that has had areas within it defined as link areas. These map areas are defined by HTML code that can be saved in file with the image(s). Clicking the map areas takes you to those links. Because image maps can be any shape, you can create link areas of any shape.

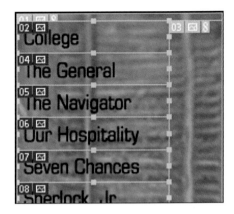

Slices: *Each area within the yellow bounding boxes is saved as a separate graphic file.*

Image Maps: *Each area within the blue bounding boxes is defined as an image map by the HTML code that is saved along with this single graphic image.*

The Shape of Slices

Slices, like all graphic files, must be rectangles. If you want to create slices that do not appear to be rectangles, you must add transparent areas to them. See Chapter 15, "Transparency," page 274.

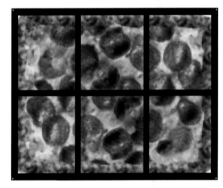

Slices must be rectangles.

---

view slices

1. **ImageReady:** Click the Slice Visibility icon on the Tool palette to turn slice edges on and off. Q is the shortcut key.

   Photoshop: Choose View>Show>Slices.

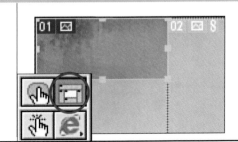

More in ImageReady:

Set slice view options by choosing Edit>Preferences>Slices.

Selecting either slice tool automatically makes slices visible.

Slice Types

Several types of slices exist that you might create or will be created for you. It is important to understand that not all the same features are available to all types of slices. Depending on what you want to do with a slice, you must create a slice of the appropriate type. Here's a rundown:

User-Slice: When you use the Slice tool to draw a slice, that slice is a called a *user-slice*. When a user-slice is selected, draggable handles for resizing exist on all its sides.

Auto-Slice: These slices are created automatically when you draw or move or alter other slices. They are a necessary part of maintaining the HTML table that the slices will be placed into. To convert an auto-slice to a user-slice, see the exercise below. Auto-slices have no handles when selected.

Layer-Based Slice: These slices adjust themselves to always be the smallest rectangle in which the contents of a layer fit. If you edit the layer, the slice bounds shift to accommodate the changes. They are created by a command in ImageReady's Slices menu. See page 200.

No Image Slice: A graphic file is not saved for any slice designated as a No Image slice. By default, the HTML table cell that would have contained the graphic file will be populated with a spacer.gif. See page 201.

Subslice: Subslices are like auto-slices in that they are automatically created. They are created when other slices overlap each other.

PHOTOSHOP OR IMAGEREADY?

Both Photoshop and ImageReady have slicing features. So, which do you use? For basic, or initial, slicing Photoshop is fine, but in general I recommend ImageReady for these operations because its tools are more convenient to use. Photoshop, for example, has no Slice palette for easy access to slice features. To access some slice options in Photoshop, double-click the slice with the Slice Select tool. Only ImageReady enables you to do things such as copy, paste, divide, distribute, and align slices.

---

change an auto-slice to a user-slice

ImageReady

Color change indicates a change from an auto-slice to a user-slice.

In Photoshop 6.0

A **Promote to User-Slice** button is available on the Slice Select tool Options bar.

1. To change an auto-slice into a user-slice, select the slice with the Slice Select tool and choose Slices>Promote to User-Slice.

After "promoting" the slice, handles appear that enable you to drag and reshape the slice bounds.

Creating Slices

There are several ways to create slices. If you want to draw them, you have two options. You can either use the Slice tool and drag rectangles, or use the Rectangular Marquee tool to drag selections and then choose Slices>Create Slice from Selection. The Slice tool is easy to use and can snap to other slices already present. This helps to prevent you from accidentally creating extra slivers of auto-slices, and all the slices are kept tightly aligned to each other. The advantages of using the Marquee tool is that it is more flexible—it's easy to add to and subtract from it—and you might have a selection already active that was the result of creating the graphic. No matter which method you use, the necessary auto-slices are created.

> ### Selections from Slices
>
> *You also can create a selection from the currently selected slice. Choose Selection>Create Selection from Slice.*

create a slice

1. Select the Slice tool from the toolbox and click and drag in the image.

   The edges and corners snap to other slices that are present. This makes it easy to keep the slices uniform. In this example, I dragged from the upper-right corner point of one existing slice to the upper-right corner point of another.

   This operation caused an auto-slice (No. 3) to be added to the right of the new slice.

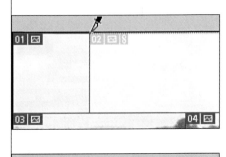
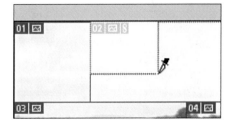
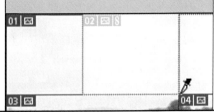
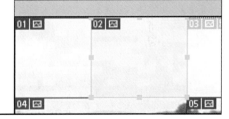

select a slice

1. Get the Slice Select tool (K is the shortcut key) and click anywhere within the slice bounds.

   Hold the Shift key to select multiple slices.

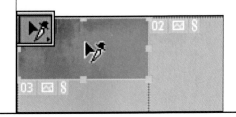

Hold the (Command) [Ctrl] key to change the Slice tool to the Slice Select tool (this works the other way, too).

Working with Slices

In the toolbox,
Photoshop's toolbox has the same slice tools as ImageReady's (shown here), with the exception of the Slice Visibility icon.

Slice tool

Slice Select tool

Slice Visibility icon (ImageReady only)

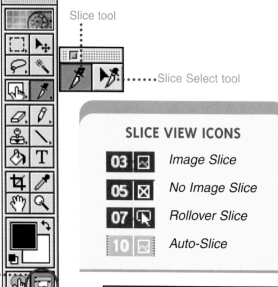

SLICE VIEW ICONS

03	Image Slice
05	No Image Slice
07	Rollover Slice
10	Auto-Slice

Yellow bounds (the default color) indicate the active slice. If the edges have handles then the y can be dragged to reshape the slice.

The slice number and type of slice are indicated in the slice. This number is used to name the slice when saving them.

Linked slices receive identical optimize settings.

Auto-slices and layer-based slices cannot be reshaped and have no handles. To reshape them, promote them to user-slices first (page 196).

SLICE OPERATIONS

To view slices:
IR: Click the Slice Visibility icon on the toolbox. PS: Choose Show>Extras>Slices.

To select a slice:
Use the Slice Select tool and click anywhere within the slice bounds.

To reshape a slice:
Use the Slice Select tool to drag the handles at the sides and corners.

To convert a slice:
IR: Select the slice and choose Slices>Promote to User-Slice. PS: Select the slice and click the Promote to User-Slice button on the Options bar (page 196).

To delete a slice:
Select the slice and press delete.

To create a no image slice:
IR: Select the slice, find the Slices palette, and choose No Image from the Type menu. PS: Double-click the slice with the Slice Select tool and choose No Image from the Type menu (page 200).

ImageReady only:

To link slices:
Select two or more slices and choose Slices>Link Slices.

To create a layer-based slice:
Select the layer in the Layers palette and choose Layers>Create New Layer-Based Slice (page 201).

Working with Slices (ImageReady only)

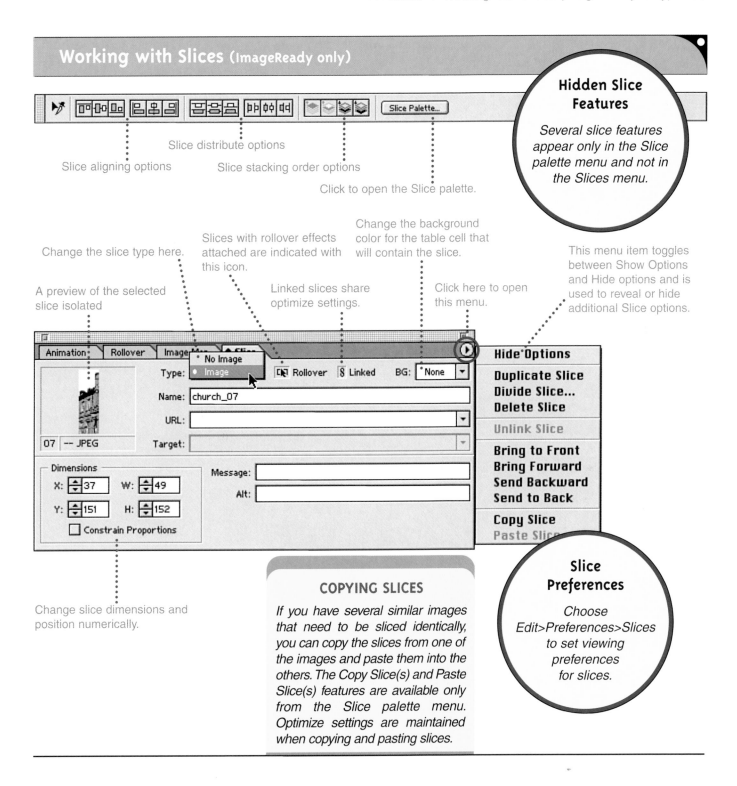

Slice aligning options

Slice distribute options

Slice stacking order options

Click to open the Slice palette.

Hidden Slice Features

Several slice features appear only in the Slice palette menu and not in the Slices menu.

Change the slice type here.

Slices with rollover effects attached are indicated with this icon.

Change the background color for the table cell that will contain the slice.

This menu item toggles between Show Options and Hide options and is used to reveal or hide additional Slice options.

A preview of the selected slice isolated

Linked slices share optimize settings.

Click here to open this menu.

Change slice dimensions and position numerically.

COPYING SLICES

If you have several similar images that need to be sliced identically, you can copy the slices from one of the images and paste them into the others. The Copy Slice(s) and Paste Slice(s) features are available only from the Slice palette menu. Optimize settings are maintained when copying and pasting slices.

Slice Preferences

Choose Edit>Preferences>Slices to set viewing preferences for slices.

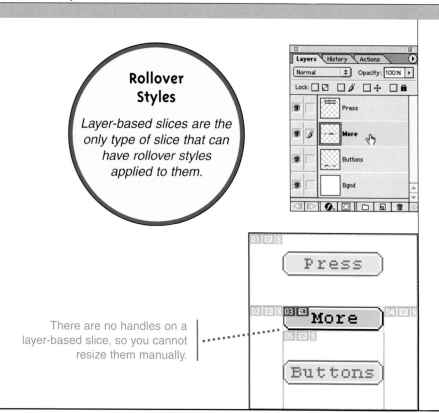

Layer-based slices automatically redraw after a layer's contents are changed.

Layer-Based Slices

Layer-based slices are created automatically by ImageReady based on the contents of a layer. The bounds of a layer-based slice are defined as the smallest rectangle in which the contents of a layer will fit. After a layer-based slice has been created, its boundaries are redrawn whenever any changes are made that affect the contents of the layer. For example, if you correct a typo in a text layer, the slice bounds reshape to the limits of the corrected text. These slices can be well suited for slices with attached links or rollover effects. Because they are based on the contents of a layer, they cannot be manually reshaped and do not have handles on them. If you want to manually reshape them, you must promote them first to user-slices. Normally, when creating layer-based slices it is difficult to avoid the addition of several small and irregular auto-slices. Be aware that they result in a more complex HTML table that will be more difficult to edit manually.

---

create a layer-based slice   *ImageReady*

Rollover Styles

Layer-based slices are the only type of slice that can have rollover styles applied to them.

There are no handles on a layer-based slice, so you cannot resize them manually.

1. Select a layer in the Layers palette.

    Fair Warning: *If you add a layer-based slice to a layer that has rollover effects applied to it, the layer's pre-existing layer effects will be deleted.*

2. Choose Layer>New Layer Based Slice.

    The layer-based slice and all the auto-slices necessary to fill in the gaps are created.

No Image Slices

Sometimes when an image is sliced, there are slices that contain only a solid color. These slices can be converted into No Image slices. This means that no graphic file is saved for that slice. The dimensions of the HTML table cell are maintained, and by default it is filled with a spacer.gif file. This is a one-pixel GIF that is stretched in the browser to fill the original table cell size. Set the background color (BG) for the No Image slice to the color you want to appear in the browser. No image slices save download time, and I recommend taking advantage of them whenever possible. You can also add text that will appear in the browser. This text does not preview in ImageReady. Use the Preview in Browser feature to see the effects.

convert a slice to a no image slice

1. Use the Slice Select tool to select a slice that is blank or you want to omit when displayed in the browser.

   If you selected the slice containing the loose peas, the peas would not be part of the page when it is viewed in a browser.

Text added to the Text box is added to the HTML code and displays in the browser, but you will not see this text in ImageReady. Valid HTML tags such as the bold tag (<b>), can be used. Be careful when using this feature—this text can cause the table cell to expand, and therefore break up the table. Alignment options for the text appear below.

2. On the Slice palette, choose No Image from the Type menu.

3. Click the BG menu to set the color you want the no image area to be filled with in the browser.

   If you use the Eyedropper to select the color from inside the slice bounds, you can select Foreground color from the BG pop-up menu.

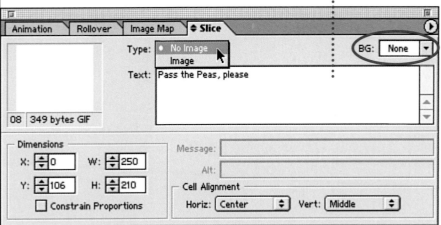

Manipulating Slices

It is a good idea to keep slices ordered and aligned. This helps to keep down the number of slices and reduces download and display time. ImageReady has tools that enable you to divide, align, distribute, copy, paste, duplicate, and combine slices. If you have a column of menu items, or a row of icons, you could draw one slice around all of them, and then divide it into identically sized slices. Take advantage of these features by selecting one or more slices with the Slice Select tool, and then choosing an option from the Slices menu. The Copy and Paste Slice(s) commands appear only in the Slice palette menu, not the Slices menu.

Manipulating Slices
ImageReady

Divide Slices
Draw one slice, and Divide it into several identically sized slices.

 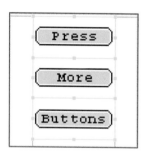

Align Slices
Select two or more slices, and Align them to each other.

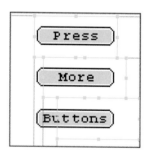 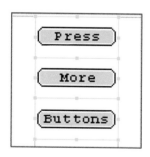

Combine Slices
Select two or more slices, and Combine them into one slice.

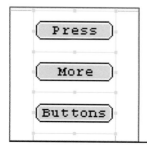 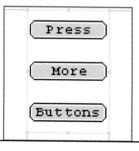

Copy and Paste Slices
Copy slices from one document, and Paste them into another. Optimize settings are maintained.

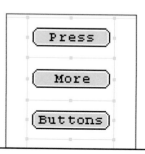 

Adding HTML Attributes to Slices

Whenever you slice an ImageReady or Photoshop file, you will probably use the HTML file that is saved along with the various images. So, as long as it's generated for you, you can take advantage of some extra items that can be added to the HTML, including a URL address to give the slice a link, a Background color for each table cell, the Target frame for the link, the Alt text that will display in case the image doesn't, and the Message that will appear in the Status bar of the browser when the mouse is on top of the slice. In addition, for No Image slices, you can add text and cell alignment options (see page 201).

Alt text is important because it is what users with text-only browsers, as well as those who have turned images off, see. It is also read aloud by browsers used by visually impaired individuals. Choosing appropriate Alt text will make those users happy.

HTML Attributes in the Slice Palette

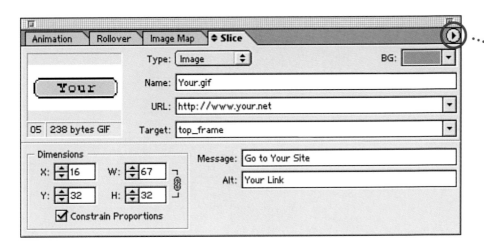

To view all Slice palette options choose Show Options from the palette menu.

BG:
Choose a background color for the slice. This color will be visible if the image doesn't load in the browser or if it is a no image slice.

Name:
Choose a filename for the slice.

URL:
Add a link to the slice by choosing a URL.

Target:
Choose the target window or frame for the URL to load into.

Message:
Choose a message to appear in the status bar when the mouse is over the slice.

Alt:
Choose text to be displayed in a text-only browser or a browser with images turned off.

Optimizing Slices

One of the primary reasons to create slices is that you can save the slices (or images) in different file formats. This enables you to save the photographic areas of a design as JPEGs and the areas that contain crisp solid colors as GIFs. Taking advantage of varied file formats improves the quality of the graphics as well as the speed of their display in the browser. To do this, select each slice with the Slice Select tool and then choose settings on the Optimize palette.

Typically, each slice in a design does need unique optimize settings. You may have two settings for the entire design: one for all the JPEGs and one for all the GIFs. You can shift-select slices and choose the optimize settings them all at one. Or, you can link slices. Once linked, changing the optimize settings for one slice changes them for all. Linking is an ImageReady-only feature. See Chapter 7, "Optimizing Graphics," for full coverage of optimizing (page 110).

Link Slices	*ImageReady*

1. Use the Slice Select tool with the Shift key to select two or more slices.

2. Then choose Slices>Link.

   The link symbol appears in the slices' icons and the icon color is made the same for all slices in the group. Slices that were linked to other slices lose those links and become part of the new group.

These red slices are linked and because they are GIFs will share the same Color Table.

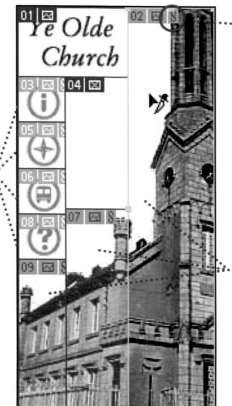

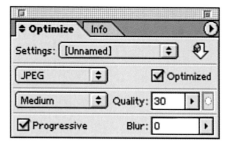

······The link symbol.

Changing the optimize settings for one of these slices changes them for all three.

Saving Slices

When you save a sliced design in preparation for browser display, an HTML document is saved along with a folder of images—one image file for each slice (plus more to accommodate rollover states). A lot of information can be involved in saving slices: slice names, optimize settings, color tables, alt text, URLs, and more. All of this information tells ImageReady or Photoshop either how to save the sliced images or what to inlcude in the HTML document that accompanies them. Saving options are available in the Output Settings dialog box. Automatic slice-naming conventions can be set in the Slices section, and if the slice has rollover effects attached, the Saving Files section controls the naming of the various states. Note that if you choose a slice Name in the Slice palette (page 203), that name overrides the automatic naming feature. In the Background section you can set a background color for the page or choose an image for background tiling.

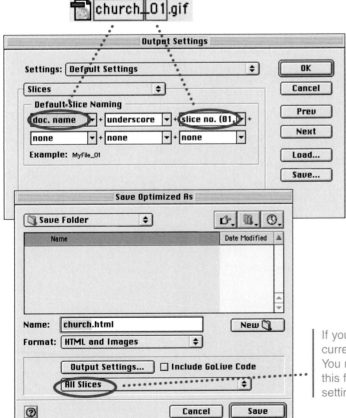

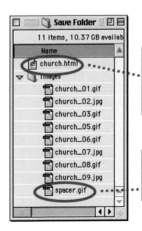

This HTML file contains a table that puts the images in the Images folder back together in the browser just as they appeared in Photoshop.

This file is created by Photoshop and ImageReady, and is used by the HTML document to maintain spacing in the table.

If you want, you can save only the slices currently selected in the image window. You might do this if you've already saved this file and want to change the optimize settings for just some of the slices.

Access Output Settings

Photoshop:

1. In the Save for Web dialog box, click the Output Settings button. After clicking OK in Save for Web, the Output Settings button is still available in next dialog box (Save Optimized As).

ImageReady:

1. Choose File>Output Settings, or click the Output Settings button in the Save Optimized As dialog box.

Slicing a Design

The following exercise pulls together some of the various slicing tasks discussed in this chapter, and applies them to a design. It is intended to show how these feature might be used in a real-world situation. Keep in mind that there are many ways to create slices. Use this exercise as a guide, and adjust it as necessary for your own designs. Get this file from the Web site if you want to follow along in the same file. Otherwise, read through the steps to get an understanding of how these features can work together.

slice a design

SLICE FROM GUIDES

Although this exercise uses alternative methods, you might find that creating slices from guides is the easiest method of dividing a design into slices. The guides may already be in place as a result of aligning elements during the design process. After placing guides, choose Slices>Create Slice from Guides. Afterward, use the Slices>Combine Slices command to combine any slices as suited for the design. This is an ImageReady-only feature.

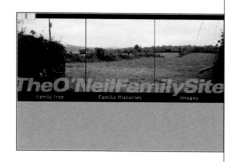

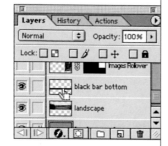

1. Create a design that has several types of graphic elements: photographs, type, icons, and so on. Keep the various elements on separate layers to better take advantage of all slicing commands.

2. To begin slicing, go to the Layers palette and select the layer that contains the black bar that runs under the three gray text layers. Hold the (Command) [Ctrl] key while clicking on the layer to load the selection for that layer's contents.

3. Choose Slices>Create Slice from Selection. There are now three slices: one user-slice and two auto-slices.

slice a design

4. Next, choose Slices>Divide Slice and enter 3 for the number in Vertical Slices. Click OK.

   If Preview is turned on, you see in the image window where the slices will be divided.

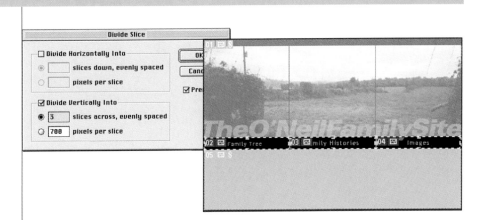

5. Repeat step 2 for the layer that contains the landscape image; then choose Layer>New Layer Based Slice to create a slice that wraps to the layer's contents.

Slice Snapping

When drawing slices manually, choose View> SnapTo>Slices to force slice bounds to snap to each other. This aids in keeping slices tightly aligned.

6. You want to divide this slice, too, but layer-based slices cannot be divided. Choose Slices>Promote to User-Slice.

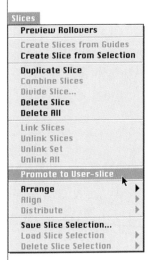

Locking Slices

Slices can be locked so that you don't inadvertently move or reshape them. Select slices with the Slice Select tool and choose View>Lock Slices.

slice a design

7. Then, choose Slices>Divide and divide this slice into 3 slices as well.

Fixed Size Slices

On the Slice tool options bar, you can choose Fixed Size from the Style menu to create a slice of an exact size.

8. Next, add rollover effects to the text links (see Chapter 12, "Rollovers," page 212).

9. Then, use the Slice Select tool with the Shift key to select the three text link slices, and choose Slices>Link to make sure they will have identical optimize settings. Do the same for the three image slices. They will all be optimized in step 13.

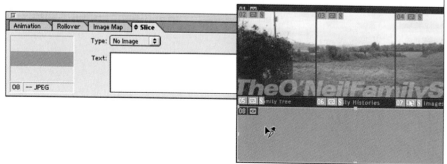

10. Two slices in this image contain only solid colors that can be generated by the HTML file that will be saved with the images. Select each of them, find the Slice palette, and change the slice Type to No Image.

slice a design

11. Then, select the top no image slice, the black stripe, and set its BG (background) color on the Slice palette to Black.

    Set the color of the other no image slice to the desired background color of your Web page design.

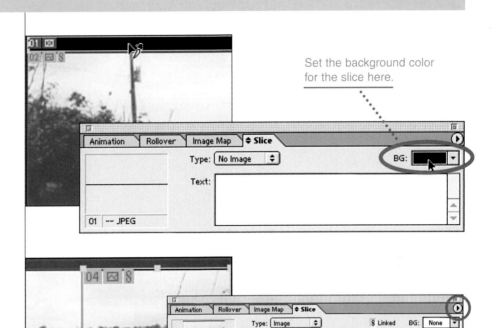

Set the background color for the slice here.

12. Use the Slice Select tool to select each of the other slices one by one (except for the no image slices) and name them and assign Alt text to them on the Slice palette.

    You can use the same Alt text for multiple slices, but be careful not to give them the same names.

To show the Dimensions, Message, and Alt slice options, choose Show Options from the palette menu.

Slice Selecting

While the Slice Select tool is active, pressing (Command-A) [Ctrl-A] selects all slices, (Command-D) [Ctrl-D} deselects all slices.

slice a design

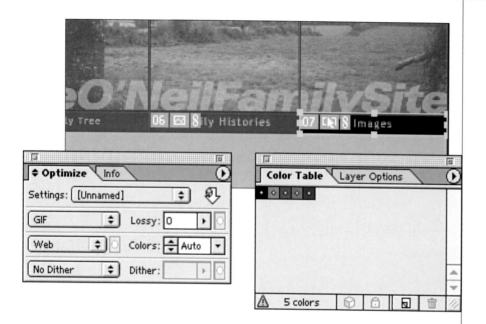

13. Select one of the text link slices, find the Optimize palette, and choose settings. The other two slices linked to it get the same settings. Choose one of the image slices and do the same. No image slices does not use optimize settings, so there's no need to set them.

Linked GIFs

Linked GIFs have identical color tables. Only link GIFs that contain identical colors. Otherwise, unnecessary colors are included in some of the files.

14. To check the settings, click the Preview in Browser button on the Tool palette.

Notice that the bottom slice does not contain any color. That is because it is a no image slice and will take on the color of the background, which will be set in the next step.

To get rid of the white margins, open the HTML file in an HTML editor and set the margins to 0.

slice a design

15. Go back to ImageReady to set the background color for the Web page. Get the Eyedropper and select the color from the bottom slice to set this color as ImageReady's current foreground color.

16. Choose File>Output Settings>Background and choose Foreground Color from the Color menu. Click OK.

    This causes ImageReady's current foreground color to be encoded in HTML as the background color for the Web page.

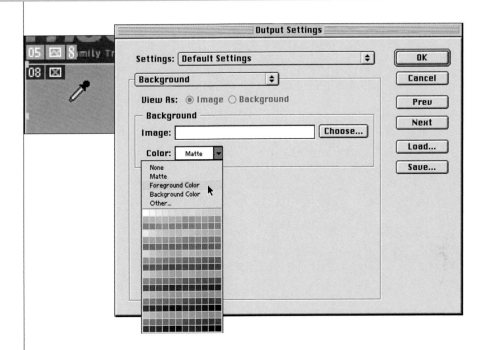

17. Choose File>Save Optimized As. Choose HTML and Images from the Format menu and click Save to finish the project.

    Here is the final design as it appears in a Web browser.

The background color chosen in step 15 fills in through the empty (no image) table cell (slice).

12

Rollovers

ImageReady gets to show off its abilities when it comes to rollovers. This chapter introduces the basic issues involved in creating rollovers, shows you how to create a simple rollover, and then builds on that knowledge to discuss and demonstrate more complex rollover effects.

What Is a Rollover?

If you move the mouse over an element on a Web page and the element changes in some way—in color, in shape, or with an added shadow—then you've run across a rollover. When you click a button and it looks like it depresses, you've found a rollover. When you run down a list and the items change color or some additional text appears below or to the side, you've found a rollover. They are one of the most common features of Web sites, and ImageReady has special features to make creating even complex rollovers easy. You might use Photoshop to help create the graphics, but rollover work is primarily in ImageReady's domain.

Rollover effects are activated by mouse events.

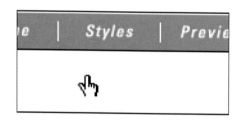 

How Do Rollovers Work?

Essentially, a rollover is a group of associated image files that are swapped depending on the current mouse event. Six possible states of a rollover image are supported by ImageReady: Normal, Over, Down, Click, Out, and Up. Typically, the Normal and Over, and sometimes the Down, states are defined. If any state is not defined then the Normal state will stand in for it. ImageReady writes the JavaScript code that controls these behaviors for you. Below is a sample of the JavaScript used for the rollover seen on page 216.

WHAT IS JAVASCRIPT ?

JavaScript is a scripting language used within HTML files. Generally, it allows greater control over events that are triggered by user interaction or unfold over time.

```
</HEAD>
<BODY BGCOLOR=#FFFFFF ONLOAD="preloadImages();">
<!-- ImageReady Slices (InfoIcon.psd) -->
<A HREF="#"
        ONMOUSEOVER="changeImages('InfoIcon_01', 'images
        ONMOUSEOUT="changeImages('InfoIcon_01', 'images,
        ONMOUSEDOWN="changeImages('InfoIcon_01', 'images
        ONMOUSEUP="changeImages('InfoIcon_01', 'images/]
        <IMG NAME="InfoIcon_01" SRC="images/InfoIcon_01
<!-- End ImageReady Slices -->
</BODY>
```

How Are Rollovers Used?

Rollovers are used to visually change a graphic link in some way as the pointer is moved over it. Think of the rollover states as a way to communicate with the person using your site. The change in states indicates to him what he's doing and what's about to happen. How many various states you create may depend on how important it is that these different user actions are differentiated. In many cases, a simple Over state is sufficient. Remember, the total size of the Web site increases as each state is added. Three states means that three graphics exist for one button.

Rollovers are generally used to create menus and navigation bars for Web sites, but they are also a useful means of displaying information dynamically—such as Melville's classification of whales: See page 234.

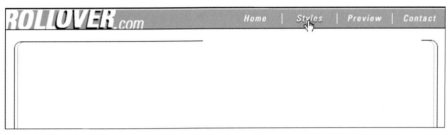

The Web page below uses rollovers in its navigation bar.

Rollovers Versus Image Maps

When you're looking at a Web page in a browser, rollovers and image maps operate similarly. Both enable you to add interactivity and links to graphics. The primary difference is that an image map is a single file that has had areas within it defined as link areas. Clicking them takes you to that link. But rollovers are composed of as many graphics as there are choices in a menu multiplied by the number of rollover states. The separate files of a menu, such as the one in the figure to the right, can be combined into a table in an HTML document.

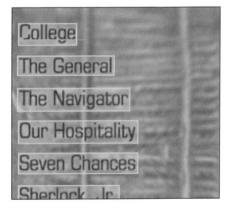

Image Maps: *Each area within the blue bounding boxes is defined as an image map by the HTML code that is saved along with this single graphic image.*

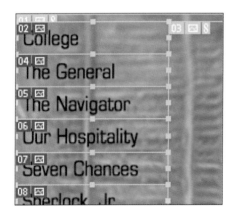

Slices: *Each area within the yellow bounding boxes is saved as a separate file.*

Working with Rollovers

When working with rollovers, use the Layers and Rollover palettes with the image window.

What you see is what you get. With Rollover Previews activated, rollover effects can be viewed inside ImageReady.

Layer effects, like the one applied to this layer, are used to quickly handle rollover effects.

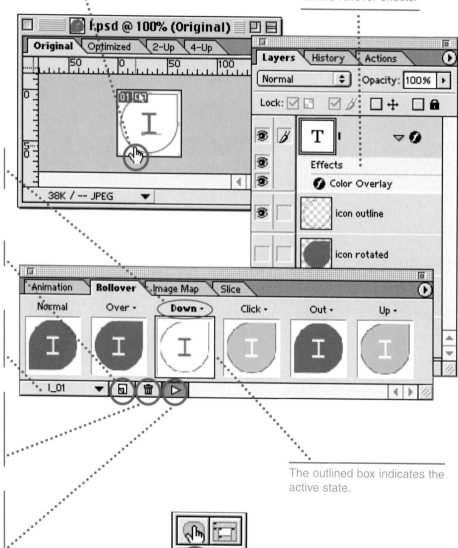

To change the rollover state, click the label above the preview to access a menu.

To add a new rollover state, click the new rollover state icon.

To choose a slice, click the slice name to access a menu of all slices. Image maps are also accessible from this menu.

To delete a rollover state, select the rollover state preview and click the Trash icon. Hold the Option key (Mac), or Alt key (Windows), to delete it without confirming.

To preview rollovers, click the Play button on the rollover palette or click the Preview Rollovers button on the Tool palette.

The outlined box indicates the active state.

create a rollover

1. Create or open an image to be used as a rollover. I simply used the Type tool to enter some text.

   It is almost always best to have the rollover element on its own layer. This enables you to be much more flexible with changes you want to make. That way, you can use layer effects and styles, use rollover styles, create layer-based slices, and make edits that will be reflected in all the rollover states. All of these things are discussed later in this chapter.

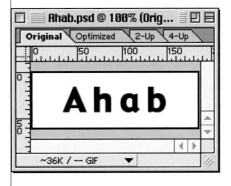

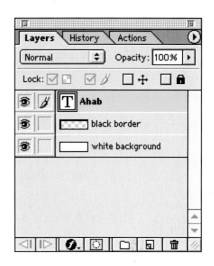

2. Click the Rollover tab on its floating palette to bring it forward, or choose Window>Show Rollover if you don't see it.

   The leftmost preview shows the Normal state of the rollover. The border around this preview indicates it is the currently active state. You should remember that what you see in the image window while that state is selected is what the rollover will look like when that state is active in the browser. (Generally, the what-you-see-is-what-you-get rule works, but in some cases it is not as accurate as you'd like due to the differences in the way browsers handle the mouse events.)

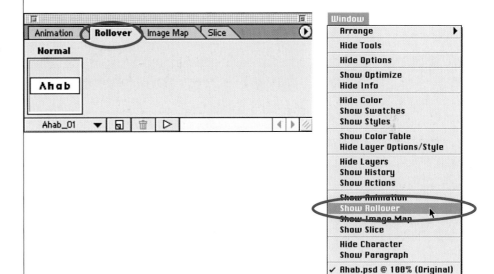

create a rollover

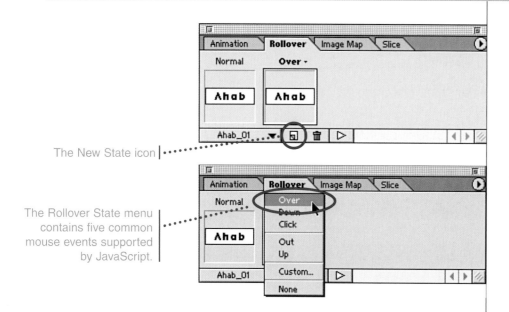

The New State icon

The Rollover State menu contains five common mouse events supported by JavaScript.

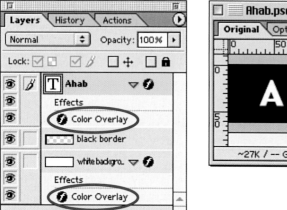

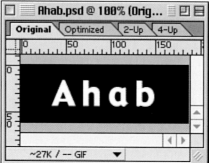

Add a Color Overlay to a layer by choosing it from the Effects menu in the Layers palette.

3. Click the New State icon at the bottom of the palette. A new state appears next to the Normal state, and the black border has now shifted to this new state.

4. Above the new state is the type of mouse event associated with that state. Click the label to bring up a menu of the options. Because it is the first available option in the list, the Over state is automatically selected. That's what you want.

   Only one of each type of state can exist for each rollover.

5. I simply used ImageReady's built-in Layer effects to add a Color Overlay to both the text layer and the background layer.

   While this state is selected, any layer change operations you peform affect only this state and none of the others. See page 226 for more details on the kinds of changes that affect only the current state of a rollover.

create a rollover

6. On the Tool palette is a Rollover Preview button. (There is also one on the bottom of the Rollover palette.) Click it once to turn it on.

7. Run the mouse over the text to test the rollover. Notice that the Layers and Rollover palettes change to reflect the current rollover state.

8. To finish the rollover, set the Optimize options. Then, choose File>Save Optimized. Use the settings you see here. An HTML file is saved along with graphic files for each rollover state.

   In this case, only two files are saved along with the HTML file. You can then open the HTML file directly in a browser or Web page authoring application such as Dreamweaver or GoLive.

   The Normal and Over states of the final rollover.

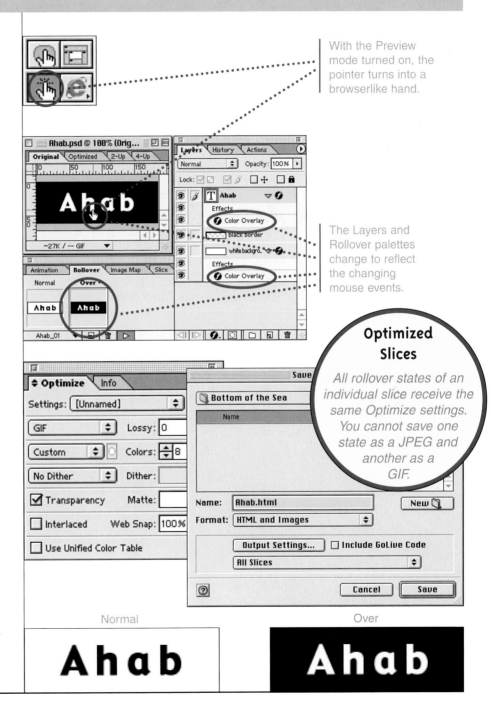

With the Preview mode turned on, the pointer turns into a browserlike hand.

The Layers and Rollover palettes change to reflect the changing mouse events.

Optimized Slices

All rollover states of an individual slice receive the same Optimize settings. You cannot save one state as a JPEG and another as a GIF.

Normal

Over

Poor pip was lost at sea.

Some Typical Rollover Adjustments

Offset up

Button up/down

Color change

Add a graphic element

Brighten or dim

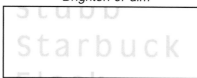

Invert colors

Roving pointer

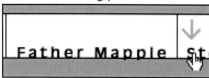

Drop shadow

Shift aside

Testing and Previewing Rollover Effects

ImageReady enables you to preview rollover effects right in the image window.

preview rollovers in ImageReady

1. Click the Preview Rollovers icon on the Tool palette, or the Preview Rollovers icon on the Rollover palette.

   Preview mode stays on until you turn it off or select a tool from the Tool palette. The keyboard shortcut y toggles the preview on and off.

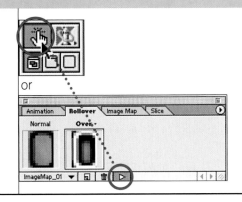

A browserlike hand is displayed when you move the pointer over a slice that has rollover effects attached.

This new feature is great, but you can't trust it completely because slight differences exist between browsers. Use the Preview Rollover mode as you build them, but when you think you've just about got what you're looking for, start previewing the effect in a browser (preferably in both browsers). Some actions will not work in the exact manner as they are previewed in ImageReady.

preview rollovers in a browser

1. Click the Preview in Browser icon on the Tool palette.

   If you click and hold, a menu of available browsers appears.

ImageReady uses the current Optimize settings when previewing rollovers in a browser. If it matters, adjust them before you jump to the browser.

You also can use the Save Optimized command to save all the rollover graphics and the HTML file; then open the HTML file in a Web page authoring application, such as Dreamweaver or GoLive.

Rollovers and Slices

Because rollovers are most often used as part of the navigation system of a Web page, usually when you create one rollover you also will make several similar ones. When building a menu, for example, normally you would construct the entire menu in a single ImageReady file and then "slice" it into its various elements (as seen in the example on the bottom of page 215). This is where ImageReady's features really show off. Before jumping into those features, however, you need to understand something about slices. Review the Slices chapter in this book if necessary (page 192).

Keep in mind that each slice will be a completely separate graphic file when it's saved for use in a browser. If you haven't defined any slices in a document, one slice is still effectively present—it is the entire document—and it is always selected as the active slice. When working with multiple related rollovers, each element must be defined by a unique slice.

Mouse events, the actions that trigger rollover effects, are actually triggered by the bounds of the slice—not what's in it. So, take care in drawing and defining slices. The effect will work a lot better if the slice is drawn very tightly to the graphic. Otherwise, the Over state, for example, will be triggered long before the mouse actually reaches the menu text, as seen in the two figures to the left.

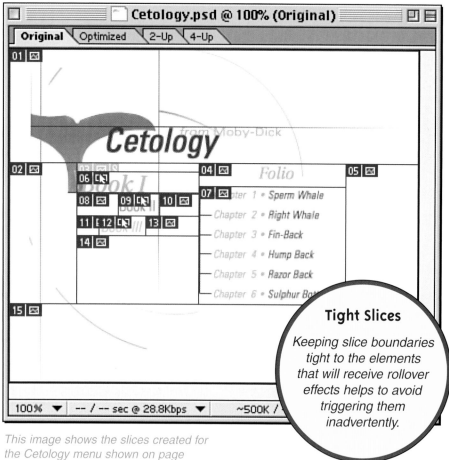

Tight Slices

Keeping slice boundaries tight to the elements that will receive rollover effects helps to avoid triggering them inadvertently.

This image shows the slices created for the Cetology menu shown on page 234. Don't be afraid of what looks complicated. ImageReady creates the HTML for this document with no problems.

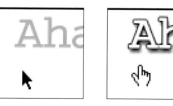

Good News: Layer-Based Slices

If the rollover element is in its own layer then you can make a *layer-based slice*. A layer-based slice will not only be the smallest rectangle in which the element will fit, but it will change its shape as you edit the content of the layer. Therefore, correcting a typo that lengthens a word causes the slice to stretch to accommodate the correction.

If you create rollover states that expand the content area of the layer then the layer-based slice expands to be large enough to incorporate all areas of all rollover states. For example, if you're adding a drop shadow to the Over state, the layer-based slice expands to include the shadow.

The problem with layer-based slices is that they produce very complex tables that are difficult to edit manually. It is often preferable to create slices such that they build the least complex table. This means making rectangles of uniform sizes and avoiding the small auto-slices that are created to fill areas that are the result of awkward-size slices.

Because slices are always rectangular, rollover effects can be applied only to rectangular areas. An alternative method is introduced on the next page.

Some Facts About Slices to Keep in Mind:

- Slices are always rectangles.

- Each slice is saved as a separate graphic file.

- Each rollover state of each slice is also saved as a separate graphic file.

- Layer-based slices wrap to the contents of the layer.

- If you add a layer-based slice to a layer that has rollover effects applied to it, the effects will be removed.

- Layer-based slices are the only kinds of layers you can use with rollover styles.

Layer-based slices wrap to the contents of the layer, enabling you to correct typos and other guffaws while maintaining all areas of the layer within the slice.

If the slice is drawn close to the content of the layer, it does not trigger the change too soon.

What About That?

A layer-based slice is a slice whose boundaries are defined by the smallest rectangle in which the layer's contents fit.

Image Map Rollovers: A Tighter Fit

One of the limitations of rollovers is that, because they are slice-based effects and slices are always rectangles, the rollover states change when the mouse rolls over any part of the rectangle. But, a way around that does exist, which uses image maps.

create an image map rollover

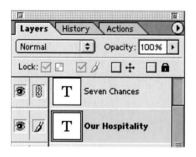

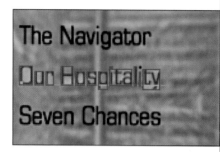

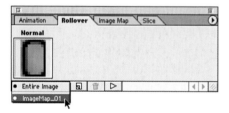

1. Select a layer and choose Layer>New Layer Based Image Map Area. An image map is wrapped tight to the contents of the layer.

   If you use this function with type and there is a little room between the letters, each letter may get its own image map section.

2. The image map shows up in the Rollover menu just like a slice. You can either select it from the list or select the image map with the Image Map select tool. Apply any effects to it just as you would with a slice-based rollover.

   Refer to the Create a Rollover steps that begin on page 217 for a full explanation of creating a rollover. After selecting the image map, you can begin with step 3.

The red outline is the image map wrapped tight to the letters.

For an even tighter fit: After creating the layer-based image map, find the Image Map palette and change the image map Type to Polygon. If you push the Quality to 100, it wraps to the shapes of the letters.

Understanding Rollover States, Layers, and Styles

A simple rollover was created earlier in this chapter, but to harness the real power of ImageReady's rollover features you need to learn about making adjustments to layers, know how changes to the content of a layer interacts with rollover states, and understand layer and rollover styles.

After you get the hang of it, creating rollovers is a quick and clean process, but it can be a little confusing at first. No doubt there will be a time when you're creating the ultimate complex rollover and you will be completely lost in the midst of an array of states, layers, and layer effects. It can be confusing simply because ImageReady is doing so much for you behind the scenes. Thanks to these operations, however, you can correct a typo and it will be reflected across all the states of all the rollovers.

What-You-See-Is-What-You-Get

The first thing to get the hang of is the What-You-See-Is-What-You-Get approach that ImageReady takes to creating rollovers (and other effects such as GIF animations). When you have a particular state selected in the Rollover palette, you will see in the image window and the Layers palette only what you would see in the browser when the pointer's action corresponds to the selected rollover state. It's a kind of real-time preview. This means that the drop shadow you added to the Down state disappears not only from the image window but also the Layers palette when the Normal state is selected. The key is to keep track of which state is selected in the Rollover palette. Always keep one eye on this palette and the other on the Layers palette.

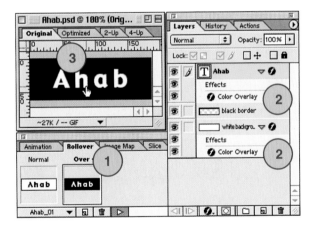

1 While this rollover state is active . . .

2 these effects are turned on in the Layers palette . . .

3 so that you see the current rollover state in the image window.

Rollover-State-Specific Versus Global Layer Changes

Some changes to layers affect only the currently selected rollover state. These include changing the position, adding (or subtracting) any Layer effects, changing the layer Blending Mode or the Opacity, and most importantly turning layers on or off.

However, changes to the pixel content of the layer—adding or subtracting any pixels, changing their colors, applying filters, and editing text—affect all states of all rollovers that use that layer.

So, depending on how you choose to alter a layer, it affects either the entire array of rollovers or just one state of a rollover. For example, if you use the Marquee tool to select an area and then fill it with a color, that color shows up in all states, However, if you use the Color Overlay layer effect to change the color, only the currently selected rollover state is affected.

Layer effects are applied to individual rollover states. For example, if you apply an Inner Bevel to the Over state of the Ahab slice, this layer effect in no way affects the Down state of the Ahab slice. The ten layer effects available include many options. Although they don't cover every type of rollover effect you might want to create, they can handle many standard effects easily.

Layer F/X

Because of the way ImageReady deals with rollover states, Layer Effects are perfect for handling the alterations of the various states of a rollover.

Some Basic Rules About How Changes to Layers Affect Rollover States

These operations change a layer in all states:	These operations change a layer in the current state:
Editing a type layer	
Adding pixels to the layer	Moving or nudging a layer
Changing the color of the pixels	Adding a Drop Shadow
Deleting pixels	Adding a Color Overlay
Making color adjustments	Adding any layer effect
Using the Transform feature	Changing the Opacity of the layer
Applying filters	Turning a layer on or off

Changing the Color of a Layer

When working with rollovers, it makes a difference *how* you work with layers. This comparison shows how to use two methods of changing the color of a layer to make different kinds of changes to rollover states.

To change the color of a layer across all rollover states:

1. Choose a new color for the foreground color.

2. Fill the contents of the layer with the new color.

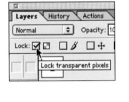

If it's a Type layer, simply press Option-Delete (Mac) or Alt-Delete [Win] to fill the type with the new color.

If it's not a Type layer, lock the layer Transparency. Then, press Option-Delete (Mac) or Alt-Delete [Win] to fill the type with the new color.

The color is changed in all the states of all the rollovers.

To change the color of a layer in a single rollover state:

1. Choose a new color as a foreground color.

2. Select a state in the Rollover palette.

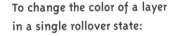

3. Then, select a layer in the Layers palette.

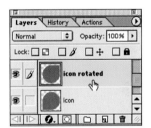

4. Add a Color Overlay effect.

The color is changed in only this specific state of this rollover.

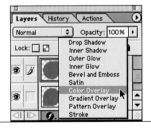

Two useful commands are available in the Rollover palette menu that enable you to make layer changes that are reflected in other rollover states.

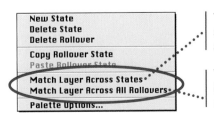

This command makes the currently selected layer look the same as it does now in all other states of the current rollover.

This command makes the currently selected layer look the same as it does now in all other states of all the rollovers.

the gamut of rollover states

The United States of Rollovers

This chart explains the names of the JavaScript mouse events ImageReady supports, what they refer to, and when they will be activated in a browser.

To change the mouse event for a state, click and hold the label above the thumbnail preview.

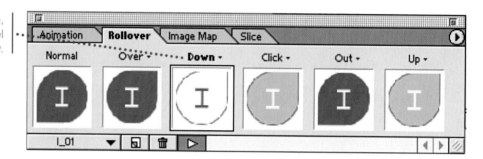

Normal	The default state—displayed in the absence of any other mouse events.
Over	Displayed when the mouse is on top of the graphic.
Down	Displayed while the user clicks and holds on top of the graphic.
Out	Displayed when the mouse moves off the graphic. If no Out state is defined then the Normal state is used.
Up	Displayed after the graphic has been clicked and the mouse is still on top of it.
Click	Displayed after the graphic has been clicked.
None	Use this as a holding place for states while you work out the nuances of a rollover, or to save alternative states you don't want to employ at the time.
Custom	Allows you to attach a custom JavaScript event to a state.

ImageReady saves the name of the state in the filename.

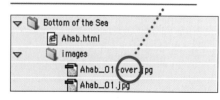

Rollover Styles

After you adjust layer effects for one rollover, you can save the settings in a Rollover or Layer Style. Rollover Styles are similar to Layer Styles, but they also add rollover states—effects are added to the layer, and the appropriate rollover states are also added to the slice. Note that Rollover Styles can only be saved from and applied to layer-based slices. For more on Layer Styles, read the Styles chapter (page 296).

create a rollover style

1. This file contains a background layer and a layer for each item in the menu. Select the layer that contains the first menu item.

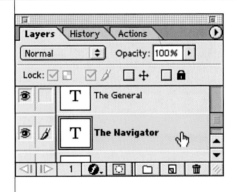

2. Choose Layer>New Layer Based Slice. Use the Slice Select tool to select the slice.

    Rollover styles can be created only from layer-based slices.

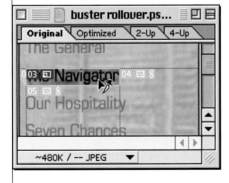

3. In the Rollover palette, create a new Over state. It will become the current state.

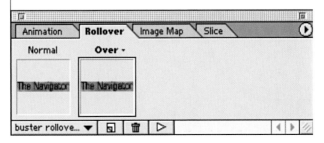

create a rollover style

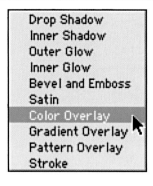

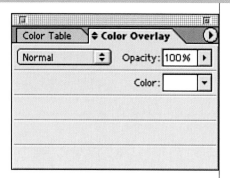

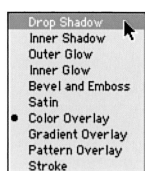

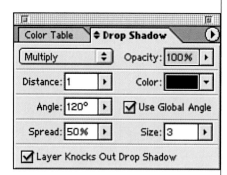

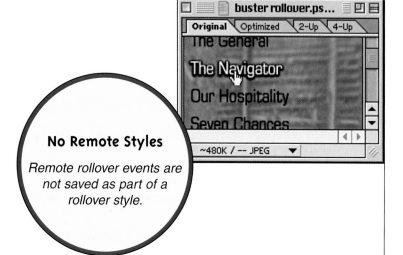

4. On the Layers palette, choose Color Overlay from the effects pop-up menu and find the Color Overlay palette. Enter the settings you want. You can see what I did here. For more control over the Layer Effect, click the double set of arrows in the Name tab of this palette.

5. Go back to the Layers palette and choose Drop Shadow from the pop-up menu; then find the Drop Shadow palette and fix up the settings.

6. Test the rollover with the Preview Rollover button.

No Remote Styles

Remote rollover events are not saved as part of a rollover style.

create a rollover style

7. Find the Styles palette and choose New Style from the palette menu. In the dialog box that opens, check all the options and name the style.

   If the selected layer does not have a layer-based slice attached, the Include Rollover States option is not available.

   The icon created in the Styles palette shows a thumbnail of the Layer styles for the Normal state applied to a gray square.

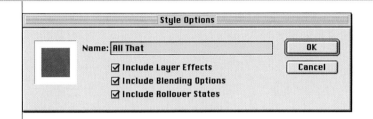

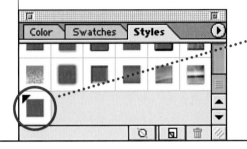

An icon with a black triangle has rollover states attached to it.

apply a rollover style

1. Select a layer in the Layers palette.

   If the layer does not have a layer-based slice attached to it then it will become a layer-based slice after the style is applied.

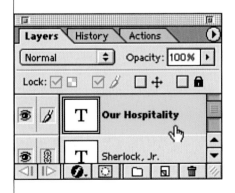

Instant rollover effects—after the style has been applied.

2. Find the Style palette and click an icon to apply the style.

   Applying a rollover style removes all other layer effects and rollover states attached to that layer.

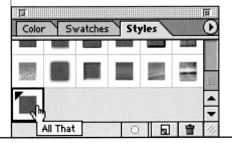

Remote Rollovers

Rollovers are not limited to only changing the slice that the pointer is on top of. They also can be used to change something in another part of the design. In terms of working with ImageReady, though, you are limited to changing what appears within a single ImageReady file.

The most common use of this feature is to provide additional information about a link. In the example to the right, as each item in the menu is rolled over, a descriptive sentence appears in a "remote" slice below the menu.

With remote rollovers, an action in one part of the image causes a change in another part.

---

create a remote rollover

To create the example above, the Over state was selected in the Rollover palette, and the layer containing the extra text was turned on.

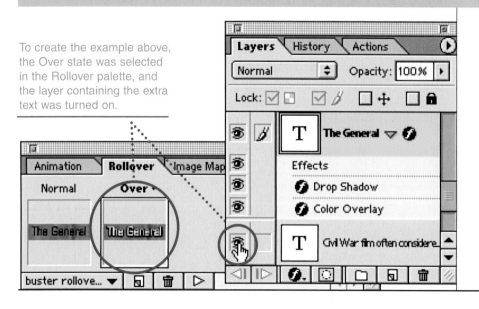

1. The only difference in building a remote rollover is that when you have a rollover state selected in the Rollover palette, instead of making a change in the Layers palette to the layer associated with that slice, you make a change to another layer—for example, turning it on.

Saving Rollovers

Okay, you've got the rollover effects you want. How do you save and use the files? When ImageReady saves rollovers, it saves a set of images plus an HTML document that organizes all the slices and rollover states into tables; it also writes the necessary JavaScript code. The HTML file can be opened directly in a browser for use or opened in a Web page authoring application for further editing or inclusion into a page design.

But before getting to the Save Optimized As or Save Optimized dialog boxes, as with all other ImageReady save operations, you need to select the Optimize settings. For more complete information on optimizing and file formats, see Chapter 7, "Optimizing Graphics" (page 110). No file format works best for rollovers—GIF, JPEG, and PNG all work. Generally, make your optimize decisions in the same way you would for any other image.

Although each slice can be saved in a different graphic file format, each state of a rollover (all the files that might replace that slice in the browser) must use the same optimize settings as every other state of the rollover. So, choose settings that work for all the states of the rollover.

In the Save Optimized As dialog box, you can choose to save the HTML file and the images, or just one or the other. You also can save selected slices only. These options can be helpful when reediting old graphics. (See Chapter 6, "Saving Files for the Web" (page 96), for more details about saving options.) From the Save Optimized As dialog box, you can access Output Settings options. In the Saving Files section you see ImageReady's system for automatically naming the files that make up rollover effects. I see no reason to change the defaults, but you have plenty of options if you want to.

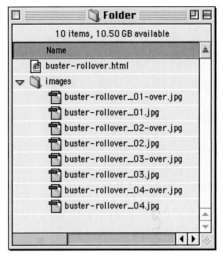

The HTML file and associated images saved in a separate Images folder.

UNIFIED COLOR TABLE

When saving rollovers as GIFs, an option at the bottom of the Optimize palette becomes available—Unified Color Table. Turning on this option creates a common Color Table to be used with all the GIFs saved for that rollover. If you can't see this option choose Show Options from the palette menu.

☐ Use Unified Color Table

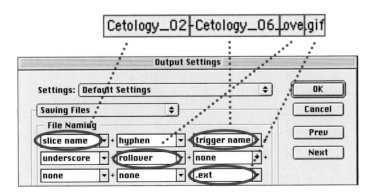

A graphic file automatically named by ImageReady and how the parts correspond to the Output Settings, Saving Files options.

Dynamic Rollover Structures

So far, rollovers have been discussed as they would be used for buttons and menus, but they also can be used simply to display information dynamically. This was the case with the remote rollover example on page 232. The example that follows uses rollovers to break down the classification of whales as described in *Moby Dick*.

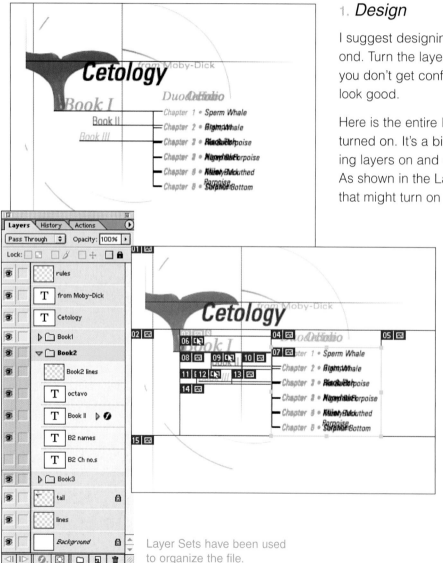

Layer Sets have been used to organize the file.

1. *Design*

I suggest designing first and defining rollover states second. Turn the layers on and off manually as you work so you don't get confused, but concentrate on making it look good.

Here is the entire ImageReady file with all the layers turned on. It's a bit of a mess until it's organized by turning layers on and off for the appropriate rollover states. As shown in the Layers palette at the left, each element that might turn on and off is on its own layer.

2. *Slice*

The next step is to draw slices for each element. The important slices here are the ones that surround the Book I, Book II, and Book III titles. These three slices trigger the rollover actions. Also, notice that only one slice is drawn around the area where the chapter names and numbers appear. This information always displays together so it's on one layer and in one slice.

3. *Define Rollover States*

Next, rollover states are defined for each of the three "Book" links. Rolling over "Book I" will make the "Book I" darken (by using a Color Overlay) and chapter numbers pop up, whereas clicking it will make the chapter names appear. All effects were created by turning layers on and off or using Color Overlays.

4. *Add Animations*

Finally, animations are added to the book titles. To make an animation that is triggered by a rollover effect, select the slice and choose or create a rollover state for it. Then, while that state is active in the Rollovers palette, switch to the Animations palette and build the animation. Animations will preview when Preview Rollovers is turned on.

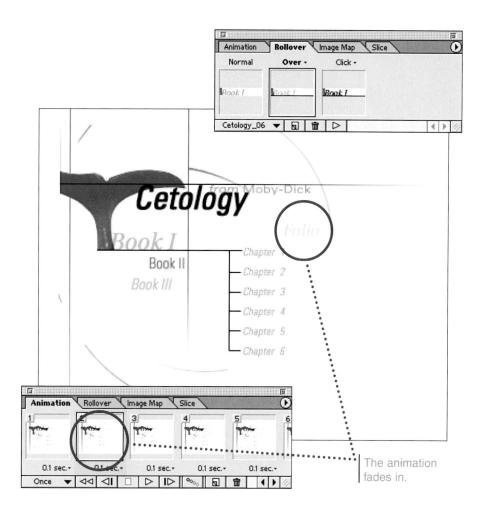

The animation fades in.

Sorry. No, You Can't.

In ImageReady, you cannot build a secondary level of rollovers. That is, you can't have one rollover that turns on an element that also has rollover effects attached to it. Effects like these can be achieved with DHTML, but are beyond the scope of ImageReady and this book.

A dynamic rollover also might pop up pictures of items in a list.

13

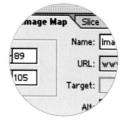

Image Maps

Image maps are HTML codes that cause discrete areas of a graphic displayed in a Web browser to act as link areas, or "hot spots." Although image maps are actually created by the HTML code, and are not part of the graphic file, ImageReady features tools that enable you to define these areas within the image, and include the code in an accompanying HTML file. This chapter gets you up and running with image maps. Note that image maps cannot be created in Photoshop.

What Is an Image Map?

An *image map* is a discrete area of a Web-ready image that has a URL attached to it. When you "roll over" an image map area in a Web browser, the pointer changes, and clicking it loads a new URL (if defined). The image itself has not been modified in any way, rather, the link area, or "hot spot," is defined by HTML code associated with the image. The code also can specify other HTML attributes, such as link information or rollover effects. The image can be in any Web-ready image format—GIFs and JPEGs work equally well.

Sliced-based rollovers, discussed in the previous chapter, are also images with links attached to them. These two types of effects behave similarly in a Web browser. With slices, though, the link is activated by the entire slice, or image. This, of course, limits them to having only one link attached to them. With an image map, on the other hand, many areas within a single image can be defined as clickable links. This is a common use of image maps, as shown in the image below.

The image maps defined in this image use Polygon and Circle image map areas. Note that their outlines will not be visible when this image is displayed in a browser.

The greatest benefit of using image maps is that the link area does not have to be a rectangle. Slices are always limited to this basic geometric shape. Image maps, however, can be virtually any shape. And they, like slices, also can have rollover effects attached to them.

If you're going to display any type of graphic guide or floor plan or chart, image maps are a great way to handle its use as a navigation map. The image at left uses a polygon image map to define the shape of the rivers as a clickable link and two circle image maps to define the area around the clovers as clickable links.

Image Map Basics

Here is a sample of the HTML code used to define an image map. It is
included in the HTML file that is saved along with the optimized version of
a file which includes an image map.

```
<!-- ImageReady Slices (map.psd) -->
<IMG SRC="map.gif" WIDTH=1135 HEIGHT=829 BORDER=0 USEMAP="#map_Map">
<MAP NAME="map_Map">
<AREA SHAPE="circle" ALT="" COORDS="588,380,40" HREF="#">
<AREA SHAPE="circle" ALT="" COORDS="844,634,40" HREF="#">
</MAP>
<!-- End ImageReady Slices -->
```

ImageReady provides two general methods of defining image maps,
and you can use both within the same image. The first is an image map
that you define by drawing it. Adobe calls this type a *tool-based image
map* because you use a tool to draw it. The second type is called a *layer-
based image map*, and is defined by the contents of a layer. Functionally,
they are identical; the difference is only in how you define them. And you
can convert layer-based image maps into tool-based image maps.

No Transfers

*Image maps cannot be
copied and pasted to other
files. Layer-based image
map information is also
not transferred when a
layer is moved to
another file.*

Tool-Based Image Maps

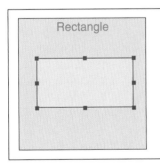
Rectangle

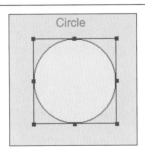
Circle

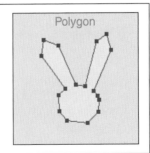
Polygon

Layer-Based Image Map

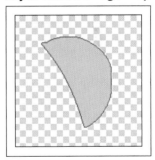

Modifying the HTML

Image maps exist only in HTML, but ImageReady is kind enough to have
tools that enable you to describe the outlines of your hot spots. On the
Image Map palette, you can add certain attributes to the HTML file, including a name for the map, a URL, a target frame for the URL, and ALT text.

Tool-Based Image Maps

There are three image map drawing tools: Rectangle, Circle, and Polygon. In the case of image map tools, Circle means precisely that—a perfect circle. You cannot create ovals with this tool. Aside from that limitation, you can draw an image map of virtually any shape.

---

create a polygon image map

1. Open the file to which you want to add image map areas.

   A typical image map operation might be to make each person in this image a clickable link.

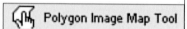

2. Select an Image Map tool. I will use the Polygon tool.

   To draw with the Polygon tool, click once to anchor the first point. As you move the mouse, a line extends from it. Keep clicking from point to point to draw the shape. This tool does not work, as you might expect it to, like the Pen tool. No Bézier curves or handles are available to drag beautiful curves—you can draw straight lines only. To use the Rectangle or Circle tool, simply drag it across the image; then use the handles to resize the map area.

AUTO-CLOSE

To automatically close an image map you are drawing, hold the (Command) [Ctrl] key. When the circle appears next to the pointer, click to close the map.

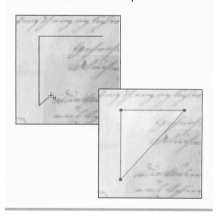

3. An image map area must be a closed shape. Make your way back around to the origination point and click it to finish the map.

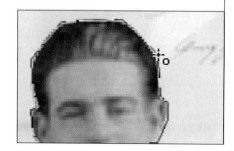

create a polygon image map

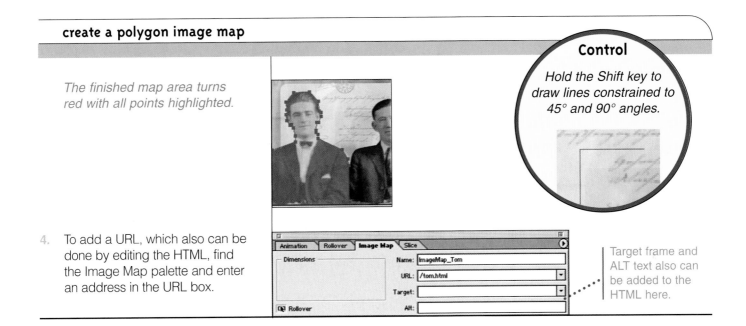

The finished map area turns red with all points highlighted.

Control

Hold the Shift key to draw lines constrained to 45° and 90° angles.

4. To add a URL, which also can be done by editing the HTML, find the Image Map palette and enter an address in the URL box.

Target frame and ALT text also can be added to the HTML here.

Editing Tool-Based Image Map Areas

Use the Image Map Select tool to edit image map areas. When you compare image map area editing to editing things such as selections and layers, or even Pen tool paths, then image maps seem a bit clunky to work with. But, you can get the job done. With the Image Map Select tool, you can move an entire map or select, subtract, move, and add individual points. You can't select multiple points; you can't resize an entire map at once; and Circle and Rectangle map areas are not editable—only resizable.

Select	*Move*	*Move a Point*	*Subtract*	*Add*
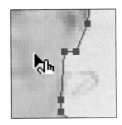	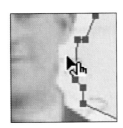	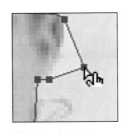	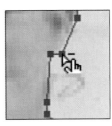	
Click inside an image map area.	Drag the map.	Click and drag a point.	Hold the (Option) [Alt] and click on top of a point.	Hold the Shift key and click on top of the outline.

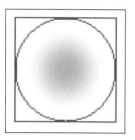

A layer-based image map will contain all nontransparent areas of the layer including very faint ones.

Layer-Based Image Maps

Layer-based image maps are generated from contents of a layer. The bounds of the image map area are defined by all areas of the layer in which there are pixels, even if they are only faintly opaque. So, a layer-based image map area attached to a layer with blurred areas looks as though it is larger than the contents of the layer. When creating layer-based image map areas, again, you have three shape choices: Rectangle, Circle, and Polygon. For the Rectangle and Circle choice, the image map area will be the smallest shape in which all nontransparent pixels can fit. The shape of a Polygon layer-based image map area depends on the Quality setting found on the Image Map palette. When it is set to 100, the image map area wraps perfectly to the contents of the layer. As the quality decreases, the area definition loosens and, depending on the layer, might become less complex, thereby providing simpler HTML coding and faster processing. Note that even if the layer's visibility is turned off, an image map area based on its contents will still be saved.

create a layer-based image map

1. Open the file to which you want to add image map areas.

2. Select the layer that contains the element you want to act as an image map area and choose Layer>New Layer Based Image Map Area.

   The initial map that is created will be a rectangle just big enough to fit all contents of the layers inside it.

create a layer-based image map

3. Find the Image Map palette and select an image map type appropriate to the layer's contents: Rectangle, Circle, or Polygon.

   If you choose Polygon, a Quality setting also must be chosen. This determines the extent to which the map wraps tightly to the layer's contents. A quality setting of 100 draws a perfect outline of the layer. The Quality can be changed at any time.

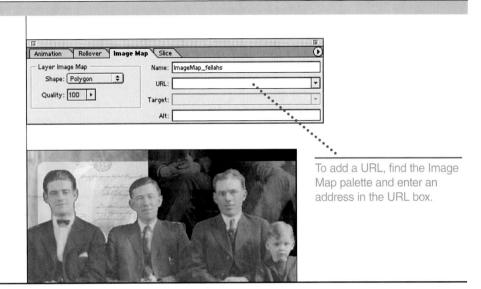

To add a URL, find the Image Map palette and enter an address in the URL box.

Editing Layer-Based Image Map Areas

Editing a layer-based image map is equivalent to editing the layer because all the changes you make to the layer are automatically reflected in the definition of the image map. Pay attention to the red outline in these images.

Deleting this part of the layer forces the image map to redraw.

Adding something to the layer forces the image map to redraw.

Transforming the layer contents forces the image map to redraw.

To edit the shape manually, the map must be converted to a tool-based map (see page 247).

Working with Image Maps

Tool-Based Image Maps

Use one of the three Map tools:

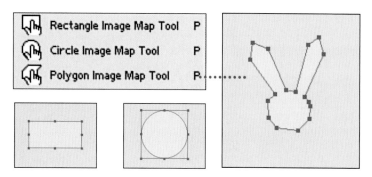

Circle and Rectangle image maps can be resized by dragging their handles with the Image Map Select tool.

Polygon image maps have editable points (see page 241).

Make fixed-size map areas by setting values on the Options bar.

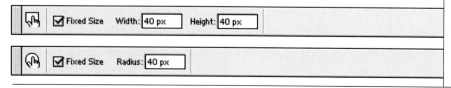

Layer-Based Image Maps

These map areas are based on layer transparency. Choose Layer>New Layer Based Image Map Area.

The Layers palette shows no sign of the layer-based image map.

Layer-based image maps have no points.

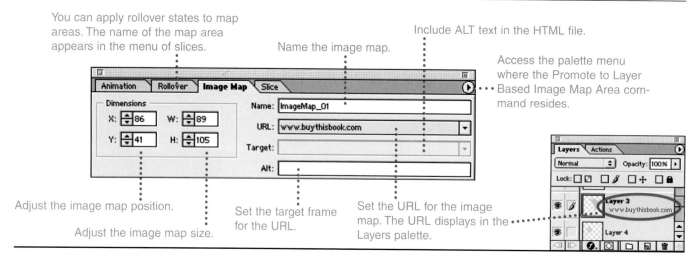

You can apply rollover states to map areas. The name of the map area appears in the menu of slices.

Name the image map.

Include ALT text in the HTML file.

Access the palette menu where the Promote to Layer Based Image Map Area command resides.

Adjust the image map position.

Adjust the image map size.

Set the target frame for the URL.

Set the URL for the image map. The URL displays in the Layers palette.

To Show or Hide Image Maps

 Click the Image Map Visibility icon on the Toolbox. Selecting the Image Map Select tool also turns them on.

To Select Image Map Areas

Get the Image Map Select tool from the toolbox and

Click inside an image map area.

Hold the Shift key to select multiple map areas.

Press (Command-A) [Ctrl-A] to select all map areas within the document.

Press (Command-D) [Ctrl-D] to deselect all map areas in the document.

To Delete Image Map Areas

Select one or more image map areas with the Image Map Select tool and press Delete.

To Duplicate an Image Map

Use the Image Map Select tool to select a map area. Then, hold the (Option) [Alt] key as you drag the map to create a duplicate.

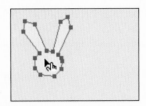

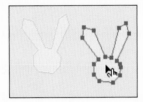

Or, select a map and choose Duplicate Image Map Area from the Image Map palette menu.

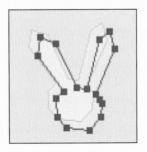

Alignment Options   Distribute Options   Stacking Options   Opens the Image Map palette

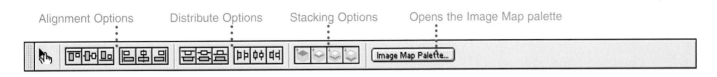

Organizing Image Map Areas

A few special features can help you organize groups of image map areas. They are useful when you're setting up a design on a grid and want the image map areas to keep in line with everything else. You can duplicate, align, and distribute map areas. These commands, though, work only with tool-based image map areas. If you want to do this with layer-based map areas, you can use the similar layer organizing commands (find them in the Layers menu). Lining up the layers lines up the the image map areas.

Use the Options Bar to Align and Distribute Groups of Map Areas

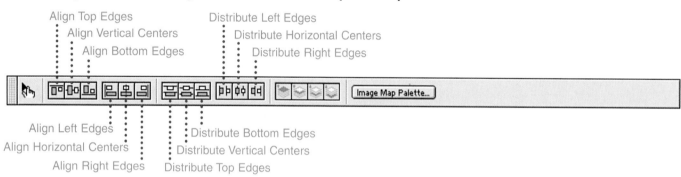

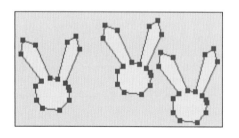
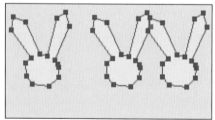

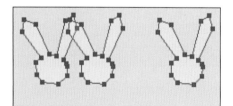
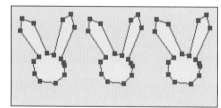

Align Image Maps

Use the Image Map Select tool with the Shift key to select multiple map areas. Then, choose an alignment option from the Options bar, such as Align Top Edges.

Distribute Image Maps

Use the Image Map Select tool with the Shift key to select multiple map areas. Then, choose a distribution option from the Options bar, such as Distribute Horizontal Centers. (To distribute map areas, you must have at least three map areas selected.)

Converting Image Map Types

You cannot edit layer-based image maps areas. They must first be converted, or "promoted," to tool-based image map areas. Keep in mind that a promoted image map area can't be converted back to a layer-based image map area (aside from using the Undo command).

convert a layer-based image map

1. Use the Image Map Select tool to select the image map area (or layer).

   If the image map area is a Polygon, you might need to adjust the Quality setting before converting it. If the Quality setting is set to 100, the map area will have countless points (on a complex image). There are so many in this image that it looks like a fat red line.

2. Set the Quality setting. Any value of 95 or below produces a reasonable number of points.

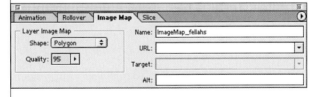

3. From the Image Map palette menu, choose Promote Layer-Based Image Map Area.

   See page 241 to learn how to edit the points.

Overlapping Image Map Areas and Stacking Order

Image map areas within a document have a stacking order. The stacking order is very important because it determines which link is used when a user clicks on overlapping areas. In addition, there is nothing to prevent map areas from overlapping. If they do, the image map area on top always wins out. If you do nothing to affect the stacking order, image map areas are stacked as they are created: The first map area created is on the bottom, and they stack up from there, so that the most recent area is always on top.

change the stacking order of an image map

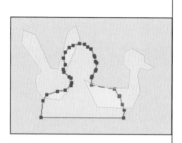

1. Use the Image Map Select tool to select a map area. Use the Shift key to select multiple areas.

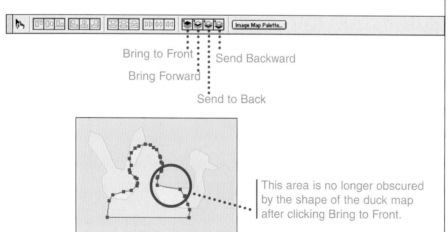

Bring to Front

Bring Forward

Send Backward

Send to Back

This area is no longer obscured by the shape of the duck map after clicking Bring to Front.

2. Then, choose a stacking option from the Image Map Select tool Options bar.

   The only noticeable change in ImageReady can be seen in the map outlines. A map on top will not have its outline broken by the outlines of other map areas. Note that when using layer-based map areas, the stacking order of the layers (in the Layers palette) does not affect the stacking order of the image maps.

Image Map Rollovers

Image maps areas can have rollover effects attached to them just as slices can. This means that you can dynamically change parts of a page design as a reaction to mouse events. The example below relies on your familiarity with creating rollovers. Review Chapter 12, "Rollovers" (page 212), if necessary.

add a rollover effect to an image map area

1. Create the image map areas for the image with any method.

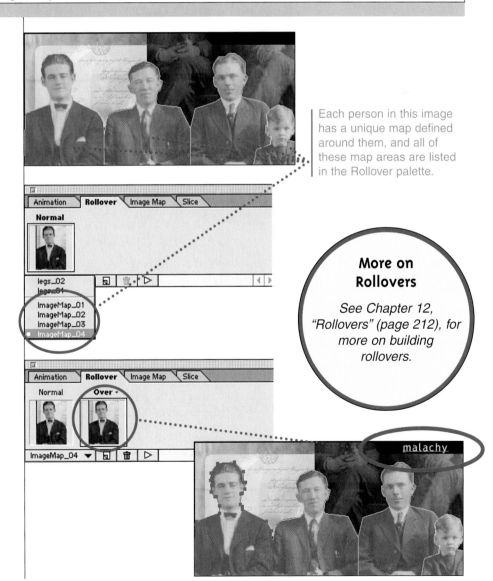

Each person in this image has a unique map defined around them, and all of these map areas are listed in the Rollover palette.

2. Find the Rollover palette and select the desired image map area from the list on the lower-left corner of the palette.

More on Rollovers

See Chapter 12, "Rollovers" (page 212), for more on building rollovers.

3. Create the rollover as you would any other rollover. I just created a new Over state and turned on a type layer in the upper-right corner of the image.

The tricky thing about image map rollovers is that you must remember that rollover effects work by replacing images (or slices). If there is only one slice in the document then the entire image must be replaced for any rollover effect.

add a rollover effect to an image map area

4. I sliced this image so it would work more efficiently.

I sliced the image in such a way that the image maps were contained within one slice and the rollover effect was in another slice. This way, only a small file is replaced as a result of the rollover, reducing the overall amount of memory that this design requires.

Slices and Image Maps

Avoid drawing image maps across slice boundaries. This can create complex files and might cause problems.

Previewing Image Map Areas in a Browser

It's a good idea to test image map areas in a Web browser to make sure they're working properly. It also gives you a chance to see whether you like how the map areas are defined. Are they too far away from the right areas of the image? Too tightly defined? To test image maps, use the Preview in Browser command by clicking on its icon on the toolbox (shown at right). As you roll over the image map areas, the pointer should change to a hand icon, and the linked URL will display in the status window at the bottom of the browser window. This also is a good chance to take a look at the HTML that ImageReady creates for the image map areas. Note that if the map areas have rollover effects attached to them, you can just click the Preview Rollover button in ImageReady to test them.

Saving Image Maps

Two special considerations should be made when saving images that contain image map areas. In the HTML dialog box is an option to choose either a client-side or a server-side image map. With client-side image maps, all the functions of the image map are handled by the browser (or client). With a server-side image map, image map information is stored on the server and shared with the browser. If you have no intention of using scripts to interact with the server then choose client-side (which is the default and more common image map type). If you choose any other option, a separate .map file is created for use by the server.

The Placement option tells ImageReady where to put the image map information in the HTML file: at the Top of the BODY section, at the Bottom of the BODY section, or Body to place the information just before the associated slice. This is a matter of personal preference.

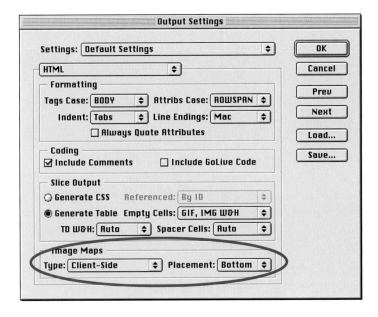

Also be sure that you do save an HTML document with the images when optimizing and saving files containing image map information. After all, it is the HTML file that contains all the image map information.

Creating Dynamic Graphics

This example uses layer-based image maps to create a dynamic graphic—in this case, a pie chart. This effect would not be possible with slices because slices must always be rectangles. Building graphics in this manner enables you to be more efficient with the display of information on a site because you are able to combine the graphics with the links. You get the kind of visual impact that sometimes only a single image can provide with the ability to redirect the user.

create a dynamic graphic

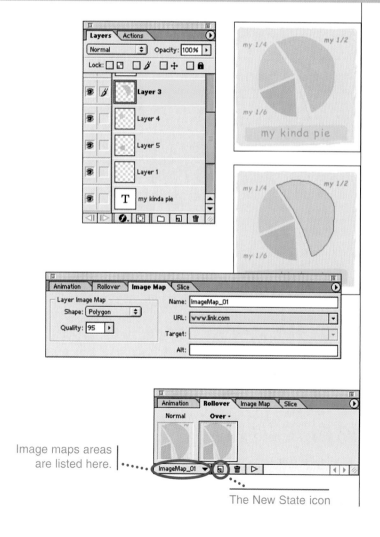

Image maps areas
are listed here.

The New State icon

1. Create the graphic first. As you do, be sure to isolate separate elements into their own new layers. This is the only way that creating the layer-based image maps will work. If it's not possible then tool-based image maps can be used.

2. One at a time, select each layer and choose Layer>New Layer Based Image Map Area. As you do, find the Image Map palette and change the Shape to Polygon, change the Quality to 95, and add a link address in the URL field.

3. After defining all the image map areas, find the Rollover palette and select one of the map areas from the pop-up menu in the lower left.

4. Click the New State icon to create a new Over state.

create a dynamic graphic

5. On the Layers palette, select the layer that corresponds to the currently selected image map. Then, from the Layer Effects menu at the bottom of the palette, choose Stroke to add an effect to the Over rollover state.

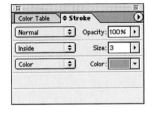

6. After adjusting the Stroke settings, hold the Control key and click (Mac) or right-click [Win] the effects icon next to the selected layer and choose Copy Style from the pop-up, context-sensitive menu. Pasting the style to each new rollover ensures consistency.

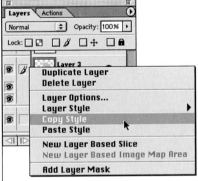

Caution!

The exercise produces a cool and useful effect, but because a new full-sized image must be replaced for each rollover, it's a memory hog.

7. Return to the Rollover palette and select one of the other image map areas from the pop-up menu. Add a new Over state, but don't add the Stroke layer effect as before. See the next step.

In the final graphic, a stroke is added to each piece of the pie as the pointer is rolled over it. Clicking it loads a new URL.

8. Go back to the Layers palette and select the layer that corresponds to the currently selected image map. Then, hold the Control key and click (Mac) or right-click (Windows) to the right of the layer name and choose Paste Style from the pop-up menu. The stroke is added to the Over state.

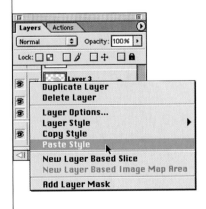
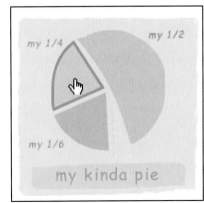

9. Repeat steps 3 through 8 for the rest of the image map areas.

14

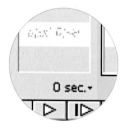

Animated GIFs

ImageReady enables you to create files that can be saved as animated GIFs for display in Web browsers. They are built on ImageReady's Animation palette, but a lot of the work must be done on the Layers palette. Learning the best way to use ImageReady to animate GIFs is largely about understanding how the Layers and Animations palettes interact. In this chapter, several animations are put together, each intended to teach a different aspect of animations.

How Do Animations Work?

The GIF file format has the capability to display mutliple frames, each with a specific duration, that "play" as an animation in a Web browser. After an animated GIF is created, it can be used in an HTML document just as any other Web-ready image. Nothing additional needs to be done in the HTML document to make them work. GIF animations are the only type of animation that you can build in ImageReady.

Building animations is an ImageReady-only activity. However, although animations cannot be built in Photoshop, you might use it to create graphics for the animation. Because ImageReady can convert a series of layers into a sequence of frames, it is might be as convenient to create the layers in Photoshop first, and then use ImageReady to turn them into an animated GIF. With animations, bear in mind, though, that the only file format that supports animation is the GIF format (GIF89a, to be exact). This means that ImageReady animations are subject to the limitations of the GIF compression scheme, which is limited to 256 colors and generally prefers graphics that contain areas of solid color.

Animated Layer Opacity Change

Animated Layer Movement Change

 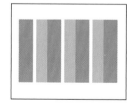  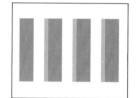 

A Series of Layers Turned into Frames

 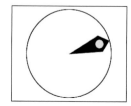 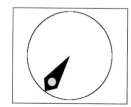 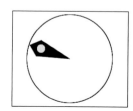 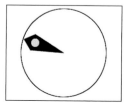

GIFs and File Size

GIF animations use the GIF compression scheme, which means that the same things that make GIFs small makes GIF animations small. See page 114 for more about what makes small GIFs. Generally speaking, GIF is best at compressing images that contain wide areas of flat color. An animation file, though, must contain graphic information for all the frames within it. Adding frames obviously increases the file size of a GIF. However, ImageReady has two optimization features that can potentially reduce the file size of a multiframe GIF file: Redundant Pixel Removal and Bounding Box. Both operate to reduce file size by limiting the graphic information of within a frame to contain only those areas of the frame that are different from the preceding frame. Repetition and redundancy are eliminated, aiding compression. Because of these optimization features, you might be able to open GIFs created outside ImageReady, turn on these optimization features, and resave the GIF as a smaller file.

Animation Strategy

You can create an animation in ImageReady that does just about anything you want, but ImageReady makes certain methods of animation easier than others. The difficulty of the operation depends on whether you are taking advantage of the types of things that ImageReady animates easily.

There are two general methods you might employ to create an animation in ImageReady. The first method, the more painstaking, is to create a new graphic for each of the frames in the animation. Typically, this is done by placing each graphic in a layer and then converting the layers to animation frames—an automatic feature in ImageReady. The second method is to use the Animation palette tweening functions to create the in-between steps of an animation for you. This feature can't morph graphics, but it can tween layer opacity, layer position, and layer effects. To morph one shape into another, you would need a more sophisticated animation or illustration application.

After you've built a couple of animations, this chapter will make more sense to you. ImageReady makes the process fairly intuitive.

Working with Animations

Animations are created by using the Animation and Layers palette.

To select frames
click it to select it. Hold the Shift key to select multiple frames.

To move a frame
click and drag it to a new location.

To set Frame Disposal Method
hold the Control key and click (Mac) or right-click (Windows) the frame preview for a menu.

An icon in this position indicates the Disposal method. See page 264 for more.

To set Frame Delay
click here for a menu.

To set Looping option
click here for a menu.

To control playback
use the Return to First Frame, Step Backward, Stop, Play, and Step Forward buttons.

To create tweening effects
select either the ending or beginning frame and click the Tween icon to open a dialog box.

To add a frame
click the new frame icon. The new frame will be identical to the currently selected frame.

In the Animation palette menu:

Copy/Paste Frames: Copies or pastes the selected frame(s)

Optimize Animation: Turns special file-size saving options on or off

Match Layers Across Frames: Makes the current condition of the selected layer the same in all frames

Make Frames from Layers: Converts a stack of layers into a sequence of frames

Reverse Frames: Reverses the order of a group of selected frames

Palette Options: Changes the size of the frame preview icons

The currently selected frame   Click here to access the palette menu.

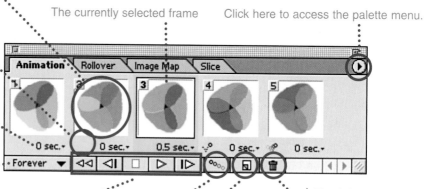

To delete a frame
select the frame and click the trash icon.

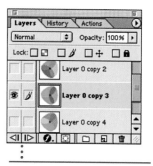

To change frames from the Layers palette
use the Forward and Backward buttons.

Building Animations

Similar to building rollovers, putting an animation together is mostly about using the Layers palette and all of its flexible powers in conjunction with the Animation palette. You might think of the Animation palette as the receptor of the changing states of the Layers palette. The one major feature the Animation palette throws into the mix is its Tween command. The first step is understanding how layer changes affect the animation. As with creating rollovers, some changes to layers affect the layer in every frame in which it appears, and other layer changes affect it in only the currently selected frame.

In the following step-by-step section, an animation is built from a series of static elements that exist in a stack of layers. This is only one method of building an animation. Other methods are used later in this chapter.

create an animation

1. Open or create a file that contains the elements for an animation on separate layers.

    This file contains a white background, a red circle, eight triangles rotated to point in eight directions, and a type layer— all in separate layers. See the Layers palette at right.

2. Find the Animation palette and notice that there is only one frame, and it is selected. Return to the Layers palette and turn layers on and off so that the image window displays only what you want visible in the first frame of the animation.

    The Layers palette at right shows which layers are turned on for the first frame.

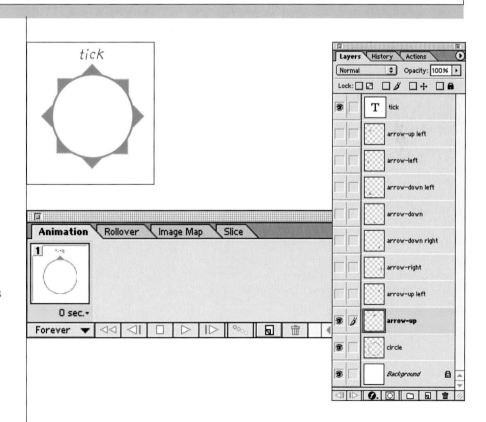

create an animation

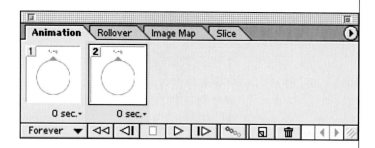

3. On the Animation palette, click the New Frame icon.

   A new frame is added that is identical to the first frame. The new frame also is the selected frame, which means that any changes you make to layers now will affect this frame.

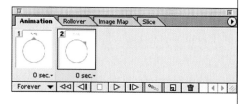

4. On the Layers palette, turn on the upper-right-pointing arrow layer and turn off the up-pointing arrow layer. Then select the type layer and change the Opacity to 50%.

   The Opacity has changed only for the current frame. If you click on the first frame in the Animation palette, you will notice that the type layer is still 100% opaque.

THINKING AHEAD

New frames are identical to the frame that is selected before creating them. When adding a new frame, select the frame most similar to the one you want to create. That way you must change little in the new frame.

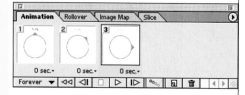

5. While the second frame is selected, create another new frame; then turn on the right-pointing arrow layer and turn off the previous arrow layer. Select the type layer and change the Opacity to 25%.

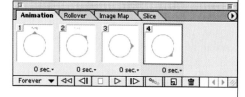

6. Create a fourth frame, and turn layers on and off to advance the arrow one more position around the circle. In this frame, turn off the type layer.

Gradually lowering the Opacity of the type layer makes it fade away in the animation. This also can be done using Tweening, which is demonstrated later in this chapter. The technique used here, though, demonstrates how changes to layers affect individual frames.

create an animation

7. Continue to create new frames, and turn the arrow layers on and off until they make a complete revolution. Leave the type layer off and don't repeat the up-arrow position of the first frame.

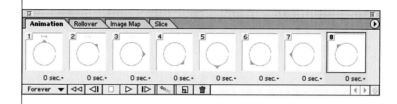

8. Click the Play button to get a sense of the animation.

   ImageReady playback of animations is slow, making the animation seem less smooth. Don't worry about that for now. Just make sure there are no glaring mistakes.

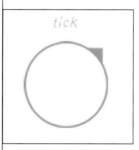

9. Take a moment to look at the Animation palette. Below each frame is a time setting. This is the frame delay time. In this case, you want all the frames to appear for a uniform amount of time, and you want it to move quickly. Leave them at 0 sec.

   Also, in the lower left of the Animation palette is a pop-up menu that currently says Forever. From this menu, you can set how many times the animation loops in the browser. Leave it at Forever.

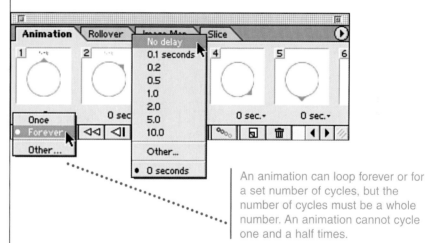

An animation can loop forever or for a set number of cycles, but the number of cycles must be a whole number. An animation cannot cycle one and a half times.

10. The animation is complete.

    For a more accurate preview, see the next section, "Previewing Animations."

    To save the animation, see page 267.

Previewing Animations

Although using ImageReady's Animation palette's Play button to preview an animation is an invaluable tool while building the sequence, it is important to also use the Preview in Browser to get a better idea of how the animation will actually behave in a browser. ImageReady plays the animations much more slowly than a browser does. An animation that looks choppy in ImageReady might look smooth, by Web standards, in a browser simply because of the faster playback. Of course, you also, at some point, need to test the animation to see how it behaves within a page as it downloads.

preview an animation

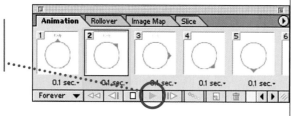

Use the Play button on ImageReady's animation palette for a crude playback preview.

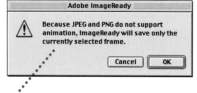

This error message is displayed when you attempt to preview a non-GIF image in a browser.

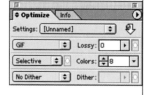

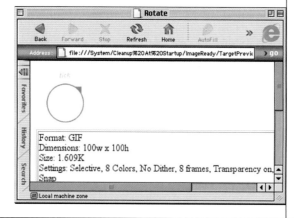

1. After creating the animation, preview it first by clicking the Play button on the Animation palette. This gives you a rough idea of the animation.

2. Find the Optimization palette and select GIF as the file format. For preview purposes, other settings are not crucial. But, if the Optimized palette is not set to GIF, the file will not animate in the browser.

3. Click the Preview in Browser icon on the toolbox or click and hold to choose a browser other than the default one.

   The browser will launch, and the animation will load and play.

Global Layer Changes Versus Frame-Specific Layer Changes

As with rollover effects, ImageReady attempts to aid you in creating some types of animations—those that don't involve the change of the pixel content of layers. You can create effects, both rollovers and animations, without changing the content of the layers. Whenever possible, this type of animation is preferable because it eliminates excessive copying of layers and keeps original graphics intact. You might refer to this kind of animation construction as *nondestructive* because the original content of a layer is never destroyed. It is only temporarily altered for the purposes of creating the animation effects.

You might have to work through this type of animation a couple of times before understanding how the concept works. Some changes to layers change the pixel content of the layer and therefore affect every frame in which that layer is visible, and other changes affect the layer only in the currently selected frame. These two kinds of changes can be broken into two categories: *global* changes (affect all frames) and *frame-specific* changes (affect the current frame only).

Essentially, each frame can "remember" the state of the layer palette while it is active. As you switch from frame to frame, layer attributes are switched. In this manner, an entire animation can be created from a single still layer.

Some Basic Rules About How Changes to Layers Affect Frames

These operations change a layer in all frames:	These operations change a layer in the current frame only:
Editing a type layer	Moving or nudging a layer
Adding pixels to the layer	Adding a Drop Shadow
Changing the color of the pixels	Adding a Color Overlay
Deleting pixels	Adding any layer effect
Making color adjustments	Changing the Opacity of the layer
Using the Transform feature	Turning a layer on or off
Applying filters	

Tweening

Tweening is ImageReady's key feature for automating animation effects. By using it, you can automate three kinds of animation effects: layer movement, layer opacity, and the application of layer effects. Text warping, a kind of layer effect, also can be animated. Layer effect tweening is perhaps the only one of these types that is difficult to immediately understand. It means that, for example, a graphic can be raised gradually from perfectly flat into a beveled graphic.

Tweening Movement: When the same layer is visible in two consecutive frames, select the second frame, and then use the Move tool to move the contents of the layer. Choose Tween from the Animation palette menu. In the dialog box, select Movement in the Parameters section and set the number of frames to add between the two original frames.

Tweening Opacity: When the same layer is visible in two consecutive frames, select the second frame, and then change the Opacity for that layer. Choose Tween from the Animation palette menu. Select Opacity in the Parameters section and set the number of frames to add between the two original frames.

Tweening Layer Effects: When the same layer is visible in two consecutive frames, select one of the frames and turn the layer's effects on or off. Then, choose Tween from the Animation palette menu. Select Layer Effects from the Parameters section and set the number of frames to add between the two original frames.

In the Tween dialog box, you can choose to Tween all layers or only the selected layer. Choose the All Layers option when you want to adjust the effects, opacity, or movement of more than one layer simultaneously. You also can use this feature to ensure that all visible layers are included in the new frames created by the Tween command. Choose the Selected Layer option to preserve the layer attributes of other layers while you tween the selected one.

DISPOSAL METHOD

Each frame has a hidden setting called its Disposal Method, identified by an icon that appears, or does not appear, below the frame preview in the Animation palette. If no icon is present, then the Disposal Method is set to automatic, the default.

The Disposal Method determines whether the content of a frame is removed when the next frame is loaded. Using this feature you can, for example, make the background layer visible in only the first frame on the Animation palette, but have it show up in all subsequent frames.

To access this feature, hold the Control key and click (Mac) or right-click (Windows) one of the frame previews in the Animation palette and choose an option. Note that the effect is viewable only in a browser; ImageReady does not preview it.

create a tweened animation

1. Open a new file and use the Type tool to enter some text.

2. Use the Move tool to move the type so that the last letters are barely visible on the left side of the image area.

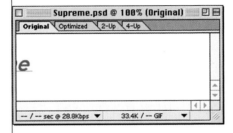

3. On the Animation palette, click the New Frame icon to create a new frame that is identical to the first frame.

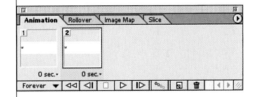

4. Use the Move tool again to move the type layer directly to the right (hold the Shift key to make sure it does not move vertically). Move it just out of view of the image area.

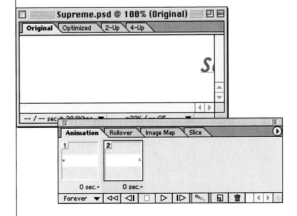

create a tweened animation

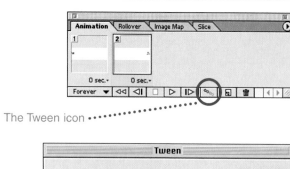

The Tween icon ••••••••••••

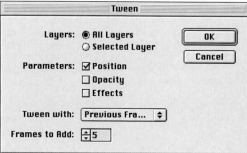

5. While the second frame is selected, click the Tween icon on the bottom of the Animation palette to open the Tween dialog box.

    By choosing All Layers, the white background will be included in the new frames that are created.

    Check Position in the Parameters List. This means that in-between states will be created for the Position of the Layer.

    Choose Tween with: Previous Frame and set the Frames to Add to 5. The number of frames affects the size and smoothness of the file. The more frames, the smoother the movement and the bigger the file.

6. Click OK to accept the settings and have ImageReady generate the new frames.

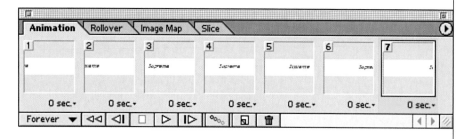

7. Make any adjustments, play the animation, set optimize settings, preview it in a browser, and save it.

Optimizing Animations

Before proceeding to optimization settings and saving options, there are two special optimization settings available for animations that can drastically reduce file size. They are Redundant Pixel Removal and Bounding Box. Redundant Pixel Removal removes pixels from a frame that were contained in the previous frame. That causes each new frame to contain only graphic information that is new to that frame. If two consecutive frames are identical then no new graphic information needs to be saved for the second frame. When file size is a big concern, design animations that take advantage of this feature—ones that introduce a minimum amount of new graphic information with each new frame. Bounding Box crops each frame of an animation to include only the pixels that have changed from the previous frame. Again, this is a great file-size saver. The only reason not to use these options is if you know you will need to open the animated GIF files in applications that don't support these features.

> ### SHRINK OLD GIFS
>
> *You can, because of these two animation optimization options, open GIFs not built in ImageReady and resave them (with these options turned on) as smaller files. Whether the file size will be smaller depends on the application that was originally used to save the animation file, but it can't hurt to try.*

turn on optimize options

1. Choose Optimize Animation from the Animations palette menu.

   Check the desired options. Turning these options off will make the animation more compatible with other GIF animation applications.

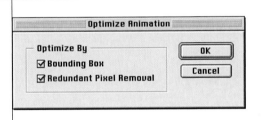

Saving Animations

Animations must be optimized and saved in the GIF file format. It is the only file format that supports animation playback. You must remember to optimize as a GIF because ImageReady will not stop you from saving a file with several frames in any other format. Use the same guidelines for saving an animated GIF as for a still GIF. Use the optimized preview windows and play the animation to ensure that the optimization settings are proper for the entire animation. There is no HTML code necessary for an animated GIF beyond what you'd use for an ordinary GIF; saving only the image is adequate.

Layers into Frames

When you are building animations manually, without aid of the Animation palette's Tweening features or effects achieved through layer manipulation, ImageReady's capability to automatically load layers into frames comes in handy. This command places each layer in the Animation palette as a frame, starting with the bottom layer as the first frame. The Animation palette will look like the Layers palette rotated by 90°. The upward vertical progression will be turned into a horizontal progression to the right.

turn layers into frames

All layers turned on

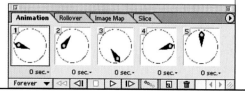

1. Open or create a file that contains a list of layers.

    This command places the frames in the same order as they are in Layers palette, starting from the bottom of the palette and working upward.

2. From the Animation palette, choose Make Frames from Layers.

Folders into Frames

You also can turn a folder of images into an animation. Proper preparation of the files makes this a smoother operation. Make sure that the folder contains only files that you want in the animation, because it's going to load them all. Name the files so their alphabetical order is the same as their sequential order. The files will be loaded one at a time, the first alphabetically becoming the first frame and the first (or bottom) layer. Also, make sure they are all saved in a file format ImageReady can open. After preparing the images, open ImageReady and choose File>Import>Import Folder as Frames. Note that there is nothing magical about this feature; it simply opens the files in order and dumps them into the Animation and Layers palettes. It won't resize images, and it won't adjust the registration of elements to make the action match from frame to frame.

ALIGNING & DISTRIBUTING LAYERS

To precisely position layers relative to each other, link the layers and use ImageReady's layer commands for aligning and distributing them. With the Move tool selected, these commands are available in the Options bar.

Animating Image Adjustments

By employing a little strategy and math, you can animate some image adjustment features. For example, you can gradually make an image get grainier and grainier by adding greater and greater amounts of noise to copies of the original image. The following step-by-step example animates a hue shift.

animate image adjustments

1. This image is created from three intersecting ovals of magenta, cyan, and yellow. The layer opacity was lowered for each, and then the layers were flattened into one layer. This effect, however, will work even on a simple colored square.

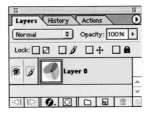

2. Make a copy of the layer.

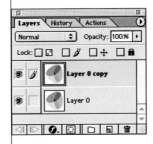

3. After the image is complete, choose Image>Adjust>Hue Saturation.

   The Hue slider ranges from -180 to +180 for a total of 360 for a full spectrum shift. This animation will consist of five frames. So, shifting the Hue by 72 for 5 times (5 x 72 = 360) shifts it back around to the original color(s).

   Enter 72 for the Hue setting.

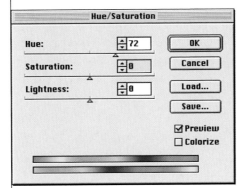

animate image adjustments

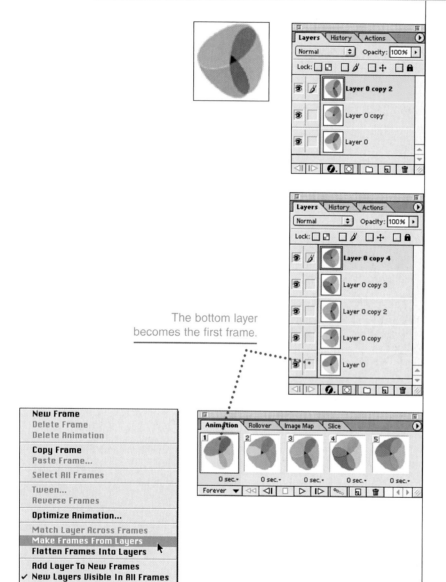

The bottom layer
becomes the first frame.

4. Make a copy of the current layer and open the Hue/Saturation dialog box again. Enter 72 for the Hue setting once more.

5. Repeat step 4 until five layers exist in the Layers palette. Each will contain the same image, equally shifted along the Hue spectrum.

6. On the Animation palette, click the arrow in the upper right to access the palette menu. Choose the Make Frames from Layers command.

   Each layer is loaded as a new frame in the Animation palette, beginning with the bottom layer and working up until the top layer is the final frame.

7. That's all there is to creating this animation. You can make any adjustments on the Animation palette, optimize it, preview it, and save it.

Rollovers and Animations

Rollovers and animations can be combined to create animations that are triggered by mouse events. For instance, you can create an animation that is activated only when the mouse rolls over it. Or perhaps create a rollover that stops the animation. Hopefully, if you are entertaining the possibility of combining rollovers and animations, you have gained an understanding of how various types of layer changes interact with rollover state selection and animation frame selection. Combining rollovers and animation, although not difficult, adds another level of complexity to these operations. It merely means that you have to pay attention to several palettes at once.

add an animation to a rollover state

1. Open or create a file that contains a menu or menu item.

    Create all layers necessary for the animation ahead of time. This file includes a layer for each menu item that will blink on and off during a rollover state.

2. The next step is to begin building the rollover effects. Slice the image so that each menu item is in its own slice.

    See Chapter 11, "Slices" (page 192).

3. Use the Slice select tool to select the slice containing the first menu item.

add an animation to a rollover state

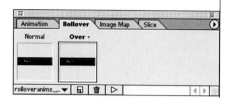

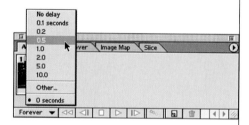

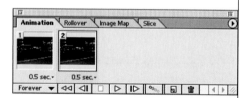

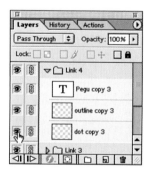

4. Find the Rollover palette and create a new state—the Over state.

   The order of operations when working with the Rollover and Animation palettes is very important. Any changes you now make will be visible in the browser only when the pointer is over the slice containing the first menu item.

5. Click the Animation tab to bring that palette forward. Set the time delay of the first (and only) frame to .5 second.

   Setting the delay now saves time because the new frame created in the next step will automatically inherit the same delay.

6. Click the New Frame icon to add a second frame to the animation. This frame is identical to the first.

7. On the Layers palette, turn on the layer that adds an orange dot to the image.

   Let's check up on where we are. The layer just turned on is the second frame of the animation that will play when the mouse rolls over the slice that contains the first menu item.

add an animation to a rollover state

8. The animated rollover is complete. To add the same rollover to the other menu items, repeat steps 3 through 7, selecting the appropriate slice each time and turning on the correct layer in step 7.

9. There are several ways to test the effect. Simply play the animation to make sure it's working. Then, turn on the Rollover Preview icon on the toolbox to ensure that the dot animates in the correct rollover state. Move the pointer over the slices to test them. Note that you might need to roll over the slices once before the animation behaves as it should. Finally, click the Preview in Browser icon to test the entire menu.

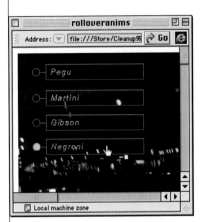

OPTIMIZING ANIMATED ROLLOVERS

Because the rollover states contain animations, the slices must be saved as GIFs. You can't save different states of a rollover in different file formats. In this case, this might present a problem because the photographic background would be better saved as a JPEG. For a better effect, you might consider making slices around the dots only, and then creating the animations as remote rollovers from the slice that contains the text.

More Animations Stuff

Because animation files can get big by Web standards, they generally are best used as highlight elements within a page. However, ImageReady itself does not limit you to these uses. GIF animations could even be used to present a slideshow of images (although the images must be GIFs) or screens of information that change automatically.

There's a lot more you can do with animations beyond the basics discussed. For example, because animations are saved as GIF files, you can create animations that contain transparent areas. See the Transparency chapter to learn more about it. Animations are also the way that you create banners that flip from one image to another. You can also import QuickTime movies as GIF animations via the Open command.

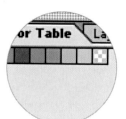

Transparency

Some of the Web file formats support the option to include transparent pixels in the image—this enables some great-looking layered graphic effects and can also aid in creating a more flexible Web page design. ImageReady and Photoshop make a quick process of transparency. This chapter sorts through the ins and outs, or ons and offs, of this subject.

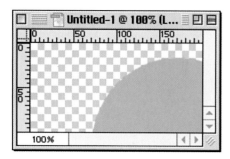

All Photoshop and ImageReady files are rectangles defined by X and Y dimensions, but they can contain transparent areas.

This checked pattern is Photoshop's and ImageReady's means of displaying transparent areas within a document. The color and scale of the checks are adjustable (see page 282).

Rectangles, Rectangles, Rectangles

What is transparency? That might sound like a stupid question, but because the same word is used to describe a number of types of images, it is important to pin down exactly what we're talking about. All graphic files saved by Photoshop and ImageReady are rectangular. They are defined by a vertical and a horizontal dimension, and all graphic or pixel information is contained within this rectangle. It is the same rectangle that is displayed in Photoshop as the image window. No matter what the shape of the images within the image window, the file is saved as a rectangle.

Creating "transparent" images, or images with transparent areas, is a way of making a rectangular graphic display as if it were not a rectangle. Areas of the image are removed, and whatever is beneath them shows through. This is parallel to the way that Photoshop layers have transparent areas through which the layers below show through. Sometimes images with transparent areas are referred to as *nonrectangular*.

Image Transparency Versus Layer Transparency

Do not confuse layer transparency with image transparency. Layer transparency is not image transparency but it is used to create image transparency. Just because there are transparent areas in the Photoshop or ImageReady image window, transparent areas won't necessarily be in the saved image. If you want transparent areas in the final image, you must first create transparent areas in the Photoshop or ImageReady image window by removing areas of layers.

Creating transparent areas in Photoshop documents is not difficult. The real key to creating this type of image lies in the Web file formats and how they are supported by browsers. After creating transparent areas in the layers of the image, you must employ the specific transparency-supporting features of the Web-ready file formats. Only one of these formats supports the full range of transparent effects these applications can create—PNG-24. For all others, you must learn how to use them for their particular strengths and according to the situation at hand.

Types of Transparency

Transparency Fakery

Look at the image at right. Does the logo have transparent areas within it? It appears to. The background shows through it. Or does it? The fact is that there is no way to tell whether this is a transparent image. It might be that the background color in the logo's file perfectly matches the background color that surrounds it. But the effect is still one of transparency, so this type of image is sometimes called a transparent image. The Matte option, an optimizing feature in Photoshop and ImageReady, is used to create this type of "transparency." It's a sort of fake transparency and is the only kind of transparency you can create in a JPEG image. GIF, PNG-8, and PNG-24 (all the rest of the Web formats) use the matte function in a slightly different manner, although the PNG-24 format can use it in the manner just described. The Matte option fills the transparent areas of the Photoshop image with a solid color in the final, optimized image. By matching this color to the background of a page on which it is placed, a transparent effect is achieved (as in the image at right).

Hard-Edged Transparency

To create true transparency, the file must be saved in the GIF, PNG-8, or PNG-24 format. GIF and PNG-8 support only hard-edged transparency. These formats use a color table to log all colors in the image. Turning on the transparency option adds "transparent" as a color in the table. *Hard-edged* transparency means that pixels can only be either on or off. They cannot be partially transparent, and you cannot blend the image or parts of the image into the background. This type of transparency makes these images very versatile, but, because pixels can be only on or off, the edges of the image are jagged. Normally, antialiasing helps maintain smooth-looking edges in pixel graphics by blending edge pixels to create the illusion of a smooth edge. But, because only one level of transparency is available, blending to transparent is impossible in GIF and PNG-8 images.

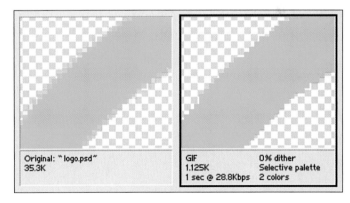

In this comparison, you can see how the antialiasing of the original image (left) is removed when the image is saved as a GIF file with transparency (right).

Multiple Levels of Transparency

And now for something truly amazing! Introducing the PNG-24 format now supported by some browsers. Currently, only Netscape version 6 or later (both Mac and Windows) or Internet Explorer 5 or later for Mac support multiple levels of transparency in PNG-24s. Therefore, use this feature of this format with caution. A file saved in this format can have multiple levels of transparency, which means it can blend into the background. For example, the logo on page 277 could have a soft drop shadow behind it and would display perfectly no matter what background it was laid on top of. Or, the entire image might be only partially opaque. And it has no jagged edges because antialiasing is preserved by the multiple levels of transparency.

The PNG-24 format can create effects like this partially transparent banana that was placed on a tiled background.

Comparing Edges: The File Formats

JPEG with matteing
The yellow was added as the matte color and blends with the red edge.

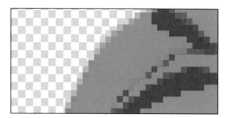

GIF with matteing
Green matte pixels are blended with antialiased red edges.

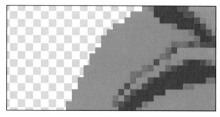

GIF, hard edged
Pixels can be only completely transparent or completely opaque.

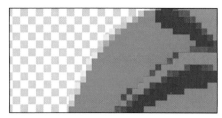

PNG-8 with matteing
Yellow matte pixels are blended with antialiased red edges.

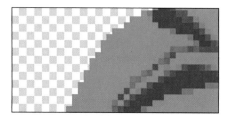

PNG-8, hard edged
Pixels can be only completely transparent or completely opaque.

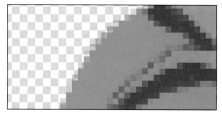

PNG-24
Multiple levels of transparent pixels are preserved and will mix with any background image.

When to Use Transparency

When would transparent images be used on Web pages? Ask yourself some questions about the image. Will it show up in various parts of the design? Do you expect it to be exchanged for new graphics? In general, transparent images aid in maintaining flexibility in a design. However, if you don't need a transparent image then don't make one. If the image is only going to be placed on a solid background, you probably don't need to save it with transparency. Just set the image background color to match the color of the page background. Don't complicate what doesn't need to be. Here's a list of guidelines for typical applications. Use transparency:

- When you want to place the same image on several different back-grounds. A logo, for example, might appear many times within a site. By using a transparent image, you can save downloading time because the same image can be reused.

- When the image is on top of a patterned or textured background and you expect that it will shift because of dynamically changing Web page content or because of browser differences.

- When incorporating images into applications such as Macromedia Flash and Director in which elements are commonly moving around and in front of or behind each other, transparency becomes very important.

- When you want the flexibility to move an image around in the HTML editor. The creation of a Web page does not always proceed smoothly from graphics creation to final implementation. The flexibility of transparent graphics that can be used on numerous backgrounds means you don't have to make a new image if the background changes.

> **TESTING TRANSPARENCY**
>
> *Want to find out for sure that the transparent effect will work as intended? Use the Preview in Browser command. After setting optimization options, choose File>Output Settings>Background (ImageReady) or click the Output Settings button in the Save for Web dialog box (Photoshop) and set a background for the preview page.*
>
> **Color:**
> *To choose a color, click the color swatch.*
>
> **Tiled Background Image:**
> *To choose an image for a tiled background, click the Choose button and go and find a file to use.*
>
> *To properly test the image, change the background color or tiled image and preview it again.*

Three types of backgrounds with the same logo positioned on top.

Basic Transparent Image

The following example shows you the most basic method of creating an image that contains transparent areas. Transparency is created in the Photoshop layers first; then the image is saved as a GIF with the transparency option turned on.

create simple hard-edged transparency

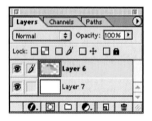

1. Open or create a file and place a nonrectangular image in a new layer.

   There should be two layers in the file: the original background layer and the new layer containing the placed image. Just scratch a few brushstrokes if you don't have an image handy.

2. Turn off the background layer. The transparent areas of the top layer are revealed, and the checkered pattern shows through.

   Conveniently, Photoshop and ImageReady work in a what-you-see-is-what-you-get method. You must see transparent areas in the image to save an image with transparency.

   Both Photoshop and ImageReady show this same checkerboard pattern. See page 282 to learn how to change it.

THE 50% THRESHOLD

Because GIF and PNG-8 formats do not support multiple levels of transparency—pixels are either 100% opaque or 100% transparent—what happens to partially transparent areas within the image? Pixels that have a transparency level below 50% are made completely transparent, whereas all pixels 50% or above are made completely opaque.

create simple hard-edged transparency

3. **ImageReady**

   Turn on the 2-Up view and find the Optimize palette.

   Photoshop

   Choose File>Save for Web and select the 2-Up view.

   Choose GIF for the file format. PNG-8 also works in the same way, but it is a less commonly supported file format.

   You will notice that a transparency option is available. If it is turned on (checked), turn it off to see the effect it has in the two previews. The Original image shows transparent areas, but the Optimized preview does not. You can see that just because there are transparent areas of the image does not mean that they will be there in the optimized file.

4. Turn on the Transparency option and set the Matte color to None. The Matte function is discussed later in this chapter. In terms of transparency, the two previews should match each other. They will not match, however, if partially transparent areas exist in the original image. See the previous page.

5. Set other Optimize options and save the file.

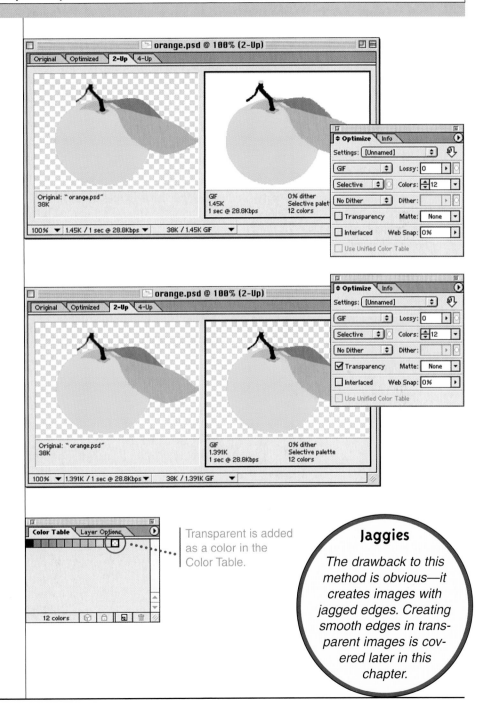

Transparent is added as a color in the Color Table.

Jaggies

The drawback to this method is obvious—it creates images with jagged edges. Creating smooth edges in transparent images is covered later in this chapter.

Layer Transparency and Opacity

The first step in creating transparent images is creating transparent areas in the Photoshop or ImageReady layers. Two things affect transparency in a layer: pixel transparency and layer opacity. *Pixel transparency* refers to the opacity of specific pixels contained in the layer. For example, you can fill a selection with a 50% opaque blue. *Layer opacity*, a specific setting on the Layers palette, refers to the opacity of the entire layer. Both things affect the final transparency of the layer's contents. As an example, a 50% opaque pixel in a layer set to 50% Opacity displays as a 25% opaque pixel.

Deleting Filling Layers and Selections

Normally, making Marquee selection and pressing Delete removes areas from a layer. But there are cases in which this doesn't work. If the layer pixel content is locked then nothing will happen. Also, if the layer is the *Background* layer, pressing Delete fills the selection with the current Background color.

Layer transparency and pixel content are lockable for layers. When pixel content is locked, pixels cannot be added, removed, or adjusted in any way; only the position can be changed. When the transparency is locked, pixels cannot be added to the layer and the relative opacity of the pixels cannot be altered. So, if you select an area with the Marquee tool and press Delete while the transparency is locked, the pixels are deleted, but if you try to fill the selection, only the current pixels in the layer would change to the new fill color—no new pixels would be added and the entire selection might not be filled. Layer opacity, on the other hand, can be changed at any time to alter the transparency of the entire layer.

CHANGING THE TRANSPARENCY GRID

You can change the default grid Photoshop and ImageReady use to indicate transparent areas. For example, if you were happening to be making a gray and white checker pattern and found this display a little confusing.

Photoshop: *Choose Edit>Preferences>Transparency & Gamut to change the grid scale or colors.*

ImageReady: *Choose Edit>Preferences>Transparency to change the grid scale or colors.*

An alternative pattern:

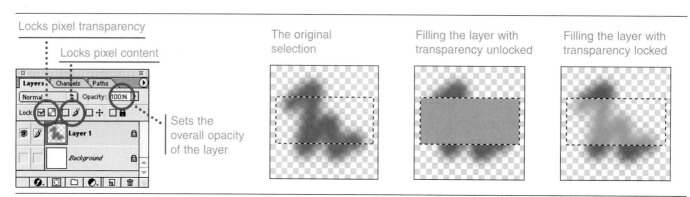

Locks pixel transparency

Locks pixel content

Sets the overall opacity of the layer

The original selection

Filling the layer with transparency unlocked

Filling the layer with transparency locked

Tools for Creating Transparency

The Eraser Tools

To save a file with transparent areas, the image must have transparent areas in its layers. Here are some tips for using the Eraser tools to create transparency. Note that all the Eraser tools work only on the currently selected layer.

Eraser

Option 1:
When erasing the *Background* layer or a layer with Transparency locked, the Eraser tool "paints" with the current Background color.

Option 2:
When erasing normal layers with transparency unlocked, the Eraser tool removes pixels from the layer, making those areas transparent.

Magic Eraser

As the name of this tool suggests, it works exactly like the Magic Wand tool. The only difference is that instead of selecting areas, it turns them to transparent pixels. This tool is not dragged across the image, but clicked on colors (just like the Magic Wand tool). Set options on the Options bar.

The Magic Eraser responds to layer transparency in the same manner as the normal Eraser tool (explained at left).

Background Eraser (Photoshop only)

This tool turns areas transparent even if transparency is locked or you are working on the Background layer. It samples the area in the middle of the brush and, based on the Tolerance percentage set in the Options bar, removes pixels from the layer. The higher the Tolerance, the wider the range of colors that are removed. Keep the crosshairs of the brush just outside the object you intend to preserve as you drag.

High-contrast edges respond well to this tool.

Part of the banana's color has been removed along with the background. Be careful when using this tool in areas where the background is too similar to the foreground object.

Fake Transparency in JPEGs and PNG-24s

ImageReady and Photoshop have a Matte option for all three Web-ready formats. Use this feature when you have an image with transparent areas and you want to add a background color to it that matches the background color of the page on which it will be placed. Effectively, it fills in the transparent areas of the image with the selected color. You can select any color, including the current Foreground and Background colors, and the effect previews in the Optimize preview windows. Partially transparent pixels in the original image are blended with the chosen matte color.

Although this function does not create an image with transparency, it gives you perfect control over the background color, and is a quick and easy way to switch its background color without changing the file. Of course, it is useful only if you know what the background color of the page will be.

use the matte function in JPEGs and PNG-24s

1. Open or create a file and place an image in a new layer.

2. Turn off the background layer or remove areas of the image to create transparent areas— revealed as a checkered pattern.

   You must see transparent areas in the image to use the Matte function.

use the matte function in JPEGs and PNG-24s

3. ***ImageReady:*** Turn on the 2-Up view and find the Optimize palette.

   Photoshop: Choose File>Save for Web and choose the 2-Up view.

   Select JPEG or PNG-24 for the file format.

   Because PNG-24 supports true transparency, the transparency option must be turned off to use the Matte feature.

   Because JPEG does not support transparency, the transparent areas of the image fill with a color, as does the PNG-24 with transparency turned off.

4. Click and hold the pointer on the Matte color swatch to pop up a menu of color choices.

   The swatches are the 216 Web-safe colors. You also can select the document's current Foreground or Background color. None sets the background to white, and Other opens the Color Picker (which can also be accessed by clicking the Matte color swatch once).

5. Set other Optimize options and save the file.

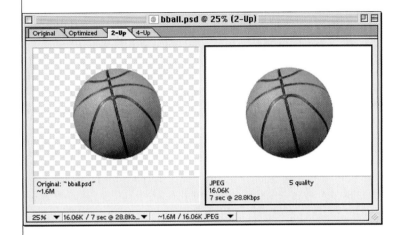

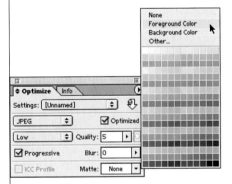

The final image

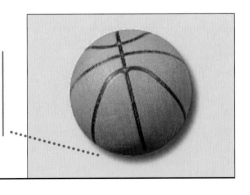

A Variation: Because this is not a true transparent effect, partially opaque colors, such as those in a soft drop shadow, can be blended into the Matte color.

Smooth Edges

This image shows how the Matte function works on an image with a drop shadow.

As you work with transparency in images, one of the first obstacles to over-come is the jagged edges that are the result of the GIF file format. There are two ways around the problem. The first, shown in the example below, uses the GIF Matte option and works well on solid backgrounds and all-over patterns. It works by blending the partially transparent pixels of the image with a matte color that matches the expected background color. This technique can get rid of the jagged edges and even enable you to include soft drop shadows, but its success varies depending on the background on which it is placed and how flexible the image needs to be. Obviously, if you include a background color in the image then the file will not work with all backgrounds. The second method is discussed on the following pages.

create smooth edges for solid backgrounds (GIF and PNG-8)

1. Open or create a file and place a nonrectangular image in a new layer.

2. Turn off the background layer. The transparent areas of the top layer are revealed as the checkered pattern shows through.

3. **ImageReady:** Turn on the 2-Up view and find the Optimize palette.

   Photoshop: Choose File>Save for Web and choose the 2-Up view.

   Select GIF or PNG-8 for the file format.

create smooth edges for solid backgrounds (GIF and PNG-8)

4. Turn on the Transparency option and set the Matte color to None.

   Take a look at the Original and Optimized images side by side. The antialiasing in the Original image is absent from the Optimized preview. The jagged edges would be noticeable in the browser.

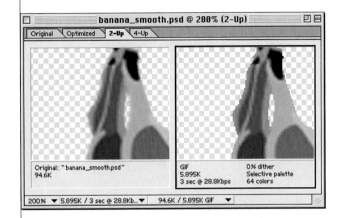

5. Choose a Matte color by clicking and holding on the Matte color swatch. Select one of the Web-safe colors from the palette, the Foreground or Background color, or Other to select another color.

   The chosen matte color is filled in and blended with the partially transparent pixels from the original image. Placing this image on a background of the same or similar color results in smooth edges.

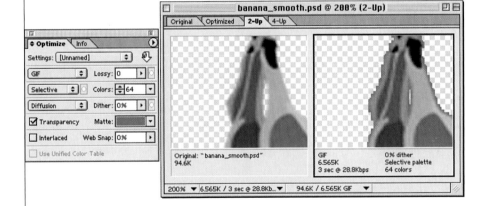

6. Set other Optimize options and save the file.

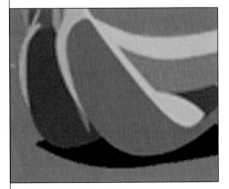
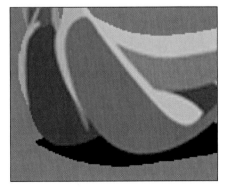

The final image   versus   A hard-edged GIF

Handling Complex Backgrounds

What do you do when you want smooth edges on an image that contains transparent areas that will be placed on a background that is not a flat color? If the Web page has a patterned tile background image, choosing a flat Matte color, as in the previous exercise, might not look very good. The matte color added to the image can create a halo effect when placed on a background. The steps that follow demonstrate a method of including a more complex background into the transparent GIF.

create smooth edges for complex backgrounds (GIF and PNG-8)

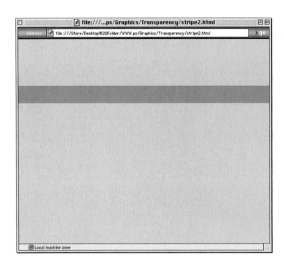

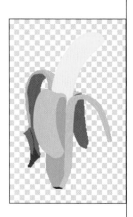

1. Open or create a file with a nonrectangular image in a layer.

   At far left is the background on which the graphic will be placed.

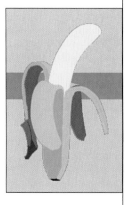

2. Before you do too much work, attempt to use the previous technique. It's a lot easier and sometimes produces an adequate effect.

   In this case, I had the choice of using either of the colors from the background. The halo that resulted was not satisfactory.

create smooth edges for complex backgrounds (GIF and PNG-8)

Timeout: Preparing the Background Graphics

This technique works by copying part of the background into the foreground image. It is necessary, therefore, to have an image of the background in Photoshop as it will look in a browser. How to do this depends on the situation. If it's a tiled background image, use an HTML editor to create a file that includes only the tiled background. Then, open the HTML document in a browser and take a screen capture of it. Finally, open the screen capture in Photoshop and place it in a layer below the foreground object you are working with. In any case, you need to construct the background image in the same Photoshop file as the foreground image, but you need only enough of it to surround the foreground graphic. All that is necessary for this example is the image at far right.

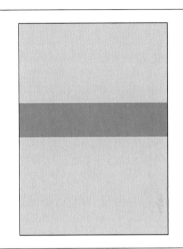

3. In this case, the vertical background tile was copied enough times to fill the background behind the banana.

   It may not be possible to know the exact position of the foreground element relative to the background, especially because of the way that graphics can shift in browsers. The only solution is trial and error. If I save this file with the layers intact, I can just return to it, shift the foreground element, and save it again.

4. After the background graphics elements are in place, load the transparency selection of the foreground element by holding the Command (Mac) or Ctrl key (Windows) and clicking the layer icon on the Layers palette.

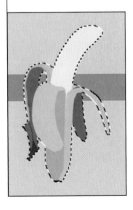

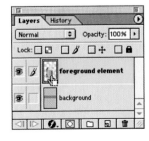

create smooth edges for complex backgrounds (GIF and PNG-8)

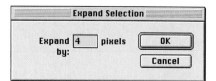

The selection expands uniformly away from the banana.

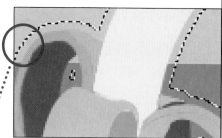

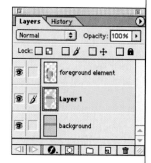

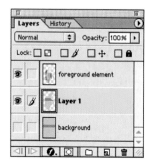

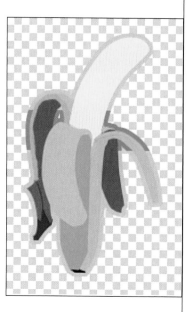

5. Choose Select>Modify>Expand. Expand the selection by 2–5 pixels. Experiment to find the correct amount. You should expand it just enough to include all the antialiased or partially transparent pixels of the foreground element.

6. Make the layer containing the background graphics active, and then choose Layer>New> Layer Via Copy.

   A new layer is created that contains only the part of the background that extends a few pixels out from the edges of the foreground graphic.

7. Turn off the layer filled with the background graphics, and deselect the selection.

   You should now see only the foreground graphic and a bit of the background peeking out from the edges. Essentially, this GIF will still have hard edges, but the edges have been shifted away from the graphic. So, the graphic will have antialiased edges and the background fringe will match the Web page background, we hope.

create smooth edges for complex backgrounds (GIF and PNG-8)

8. **ImageReady:** Turn on the 2-Up view and find the Optimize palette.

   Photoshop: Choose File> Save for Web and choose the 2-Up view.

   Select GIF or PNG-8 for the file format.

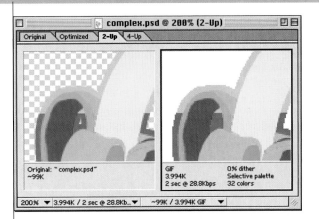

9. Turn on the Transparency option and set the Matte color to None.

   The outside edge in the Optimize view should show hard edges.

10. Set other Optimize options and save the file.

    Including the background fringe in the graphic increases the number of colors in the image. You might need to raise the number of colors in the GIF Color Table for the graphic to look the way you want.

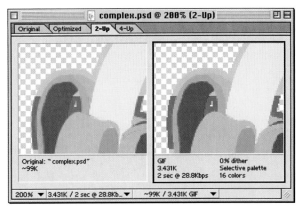

11. Use an HTML editor to place the graphic on the background as it will be in the final design. If it aligns with the background then you're finished. Otherwise, return to the Photoshop or ImageReady document, shift the foreground graphic relative to the background, resave it, and preview it again.

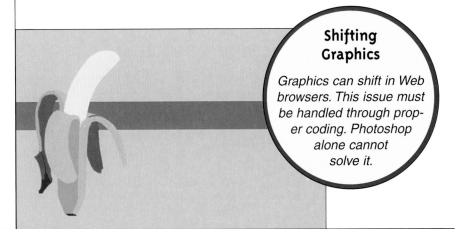

Shifting Graphics

Graphics can shift in Web browsers. This issue must be handled through proper coding. Photoshop alone cannot solve it.

Multiple Levels of Transparency: PNG-24s

The PNG-24 format is the only one that supports multiple levels of transparency—256 levels to be exact. This means the drop shadow of a single graphic could successfully blend onto various backgrounds of various Web pages. This effect is easy to achieve, but watch out for file size and compatibility because the PNG format is not as efficient at compression as GIFs and JPEGs, and multiple-level PNGs are supported only by the newest browsers—Netscape version 6 or later (both Mac and Win) or Internet Explorer 5 or later (Mac only).

create multiple levels of transparency

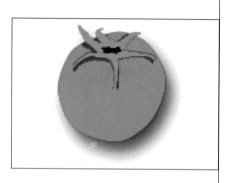

1. Open or create a file and place a nonrectangular image in a new layer. Use an image that has partially transparent pixels. Adding a drop shadow to a layer is a common use of this feature and a good example to work with.

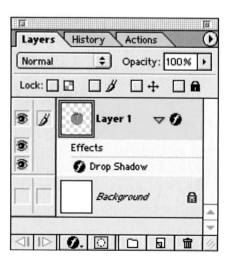

2. Turn off the background layer, or create transparent areas in the image so the checkered pattern displays.

   Don't neglect this step. You must see transparent areas in the image to save an image with transparency.

create multiple levels of transparency

3. **ImageReady:** Turn on the 2-Up view and find the Optimize palette.

   Photoshop: Choose File> Save for Web and select the 2-Up view.

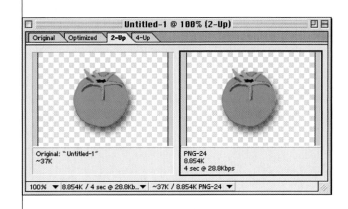

4. Select PNG-24 as the file format, and make sure that the Transparency option is on.

   The Original and Optimize views should look exactly alike—love the PNG-24.

5. Set other Optimize options and save the file.

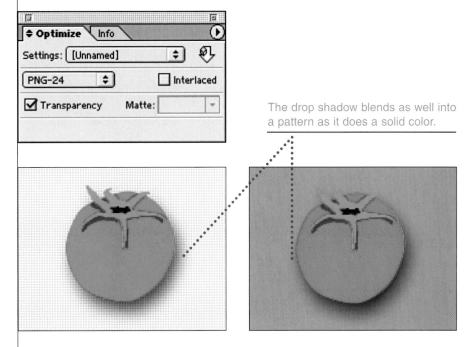

The drop shadow blends as well into a pattern as it does a solid color.

Besides drop shadows, the image itself can have transparent areas. This blurred type was placed on an orange background.

WWW.PHOTOSHOP.IMAGEREADY

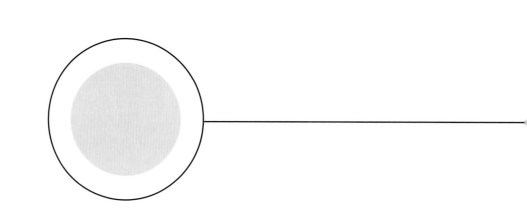

Part V

The Bigger Picture

16

Top Shadow
Inner Shadow
Outer Glow
Inner Glow
Bevel and Embo
Satin
Color Over

Styles

Styles and effects apply graphic treatments to the contents of a layer with the click of a button or the drag of a mouse. And, they do this without affecting the pixel content of that layer. The duties of a style can range from applying a simple drop shadow to handling various states of rollover effects. You might use them for their convenience, or might you use them for consistency among a set of images. Learning to use effects and build styles can surely make your Web production quicker and smoother.

Is That Style or Just Effect?

The way that Photoshop and ImageReady seem to interchange these two terms might be a bit confusing, but it really doesn't matter what you call them. Think of them this way: An *effect* is any of the 10 types of special effects that can be applied to a layer and are accessible in the Layer Effects (ImageReady) or the Layer Styles (Photoshop) menu on the bottom of the Layers palette. A *style*, on the other hand, is the sum of all the layer effects applied to a layer. This means if you've applied the drop shadow effect to a layer and no other effects, the drop shadow constitutes the effect and the style.

Styles, once composed, can be saved and reserved for later use. This is their official entrance into the world of Styles with a capital "S." Saved styles are handled by the Styles palette where they reside and are displayed as icons that provide a thumbnail preview of the effects they contain.

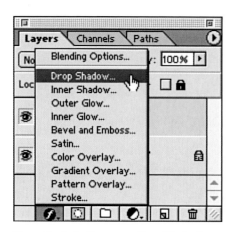

The effects in the menu that Photoshop refers to as the Layer Styles menu and ImageReady refers to as the Layer Effects menu.

Photoshop Versus ImageReady

Styles and effects are shared and supported completely by both Photoshop and ImageReady, but each application has a different way of dealing with them. For example, ImageReady styles can contain layer effects for rollover states—a feature not available in Photoshop (but Photoshop will not remove them, either).

As typical of other ImageReady features, effects and styles are handled by palettes. If you're just adding a simple drop shadow, ImageReady is a little more convenient to use for styles and effects because they are taken care of right there on a floating palette without having to open a dialog box.

Looking for Rollover Styles?

A style can contain layer effects not only for one layer, but for all rollover states of a layer. See page 229 for more.

In Photoshop, styles and effects are handled in one very large dialog box in which for one brief moment you become commander-in-chief of the united forces of all layer effects. Mastering this interface is a feather in the cap of any Photoshop user. Despite the potential initial fright of being faced with so many options, generally, I think that Photoshop is the better application for building styles because of the all-in-one nature of this dialog box, its capability to scale effects independently of the layer's contents, and its option to edit and create new gradients and contours.

Manual or Automatic?

Now that you know that you can create drop shadows with the click of a button, I must break it to you that there are better ways of doing this. Layer effects are great and work well in many cases, but they don't do everything. To have complete control over an effect, you must build it yourself. Alternatively, you could use layer effects to build the style and then generate layers from the effects (see page 309.) and make adjustments to those new layers. For example, when building a drop shadow manually, Photoshop's full range of features is available for adjusting and fine-tuning it. Many designers forsake the automatic drop shadow effect and build it themselves because they find setting the variables of the Drop Shadow effect cumbersome.

The Gradient Overlay effect (right) is layed on only the nontransparent areas of the layer.

Working with Styles

Effects and styles are simple and intuitive to use: Select a layer, choose an effect from the Effects menu, and make a few adjustments if necessary. But understanding how they work will help avoid confusion when you start piling them on in multitudes. The first concept to understand is how effects interact with the content of layers. They care less about what's in the layer than they do about the transparent and nontransparent pixels of a layer.

The Inner Bevel effect (right) uses the edges of the the nontransparent areas of the layer to determine where the effect is applied.

Let's divide the effects into two categories: surface and edge effects. Surface effects include Satin and the three Overlays, and they are simply evenly laid across the nontransparent areas of the layer (as in the figure at right). The edge effects, on the other hand, use the edges of a layer's contents to build the effect. For example, the Inner Bevel effect uses the edges of the the nontransparent areas of the layer to determine where the highlights and shadows are applied.

Things get hairy when the edges of the layer content contain partially transparent pixels. For example, if a drop shadow, an effect with transparency of its own, is applied to a layer that has partially transparent edge pixels, the effect will not be as expected. The layer contents and the drop shadow blend in an awkward mix, as shown in the figure at right. Besides these factors about the layer content, both the layer and the effect applied to it can have their own Opacity and Blending mode settings. This situation can produce both horrible confusion and very cool layered graphics.

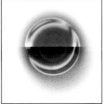

Left: A bold stroke mixing with a blurred layer.

Right: A whole lot of effects piled on top of a simple gray circle.

Applying Effects

Applying effects is as easy as choosing one from a menu and then adjusting its parameters. Some effects are built on top of the layer, such as the stroke effect, and others are layed underneath, such as the drop shadow. Keep in mind that effects are applied to layers, not selections or individual objects. If you want to apply an effect to only a part of a layer, copy that area into a new layer first. This is done on the next page. Also, effects are not applied to effects. So, if there are two effects applied to a layer, they are simply laid on top of each other; the one will not take the other into account. Finally, effects will show up in transparent areas even if layer transparency is locked.

Missing Something?

To access hidden layer effect options in ImageReady, choose Show Options from the layer effect palette menu *(see page 305).*

---

apply a layer effect: ImageReady

1. In a file, place or create an element in a layer. Make sure to select this layer.

   The layer must have transparent areas for some effects to show up.

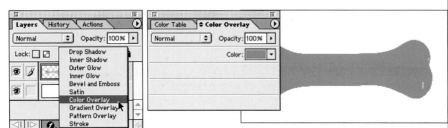

2. Click the Layer Effect icon at the bottom of the Layers palette and make a selection from the menu. When you do this, the layer effect palette comes forward and displays the parameters for the selected effect.

   I chose Color Overlay. Initially, the content area of the layer was filled with overlay color.

Set the Color Overlay effect Blend Mode here.

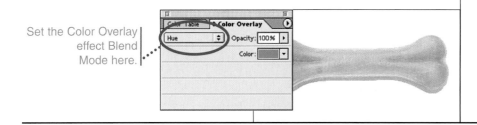

3. Make adjustments to the effect.

   I switched the Blend Mode to Hue so the chosen color would shift only the hue and leave all other image qualities alone.

apply a layer effect: Photoshop

1. Place or create an object on a layer.

   To isolate part of a layer, select that area with a Marquee tool and press (Command-Shift-J) [Ctrl-Shift-J] to cut it from the original layer and place it in a new one.

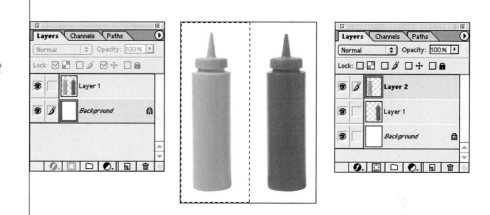

2. Click the Layer Style icon at the bottom of the Layers palette and make a selection from the menu. When you do this, a dialog box opens that displays the parameters for the effect.

3. Make adjustments to the effect.

   To choose a gradient, click the arrow to the right of the gradient. To edit the current gradient, click on top of the gradient.

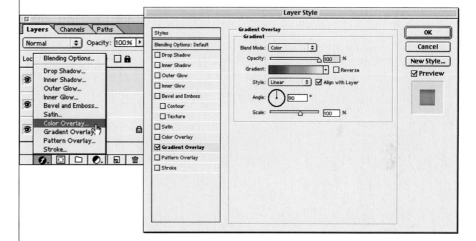

   When it's complete, the effect is displayed in the Layers palette just as it is in ImageReady. Use its visibility icon (the eye) to turn the effect on and off. If a layer has more than one effect, they can all be turned on and off by clicking the visibility icon next to the word "Effects" under the layer name.

A Rundown of the Layer Effects

Drop Shadow

This effect is a standard and takes the work out of creating this common treatment. You can change the color, size, direction, and distance.

Inner Shadow

The opposite of a drop shadow, it creates the illusion that the layer contents are cut out from the background.

Outer Glow

Adds a glow around the layer. Similar to drop shadows, glows are blended with what's in the layers beneath.

Inner Glow

Applies the glow to the inside of the layer's contents. This effect can create the illusion of three-dimensionality or just add a soft edge inside the rim of the object. The effect is also reversible so that it glows from the center outward.

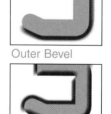

Outer Bevel

Emboss

Pillow Emboss

Stroke Emboss

Bevel and Emboss

Five versions of this effect exist: Inner Bevel, Outer Bevel, Emboss, Pillow Emboss, and Stroke Emboss. This example shows a basic Inner Bevel with a contour applied to the highlights and shadows. The Contour feature enables you to control the lighting highlights. With the Texture feature, you can choose an image to be used as a texture map for the layer. So, instead of raising the layer using the boundaries of its contents, it bevels or embosses according to the light and dark areas of the texture. Stroke Emboss works in tandem with the Stroke effect to emboss edges.

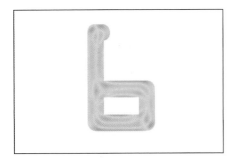

Satin

This effect applies a sheen with swirling highlights to a layer. Many options are available to affect the swirling. Used subtly, it works well to produce illusionistic resemblances of light reflections.

Color Overlay

Lays a color over the layer's contents. Although the example here shows a simple solid overlay, you can adjust the Blending Mode and Opacity to subtly adjust layers below. It's great for making color variations to design elements.

Gradient Overlay

This is similar to Color Overlay. You can use any of the preset gradients as they are, adjust them, or create your own.

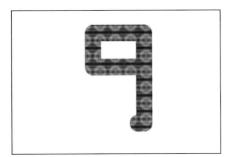

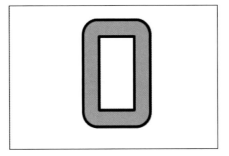

MULTIPLE EFFECTS

Of course, it's much more fun to put together several effects. This image combines the same Drop Shadow, Inner Bevel, Color Overlay, Gradient Overlay, and Stroke effects seen separately on these two pages.

Pattern Overlay

This is similar to Color Overlay. You can use preset patterns or create your own. All patterns are scalable.

Stroke

Adds a stroke around the edge of the layer. This effect has many variations. The stroke can be solid as above, a pattern, or a gradient.

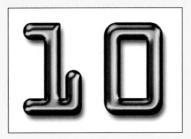

Working with Layer Effects

In Photoshop,
effects are handled in the Layer Style dialog box. Check the boxes to turn effects on and off. Click the name of an effect to access its settings in the area to the right.

To turn effects on or off, click the check box. When you turn off an effect, it retains its settings.

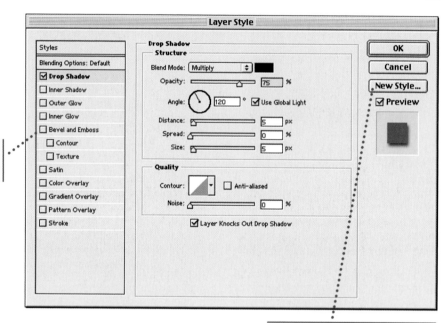

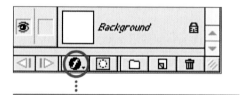

Click here on Photoshop's Layers palette to access the menu of effects and open the Layer Style dialog box.

To save the current set of effects settings as a Style, click here.

Context-Sensitive Menus: Right-Click (Windows), Control-Click (Mac)

In Photoshop, Control-click (Mac) or right-click (Windows) any single effect or the effects icon next to the layer name to open this useful menu.

In ImageReady, click a single effect to open this short menu

or

click the effects icon to open this longer menu that has a submenu.

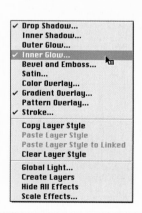

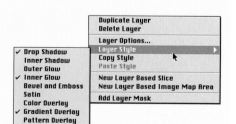

PHOTOSHOP'S SUPERIOR EFFECTS TOOLS

- More dynamic previews
- Layer Style box, which enables you to build a style from multiple effects all at once
- Scale Effects command (see page 308)
- Ability to edit and create new gradients
- Ability to edit and create new contours

In ImageReady,

effects are handled on a palette. Choose effects from the menu at the bottom of the Layers palette and change the settings on the palette that jumps forward.

This palette changes dynamically according to the currently selected layer effect.

To show the expanded set of options, choose Show Options from the palette menu.

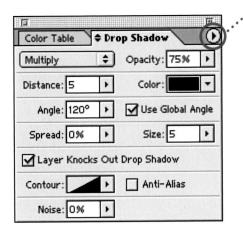

STACKING ORDER

The stacking order of effects, seen in Photoshop's Layer Style dialog box at left, makes a differ-ence. For example, you cannot see a Gradient Overlay if there is a 100% opaque Color Overlay on top of it. The order cannot be changed.

SOME GOOD REASONS TO USE IMAGEREADY

- Palettes allow easy access for making adjustments to effects.
- You can include rollover states in Styles.

In ImageReady, click an effect to reveal its parameters on the floating palette shown above.

To open or close the list of effects, click this arrow.

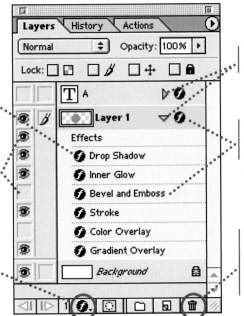

Effects can be turned on and off by using their visibility icons.

Control-click (Mac) or right-click (Windows) the effects icon or an indi-vidual effect to open a useful context-sensitive menu.

To add an effect, click this icon and select the effect from the pop-up menu.

To delete an effect, drag it to the Layers palette trash can. To delete all effects applied to a layer, drag the word "Effects" that is below the layer icon to the trash can.

More Ways to Apply Effects and Styles

Layer effects are designed to be easily shared among layers. Several ways exist to copy effects and styles to other layers and images.

• *Drag an effect from one layer to another*

Click a single effect and drag it on top of the target layer. Visual feedback indicates that it will be accepted by the layer.

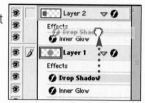

• *Drag a set of effects from one layer to another*

Click the word Effects just below the layer icon and drag it on top of the target layer.

• *Copy a style*

Control-click (Mac) or right-click (Windows) the Effects icon to the right of the layer name. Choose Copy Style (ImageReady) or Copy Layer Style (Photoshop) from the menu.

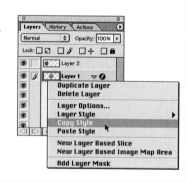

• *Paste a style*

Control-click (Mac) or right-click (Windows) the Effects icon to the right of the target layer name. Choose Paste Style (ImageReady) or Paste Layer Style (Photoshop) from the menu.

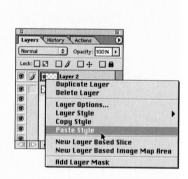

• *Drag an effect or a style onto the image window*

Click and drag an effect from the Layers palette onto an element in the image window. The effect will be applied to the topmost layer that contains pixels underneath the point where you release the mouse.

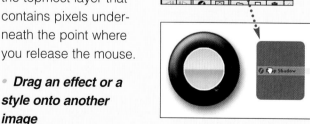

• *Drag an effect or a style onto another image*

Drag the effect onto another image window.

• *Paste a style to several layers at once*

Link all target layers, and then choose Paste Style to Linked (ImageReady) or Paste Layer Style to Linked (Photoshop) from the Layers palette menu.

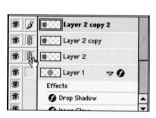

Global Light

This is not the peacekeeping mission it might sound like, but it is valuable nonetheless in ensuring the harmony of a page or set of graphics. Any effect that involves a faux light source, such as drop shadows and effects that create the illusion of three-dimensionality (bevels and embossing), has a setting for the direction of the light. The position of shadows and highlights is determined by this degree setting. And next to each of these settings is a check box labeled Global Light. If you check this box, the light source for that effect will match all other effects that have this option turned on. But there is something potentially irksome here. If you turn on the option and change the setting, all other effects with this option turned on will also change. So, it is very important to pay attention to this little check box. Otherwise, you might end up changing effects that you had no intention changing.

When you don't use Global Light for all effects, mismatched lighting can produce an awkward result.

set the global light

1. Apply two effects to a layer that use Global Light, such as a Drop Shadow and a Bevel. Turn on the Global Light option for both.

2. Click the Drop Shadow effect on the Layers palette (double-click in Photoshop) and take a look at the Global Light setting. Click the arrow next to the Angle degree and move the radial pointer to select a new lighting angle.

    The dial indicates the direction from which the light shines. Therefore, a drop shadow will spread in the opposite direction.

Notice that the lighting angle for both effects has changed. Maintaining this consistency creates a truer three-dimensional effect.

All or None

Scale Effects applies to all effects attached to a layer. To avoid scaling an effect, move it temporarily to another layer and then move it back after scaling.

Scaling Effects

The parameters for an effect can be altered only by manually changing the settings. They are static. Therefore, if you scale up the contents of a layer that has a drop shadow applied, the drop shadow does not grow in proportion to the resized object. It spreads the same pixel amount it did before. No way exists to link the scaling of an effect to the scaling of a layer's contents. But, in Photoshop, you can scale the effects separately by using the Scale Effects command in the Layer Style submenu of the Layers menu. Unfortunately, this feature is not available in ImageReady.

scale an effect

1. Open a file and apply an effect to a layer.

The Info palette displays Transform stats.

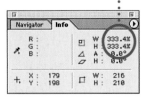

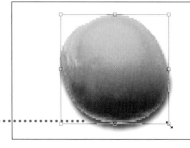

Notice that the shadow looks as if it does not spread as far from the giant pea as it did from the mini pea.

2. Select the layer in the Layers palette and press (Command-T) [Control-T] to access the Transform bounding box.

   Hold the Shift key to constrain the proportions of the layer contents and drag a corner handle away from the center to enlarge the object. Notice that the layer effect is expanding, too, but not in proportion. As you transform your pea, watch the Info box; It reveals the transform percentage needed in the next step.

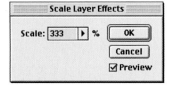

3. Choose Layer>Layer Style>Scale Effects. Enter a scale percentage.

   What percentage? Use the one displayed in the Info box in the previous step.

Creating Layers from Effects

Directly editing the pixel content of a layer effect is impossible. You are limited to adjusting the given settings. However, with the Create Layers command you can generate editable layers from the effects. Sometimes, it's useful to use the layer effects to create an element, use Create Layers to convert them to pixel data, and then use Photoshop's other tools to alter the effect. This enables you to delete unwanted parts of effects. After conversion, the effect becomes a normal layer, and no longer can be adjusted by settings.

create layers from effects

Warning

Sometimes when splitting effects into layers, the result does not match the original effect. This is an unfortunate and unavoidable aspect of this command.

1. Open a file that has effects applied to a layer.

   This file has three effects applied to it. You will see how they react differently to being made into layers.

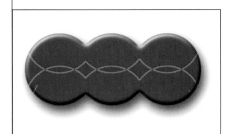

2. Select the layer and choose Layer>Layer Style>Create Layers (in Photoshop).

   The effect layers disappear and are replaced by content layers. Some of them move above the original layer, and some below. Turn them on and off to get a better understanding of how layer effects work.

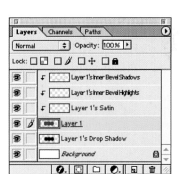

3. Everything looks the same, but the former effects are now editable layers.

Using Styles

As discussed previously, a Style is the sum of layer effects applied to a layer. As such, they can be saved as Styles and placed in the Styles palette. When effects become styles, you can apply them to a layer with a single click and they are available to all your image files. You can even share the Style file in which they exist with other computer users.

apply a preset style

Styles also can be dragged from the Styles palette onto a layer or right into the image window.

The None icon removes all effects from a layer.

RETAINING EFFECTS

Hold the Shift key while clicking a style in the Styles palette to retain any effects currently applied to the selected layer. However, if the Style being applied shares an effect with the target layer, the effect that is part of the Style is applied. Therefore, a drop shadow as part of a Style will replace an existing drop shadow.

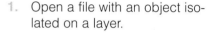

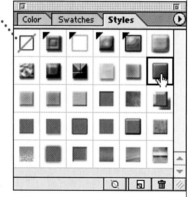

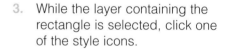

1. Open a file with an object isolated on a layer.

   Start with a simple shape so you can tell what the style is doing. I used the Rounded Rectangle tool to draw this shape.

2. Find the Styles palette. This image shows the default preset styles for ImageReady.

3. While the layer containing the rectangle is selected, click one of the style icons.

   The style is automatically applied, and all the effects show up in the Layers palette. Double-click any of them to fine-tune the settings. Changes made do not alter the Style in the Style palette, only this particular application of the Style.

Built-In Styles and Custom Styles

Seven sets of styles (including the default set) are included with and accessible from both Photoshop and ImageReady. Apply these styles to random layers to get an idea of the possibilities that lurk in the world of styles. When building your own style, you can apply one of the built-in styles and then adjust it to your needs.

The Shaded Red Bevel style from the Text set.

The Teal Glass style from the Glass Button set.

The Normal and Over states of the 2-state Plastic Button style from ImageReady's default set.

load a set of styles

1. Find the Styles palette and open the palette menu. Do one of the following:

   A. Choose Load, Replace or Append Styles from the palette menu. A dialog box automatically opens Photoshop's Styles folder, in which its sets of styles reside. Select one and open it, or navigate to a set that you have saved elsewhere.

   B. Choose a set from the bottom of the menu. These are the sets that were in the Styles folder when you launched Photoshop or ImageReady.

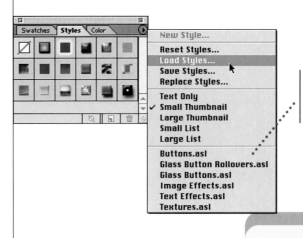

These are the sets that were in Photoshop's Styles folder when the application was launched.

YOUR STYLES HERE

If you save style sets in the same Styles folder, they show up at the bottom of the list, too. See page 315 for more on saving Styles.

Creating Custom Styles

The preset styles are useful for understanding how styles work, but the only way to really learn is to build them yourself. Styles can be useful in setting up a design that you will return to from time to time to add new elements. The following example builds a style in Photoshop, which I recommend, but the process is similar in ImageReady.

---

create a custom style *Photoshop*

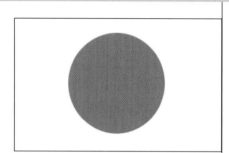

The ramp Contour means that the shadow grades perfectly from 100% solid to 100% transparent in a smooth linear blend.

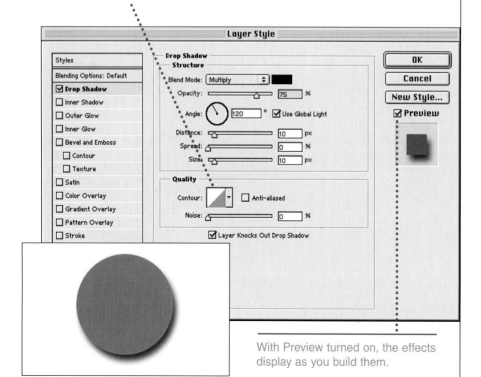

With Preview turned on, the effects display as you build them.

1. Open a file with an object isolated on a layer.

   I started with a simple circle to show just how much styles can do. I also used Photoshop for this exercise because I find it easier to work with when running through many combinations of effects.

2. Open the Styles palette by double-clicking the layer in the Layers palette. Then, click Drop Shadow in the effects lists to turn it on and reveal its parameters.

   (In ImageReady, choose effects from the menu at the bottom of the Layers palette and adjust them on their palettes.)

3. Make adjustments.

   I changed the Distance and Size settings both to 10.

create a custom style

4. Add a 32-pixel solid black Stroke (Position: Inside), and then click Bevel and Emboss. From the Styles menu, choose Inner Bevel. Basic settings are in the top Structure box. Tune the shading in the box below.

    Swing the light angle around to 120°. Remember that keeping Global Light turned on means that changing the lighting here also affects all other effects on all other layers that have Global Light checked—such as the drop shadow in this case.

The Contour controls the shape of the highlights. The glossiness in the rollover button on page 311 was created with a complex contour.

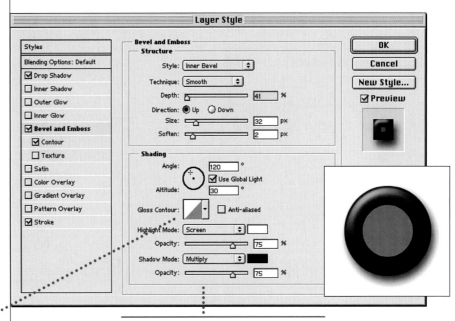

Adjust the strength of the highlights and shadows here.

5. Click Gradient Overlay.

    Click the arrow to the right of the gradient and choose a gradient from the list. To load other sets of gradients, click the arrow to the right of the menu of gradients, and choose Load, Append, or Replace Gradients. To edit a gradient, select it, and then click it once to open the Gradient Editor window. I also swung the gradient Angle around to -90°.

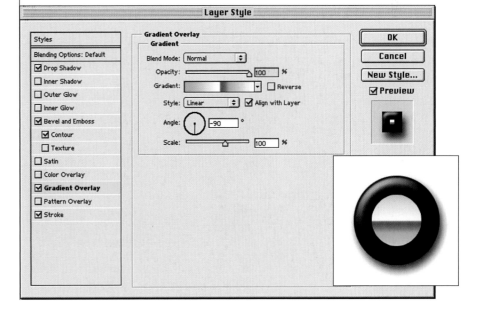

create a custom style

The effects show up in the Layers palette. You can use the Visibility icon to turn individual effects on and off.

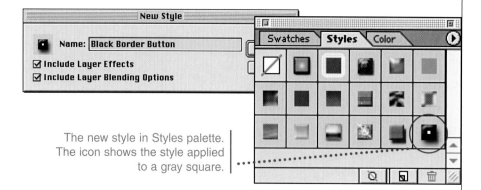

The new style in Styles palette. The icon shows the style applied to a gray square.

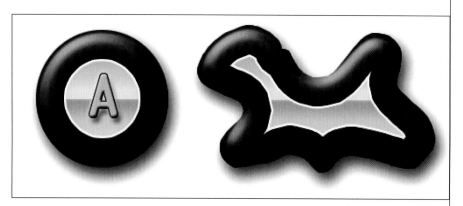

6. I also used the Inner Glow to add a white stroke outside the gradient and a Color Overlay over the top of the Gradient.

   You cannot change the stacking order of effects. For the Gradient to show through the Color Overlay, you must lower the Opacity of the Color Overlay.

7. If you're still in the Layer Style dialog box when finished then click the New Style button. Otherwise, find the Styles palette and choose New Style from the palette menu.

   In the dialog box that opens name the style. An icon for the new style displays at the bottom of the Palette.

8. The style is now ready for use.

   Try it out on other layers to see how flexible it is. You should test a style on various layers before putting it into production use.

   If you create numerous styles, you can save them as a set by choosing Save Styles from the Styles palette menu.

Saving Styles

Styles are saved as sets, which can include from one to more than 200 styles. When you use the Save Styles command, all styles currently in the Styles palette are saved in the new set. So, if you are going to save your own set of styles, I recommend that you clear the other styles from the Styles palette before saving the set. This way, when you load the set of styles, you can append it to the current set without adding a lot of unnecessary styles. If you want to save only a single style, remove all other styles and save it as a set of one.

Style Woes

Deleting styles does not delete them from their saved sets, but if they were not saved to a set before deleting them, they cannot be retrieved.

save styles

1. Create a style as described in the steps beginning on page 312. After completing step 7, the Style will be in the Styles palette.

2. Delete all unnecessary styles from the palette:

   Photoshop:
   Option (Mac) or Alt (Windows) click a style to delete it.

   ImageReady:
   Command-Option (Mac) or Ctrl-Alt (Windows) click a style to delete it.

3. From the Styles palette menu choose Save Styles. Choose a location to save the style. If you save it in the Styles Presets folder (Adobe Photoshop>Presets>Styles), it will be listed at the bottom of the Styles palette menu the next time you launch either application.

   Saved Style sets are accessible in both Photoshop and ImageReady.

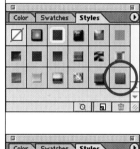

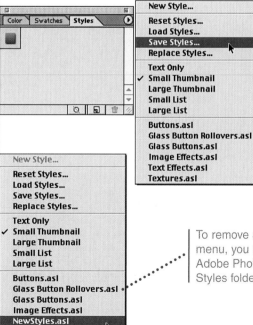

To remove a set of styles from this menu, you must remove it from the Adobe Photoshop>Presets>Styles folder.

Automation

Photoshop and ImageReady both have some great features for automating tedious operations. They share many functions, but Photoshop has the fuller set of features for full-powered automation. ImageReady, on the other hand, makes automating optimization of Web graphics a bit more convenient.

What Types of Things Can Be Automated?

Photoshop and ImageReady's most powerful automation tools are *actions*—series of commands that can be executed with a single click. Actions can, in turn, be used to apply a series of commands to a batch of images. Actions also can be run from outside these application by turning them into droplets. Besides actions and batch processing, Photoshop includes a few miscellaneous automation features, including a way to produce an HTML gallery of images ready for the Web.

Styles and Effects

The simplest type of automation is a Style. Styles are, after all, a group of effects that are applied with a single click or drag.

Actions

Actions are the heart and soul of Photoshop automation. They're easy to use via the control panel at the bottom of the Actions palette and are very powerful. They can contain almost any command and have the capability to halt and request input. After you set up and successfully run an action on a batch of images, you'll feel like you are a general in charge of your troops. Imagine watching Photoshop or ImageReady chug away while you sip your cappuccino, occasionally tapping a key to keep it all going.

Predefined Actions

Photoshop and ImageReady ship with preset sets of actions that will give you an idea of what you can accomplish with an action. If you're new to actions, I suggest running a couple of these actions first.

Making Actions

Actions are built by recording commands. Almost everything you can do in these applications can be recorded. And after a command has been included in an action, its parameters are manually editable. When an action is used to run a batch processing operation, there are additional options you can set to control which folder the target images are in and which folder the finished images are going to.

Action Uses

Use actions to automate repetitive tasks. You can use them to take care of the entire process of preparing an image or just a part of it. For example, you can open an image, make adjustments to the image where necessary, use an action to reduce it to a size that will fit into a specific table cell, optimize it, and save it—all with just a single click.

ImageReady Versus Photoshop

Like many other features shared by these applications, Photoshop actions are the more versatile and powerful. ImageReady's version is somewhat reduced and less fully featured, although it's adequate for most action operations. And, if you're creating actions to prepare graphics for the Web, ImageReady has the upper hand. Droplets can be created just for the purpose of converting files to Web file formats (see page 334).

ImageReady and Photoshop actions are not compatible. Their predefined actions are saved in folders very distant from each other, seemingly to reduce the risk of their confusion.

Action Alert

Photoshop and ImageReady actions are not compatible. You must re-create the action in the other application to use it.

Some Action Tips

Use Percentages:
Consider using percentages when resizing images (or whenever the option is available). This can make the action applicable to a wider variety of images.

Unrecorded Commands:
Some action steps are recorded only when they actually make a change to the image being used. While using an image to record an action, it may be necessary to stop recording the action and alter the image in a way that a command will make a change to it, and then resume recording the action.

Using the Save Command:
When recording Save commands in an action, be careful about changing the filename. It will be recorded and the action will rename all files to the same name.

Applying Actions

When you run an action on an image, you must make sure that the file is ready for the action. An action often requires that a certain layer is selected or a selection is active. The preset actions indicate in parenthetical words following their names how you should prepare for the action. If the action is followed by "(selection)" then a selection must be active for this action to work properly. (Color) indicates that the action will use the Foreground color. (Type) indicates that the action is intended for a Type layer.

play an action

What's Going On?

If you want to see each action step performed then choose Playback Options from the Actions palette menu and click Step by Step or Pause.

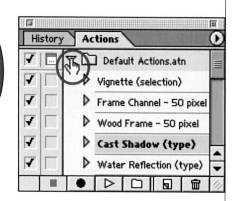

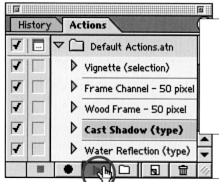

1. Open a new file and use the Type tool to enter some text. Make this new layer the active layer.

   This example uses one of Photoshop's built-in actions.

2. Find the Actions palette and open the Default set of actions by clicking the arrow next to its name. If the Default set is not loaded then select it from the bottom of the Actions palette menu.

3. Select the Cast Shadow action and click the Play button at the bottom of the palette.

   That's all there is to it. If you want to revert to the preaction state of the image, you will notice that a Snapshot was created in the History palette. Click it to revert to the image.

Playback Speed

When you run an action, there are three different playback modes you can choose. From the Actions palette menu, choose Playback options. The three options are Accelerated, Step by Step, and Pause. Most of the time, Accelerated is the best option because it runs through the steps the most quickly. The downside is that you don't see what's happening. If you want to watch what each step does then select Step by Step. For super slow playback, when you're troubleshooting an action that isn't quite working correctly, select Pause and set a delay.

Be careful when playing back actions because they are not immune from interruptions. Anything you do while running an action will affect the image.

Button Mode and Keyboard Shortcuts

If you really get into actions and use them a lot then you have two other quicker ways to play an action. First, you can set a keyboard shortcut for the action, and second, you can place the Actions palette in Button Mode. Assign keystrokes for the most common tasks and use buttons for frequent but less common tasks.

To switch the palette to Button Mode: Choose it from the palette menu. In Button Mode, actions are applied simply by clicking a button. This is a very convenient method. Keep the palette open on the side of the screen and access the commands as necessary while you work on images.

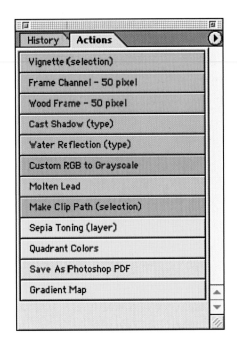

To assign a keyboard shortcut to an action: Double-click the action to open the Action Options dialog box and select a keystroke. Be careful that you don't select a keystroke that is otherwise used. Note that you must not be in Button Mode when you double-click the action.

Working with Actions

Photoshop's Action palette (shown here) is similar to ImageReady's, although ImageReady does not support sets.

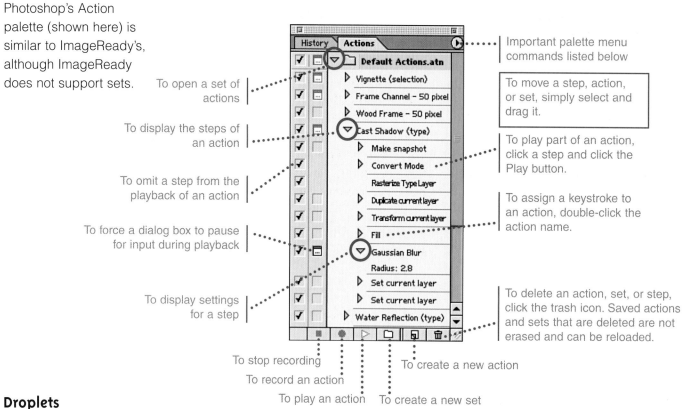

To open a set of actions

To display the steps of an action

To omit a step from the playback of an action

To force a dialog box to pause for input during playback

To display settings for a step

To stop recording

To record an action

To play an action

To create a new set

To create a new action

Important palette menu commands listed below

To move a step, action, or set, simply select and drag it.

To play part of an action, click a step and click the Play button.

To assign a keystroke to an action, double-click the action name.

To delete an action, set, or step, click the trash icon. Saved actions and sets that are deleted are not erased and can be reloaded.

Droplets

Droplets are actions that have been turned into icons. Typically, the icons are saved to the desktop. After creating and saving a droplet to the desktop, apply the action to file(s) simply by dragging files or folders onto it.

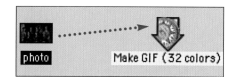

Useful Features Accessed from the Actions Palette Menus:

Photoshop	ImageReady
Inserting menu items	Inserting stops
Inserting stops	Setting Optimization Settings
Switching to Button Mode	Setting an Output Folder
Loading a set of actions	Setting an action's batch options
	Turning an action into a droplet

Predefined Actions

Photoshop has gobs of predefined actions. They are grouped into six sets, plus a default set that is a miscellaneous selection from the others. New actions are added to these sets or new sets you create. Any new set saved in Photoshop's Actions folder will also show up in the Actions palette menu.

ImageReady has a small group of predefined actions that are always in the Actions palette, as long as you don't remove them. New actions also are retained there. But, there is no load command in ImageReady's palette. Instead, actions must be dragged to a folder outside ImageReady. To make an action available to ImageReady, drag the .isa file (the ImageReady action extension) into the ImageReady Actions folder inside the Adobe Photoshop 6 Settings folder. If ImageReady is open while you do this then choose Rescan Actions Folder from the Actions palette menu to load the action in the palette.

load a set of actions   *Photoshop only*

A. From the Actions palette menu, choose one of the sets at the bottom.

Use this method when loading Photoshop's predefined sets or other sets that have been saved in Photoshop's Photoshop Actions folder.

or

B. Choose Load Actions from the Actions palette menu. In the dialog box that opens, go and find an actions file. Photoshop actions files carry an .atn extension.

Use this method when you have saved actions outside of Photoshop's Photoshop Actions folder.

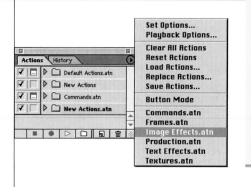

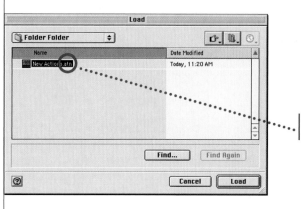

Photoshop action files have an .atn extension.

PRESET ACTION SETS

Photoshop:

Commands—*Attaches function keys to simple menu commands*

Frames—*Creates frames around the perimeter of an image or adds texture to the image's edges.*

Image Effects—*Adds special effects to images including color adjustments and textures*

Production—*Various actions to set up and save files*

Text Effects—*Various special effects for type*

Textures—*Actions that create textures from scratch*

ImageReady's default set contains a miscellaneous variety of production actions.

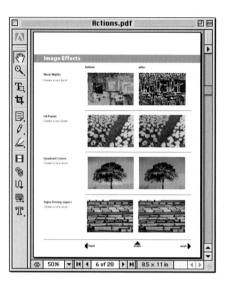

Actions Previews

To take a look at what Photoshop's predefined actions can do, find the Photoshop Actions folder (Adobe Photoshop 6.0>Presets>Photoshop Actions) and open the Actions.pdf file in Adobe Acrobat. This is a navigable database that displays examples for all the predefined actions.

A Selection of the Predefined Photoshop Actions

Frames: Brushed Aluminum

Text Effects: Die Cut

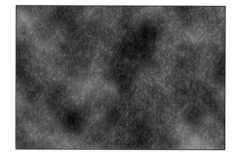

Textures: Rusted Metal

Image Effects: Blizzard

Image Effects: Quadrant Colors

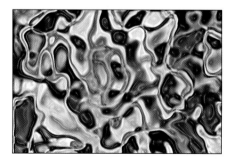

Textures: Green Slime

Recording an Action: Photoshop

You might wonder whether it's worth your time to create actions. The answer is definitely yes. Why? Because they are so easy to create. It is simply a matter of recording a series of commands and then editing, if necessary, to fine-tune it. And after an action is recorded, you can save it and always have it on hand when you get back into the same situation. The following steps detail the creation of a typical action in Photoshop that prepares and optimizes images for the Web.

record an action: photoshop

1. Open any image. The image will only be used as a sample for creating the action. If the image is important, make a duplicate of it.

2. Click the New Set icon on the bottom of the Actions palette. Name the set and click OK. While the new set is selected, click the New Action icon on the Actions palette. Name the action. If you want to set a keyboard shortcut or a color, set it now. Giving the action a color helps it stand out when you set the Actions palette to Button Mode. Click Record to start recording the new action.

    If you don't create a new action before recording, the steps will become part of whatever action was selected when you began recording.

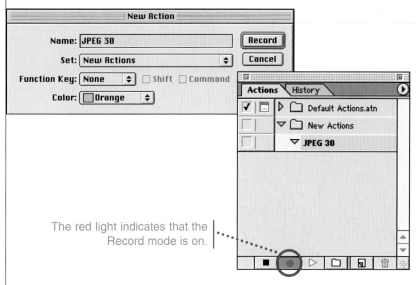

The red light indicates that the Record mode is on.

record an action: photoshop

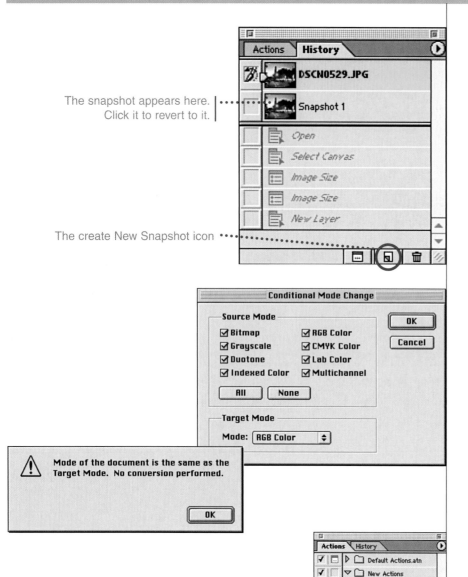

The snapshot appears here. Click it to revert to it.

The create New Snapshot icon

3. The first step in any action should be to use the History palette's Snapshot command.

   This ensures that you can quickly revert to the state of the image prior to running the action. Otherwise, you must undo each step of the action. Switch to the History palette, and click the New Snapshot icon on the bottom.

4. Choose File>Automate> Conditional Mode Change.

   Click the All button and select RGB for the Target mode. Click OK. If the image is already an RGB image, a message appears saying that no change was made because the image already is an RGB image. Click OK, and then click Cancel. No step was added to the action. To get around this, temporarily switch the image mode to CMYK by choosing Image> Mode>CMYK. This command is added to the action, but we don't want it there. Leave it for now, and we'll delete it later.

5. Choose File>Automate> Conditional Mode Change again. Use the same settings as in step 4. This command forces any image into RGB mode.

record an action: photoshop

6. Choose File>Automate>
Fit Image.

This forces the image to fit within a specific dimension rectangle, without distorting it. I set the dimensions to 100 pixels wide and 100 pixels high, which means that the image will be resized until both dimensions are 100 pixels or less. One dimension is guaranteed to be exactly 100 pixels.

7. Choose File>Save for Web.

Set Optimize settings for the image. You can see in the figure what I used. Click OK and select settings in the Save box.

8. Click the Stop button on the bottom of the Actions palette or press (Command-.) [Ctrl-.] to finish the action.

In the Actions palette, the last command is listed as "Export." Continue with the next exercise to edit this action.

Take a Break

At any time, stop recording to make a change to the image and then click Record to resume creating the action.

Editing Actions

Delete a Step

Select it and either click the trash icon or drag it to the trash.

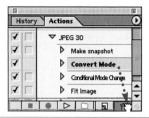

Insert a Menu Item

Click the step after which you want the menu item to appear. Then choose Insert Menu Item from the palette menu. After the Insert Menu Item dialog box opens, choose an item from the Photoshop or Image-Ready menubar, and set options in any dialog box. After choosing the item, it is listed in the Insert Menu Item dialog box. Click OK to add it to the action.

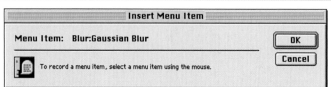

Insert Stops and Messages

With a Stop, you can display a message and cease the progress of an action. To insert a stop, click the step after which you want the stop or message to appear. Choose Insert Stop from the palette menu. Type in a message. If you turn on the Allow Continue option here, then, while the action is playing, you can click Continue in the Stop box to resume it. Stops are useful means of directing the person using the action.

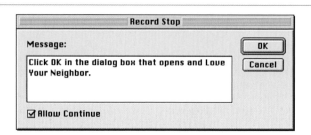

Record More Steps

Select the step after which you want new actions to be placed and click the Record button on the Actions palette. Click the Stop button to stop.

Move or Copy a Step

Click and drag the step up or down. Steps can also be dragged into other actions. Hold the (Option) [Alt] key as you drag to copy the step.

Edit Dialog Box Settings

Double-click a step to open its associated dialog box. Make any desired changes. This will change the current image, not just the settings for the step.

Ask for Input

Turn on the dialog box icon next to the step. When the action is played, it will pause and let you enter values in the dialog box. Clicking OK resumes the action.

Embed Actions

An action can call another action. While recording one action, select another and click the Play button.

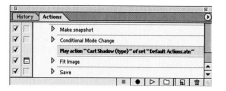

Insert History States & Layer Effects

In ImageReady, history states and layer effects can be dragged into actions for use as steps. This enables you to build an action from commands you just used to adjust or create an image.

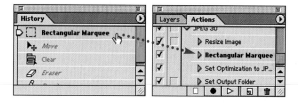

Insert Optimize Settings

In ImageReady, you can drag the Droplet icon into the Actions palette to add the current Optimize settings to the action as a new step. Choosing Insert Set Optimization Settings from the Actions palette menu does the same thing.

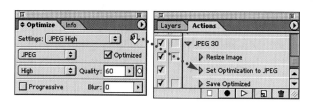

Set Output Folder

In ImageReady, choose Insert Set Output Folder from the palette menu to change or add a destination folder for a saved file. Place it before any Save command.

Recording an Action: ImageReady

The same action created for Photoshop on page 325 can be created in ImageReady, but you must create it differently because of the differences in Photoshop's and ImageReady's commands.

record an action: Imageready

1. Open an image.

   ImageReady can open only RGB images, so you don't need to include a mode change step in this action. Note that Non-RGB images cause ImageReady actions to stop; you may encounter this when using droplets (page 334).

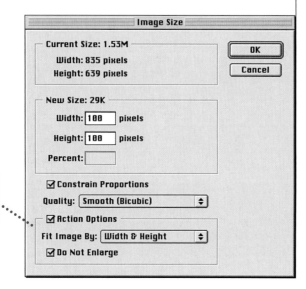

2. Click the New Action icon on the Action palette, name the action in the dialog box, and click Record.

3. Choose Image>Image Size.

   ImageReady's Image Size dialog box has a section just for actions. Turn it on and choose Width & Height from the Fit Image By menu. Then, set both the Width and Height values to 100 pixels. The image will be resized to fit within a 100-by-100 box. If Do Not Enlarge is checked, images smaller than the specified size are not resized.

This feature in the Image Size dialog box replaces Photoshop's Fit Image command.

record an action: imageready

4. Find the Optimize palette and set optimize settings. Use the Optimize, 2-Up, or 4-Up views if helpful.

Alternatively, the Droplet icon can be dragged right into the action to add it as a step.

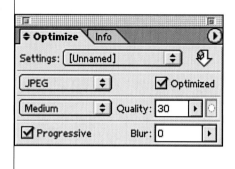

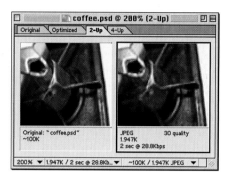

5. Choose File>Save Optimized As and select a folder to save the file. Click Save.

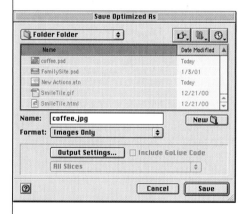

6. Click the Stop button on the Actions palette.

This image shows the action with each step's settings displayed.

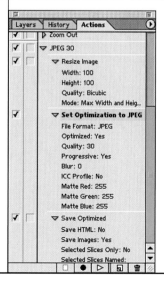

IMAGEREADY SPECIALS

Two special commands in ImageReady's Actions palette menu are very useful for Web graphics preparation. Insert Set Output Folder allows you to choose a folder in which to save processed images, and Insert Set Optimization Settings inserts the current settings from the Optimize palette as a step in the action.

Set Up and Run a Batch

The Batch command (Photoshop only) enables you to process an entire folder of images according to an action. It has great features for setting up this procedure, including letting you rename the files automatically and allowing you to override some commands within the action. Although ImageReady has no Batch command, you can use droplets to batch process images (see page 335).

---

process a batch　　　　　　　　　　　　　　　　　　　　　　*Photoshop only*

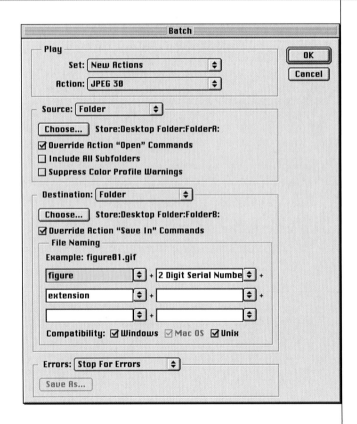

1. After creating the action for the batch, choose File>Automate>Batch.

   Despite the size of the dialog box, there are only a few things to do here. Choose an action, tell Photoshop which images to use, select a folder to save them in, and tell Photoshop what to do in case of errors.

   Play:
   Select an action from the menus.

   Source:
   You can process all open images (Opened Files) or choose a folder of images. If you are processing a folder of images, click Choose and go and find the folder that contains the original images. If the action contains an Open command then turn on Override Action "Open" Commands to use the folder you chose in this dialog box instead of the one in the action.

process a batch

Destination:
*Select a Destination folder.
Note that if you choose to override the "Save In" commands,
only the folder and name will
be overridden. Other save
options, such as format, will
still be used. The automatic file-
naming option can be helpful
for renaming the batch images
into uniformly sequentially
numbered files. I suggest
always choosing a Destination
folder so you know exactly
where the saved images are
going. Otherwise, to keep all
processed images open in
Photoshop, select None.*

Errors:
*Select an option for handling
errors. If Photoshop stops for
an error, you can choose to
resume the action if desired.
Also, some errors will stop the
action even when you have
chosen Log Errors to File for
error handling. Test the action
before leaving it to run a large
batch of images.*

Click OK to commence the
batch process.

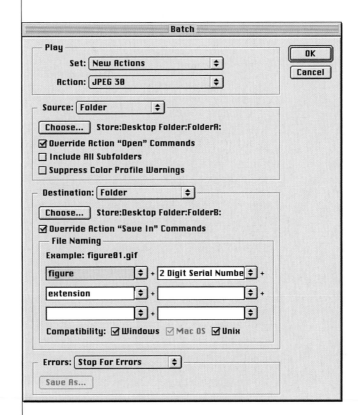

Some Batch Processing Tips

Running Multiple Actions on a Batch:

If you want the batch command to call more than one action then create an action that plays several actions within it and select the new
action in the Batch dialog box.

Using Aliases and Shortcuts in the Source Folder:

Photoshop honors aliases (Mac) that are placed within the chosen
Source folder. This can cut down on how much moving and copying of
files you have to do when setting up to run an action. Create aliases
(Mac) of folders or images and place them in a common, easily accessible folder on the desktop.

Creating Droplets

A *droplet* is an application created by Photoshop or ImageReady that plays an action on a file (or group of files) that is dragged on top of it. Need to quickly make an image a 60-Quality progressive JPEG? No problem; just drag it on top of a droplet and it's automatically processed. In ImageReady, you can use droplets as a way to batch process files.

create a droplet: photoshop

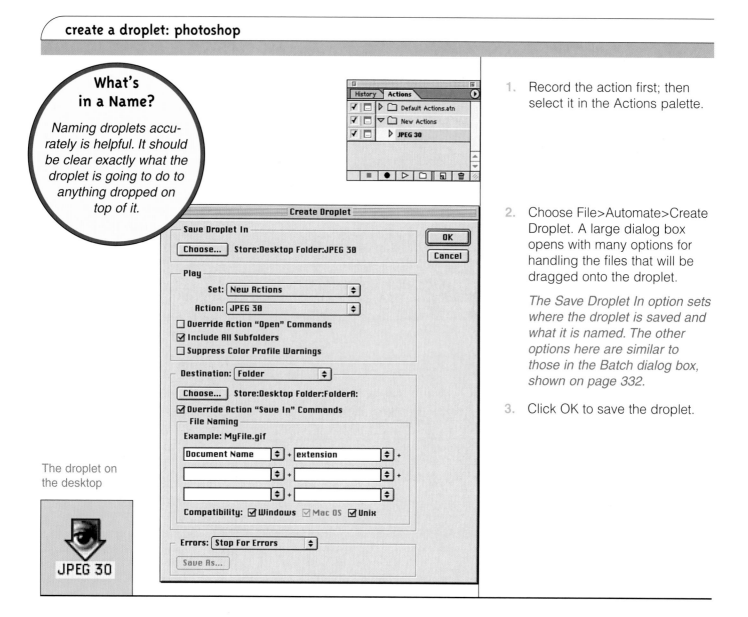

What's in a Name?

Naming droplets accurately is helpful. It should be clear exactly what the droplet is going to do to anything dropped on top of it.

The droplet on the desktop

1. Record the action first; then select it in the Actions palette.

2. Choose File>Automate>Create Droplet. A large dialog box opens with many options for handling the files that will be dragged onto the droplet.

   The Save Droplet In option sets where the droplet is saved and what it is named. The other options here are similar to those in the Batch dialog box, shown on page 332.

3. Click OK to save the droplet.

create a droplet: imageready

Actions

1. Record the action first, select it in the Actions palette, and choose Batch Options from the palette menu.

   The Batch Options dialog box enables you to set options for how files are saved after the droplet action processes them. Select settings and click OK.

2. Choose Create Droplet from the Actions palette menu.

   Choose a location and a name; then click Save to save the droplet.

   Alternatively, you can just drag an action from the Actions palette to the desktop, where it will be saved.

Optimization Settings Only

In ImageReady, you also can create a droplet just for the purpose of optimizing files.

1. Set all optimization settings on the Optimize palette.

2. Click the Droplet icon on the Optimize palette. In the dialog box, select a name and a location and save it.

   Or, grab the Droplet icon on the Optimize palette and drag it to the desktop to save it there.

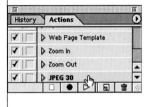

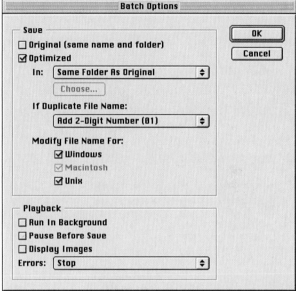

The droplet on the desktop

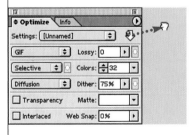

OPENING DROPLETS

An ImageReady droplet can be opened via the File>Open command. It appears in a new window that displays both the complete steps of the action as well as a line for the Batch Options. Double-click this line to edit your settings. You can make alterations and resave it via the File>Save As command or drag it to the Actions palette.

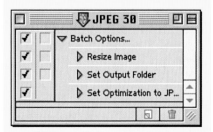

Using Droplets

After a droplet has been created, using it is simply a matter of dragging files or folders on top of it. The desktop is a great, convenient place to keep droplets. If you create a lot of them and don't want to clutter the desktop, create a folder on the desktop just for the purpose of holding droplets.

---

use a droplet

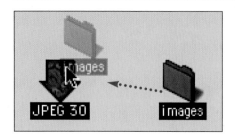

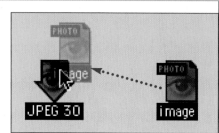

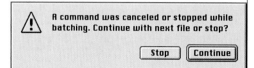

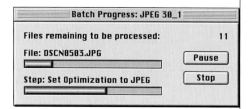

1. Locate the droplet. Then, drag a file, a group of selected files, or a folder on top of the droplet until it is highlighted. Release the mouse to activate the droplet.

2. The appropriate application launches if it is not already open and remains open after processing is complete.

   Photoshop:

   On a Mac, you can press Command-. to stop the processing.

   This enables you to skip the current file and continue or stop the processing completely.

   ImageReady:

   A progress dialog box opens with buttons for pausing or stopping the processing.

   If you pause the action, you can't do anything in ImageReady until the action is either resumed and completed or stopped. If you click Stop, however, you have the option of skipping the current file and resuming or stopping all processing.

Creating Web Photo Galleries

This command takes a folder of images and sets up HTML pages to view them as a gallery on the Web. There are four different layouts to choose from, but each creates a page (or pages) of thumbnail images with links to full-size images. Even if you don't intend to use these galleries on the Web, they are a great way to view a set of images. Before using this feature, put all the images in a single folder.

Custom Designs

Design your own photo galleries by customizing the files Photoshop uses to create these galleries. See Photoshop's Help Guide for details.

create a Web photo gallery

Photoshop only

1. Choose File>Automate>Web Photo Gallery. Choose a Style from the menu by watching the preview on the right. Then, make any of the following adjustments in the Options section:

   Banner:
   Title Information and Font

   Gallery Images:
   Image Size and Quality
   Border Size
   Caption Info
   Column and Row Numbers

   Gallery Thumbnails:
   Image Size and Quality
   Border Size

   Custom Colors:
   Background and Link Colors

2. Choose a Source folder where the images are stored and a *different* Destination folder for the resulting images and HTML file. Click OK to build the gallery.

   Photoshop does the rest. After processing the images, the gallery opens in a browser. Press (Command-.) [Ctrl-.] to stop the processing.

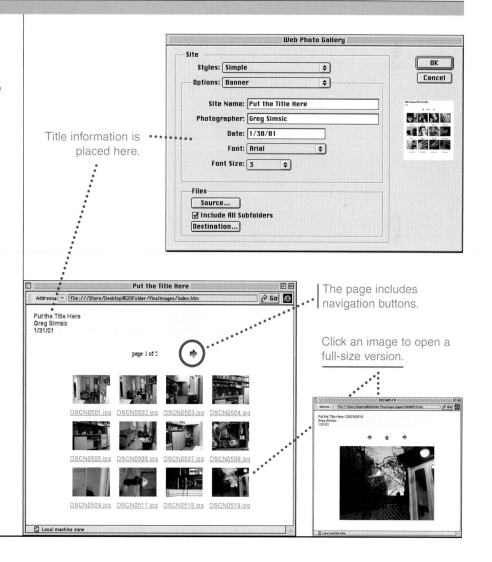

Title information is placed here.

The page includes navigation buttons.

Click an image to open a full-size version.

18

Making a Web Page

This chapter takes you through the process of putting together a Web page. It is typical in the sense that it covers the graphics issues that must be dealt with to create a working page. It is not typical in the sense that this chapter has been planned out to anticipate those issues. Your own designs will present unique challenges, but this example demonstrates how to bring together some of the various issues discussed throughout this book.

The intention of this chapter is to gather the skill, concepts, and techniques discussed in this book into a practical example—creating a complete Web page. Although you might use ImageReady and Photoshop only to produce pieces for Web pages, the example on the following pages demonstrates how these individual elements might work together in one design.

The Downloadable Photoshop File

The chapter begins with the graphic and type elements in place in a layered Photoshop file. To work along with the example, you can download the makepage.psd file that it starts with by following the link to this book found at the following URL:

www.quepublishing.com

Download the file and open it in Photoshop. Note that the type layers in the online version have been rasterized and are therefore no longer editable. This is to avoid any font substitution problems that might occur because the fonts in the file are different from those installed on your machine. You will still be able to follow these steps.

In fact, even if you don't have the .psd file, following along with the steps can help you understand the nature of working with Web graphics in the context of an entire design.

64 Easy Steps to Bliss

Taking this .psd file from its current state to the final stages of saving out the slices and HTML file consumes the entirety of this chapter in one long example. The design contains photographic images, type, some "flat" art, rollover effects, a navigation menu, and an animation. The chapter is divided into six sections: adding the menu, building the animation, slicing the design, adding the rollover effects, optimizing the slices, and previewing and saving the final images. The order of these operations is meant to represent a typical order of working on a design.

It's easy to get caught up in the details of producing a single effect or mastering a technique, but you always should have in mind the final goal of your work. And that is to produce images for Web pages and designs themselves. This chapter employs this broader perspective.

To Begin—The End

This is the final result of this chapter:

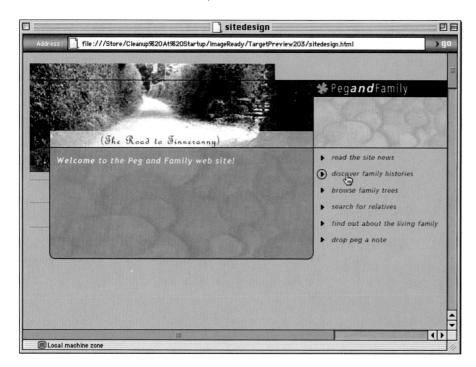

It doesn't look a lot different from the initial image, seen on the next page, but along the way several effects are added and it is transformed from a static Photoshop image into a functional, if somewhat less-than-complete, Web page viewable in a browser.

The layers in the final ImageReady file are organized into several layer sets.

Taking a Look at the Initial Photoshop File

Open Photoshop and open the makepage.psd file. Before getting to work, let's look at a few things. Turn on the rulers and set the units to pixels. The file size of this document is 650 by 450 pixels. Take note of the guides in the document. The vertical guides divide the page into three equal columns. This establishes some structure for the design. There is also a horizontal rule placed at the 350-pixel line. This rule is a reminder of the limited viewing area of monitors with a 640x480 display. Ideally, all important elements of the design are above this line, as in this example.

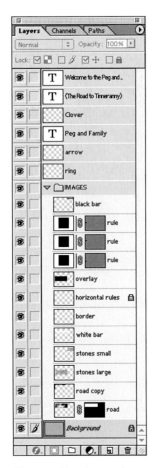

The graphics that make up the background are in a layer set titled IMAGES.

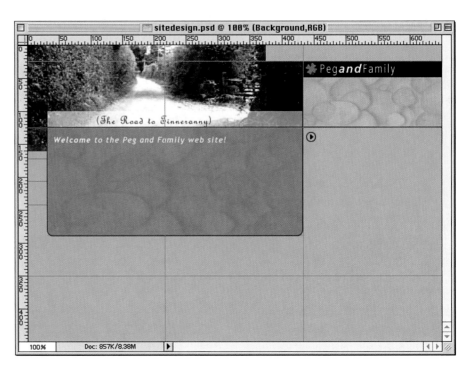

Refer to Chapter 2, "Preparing Photoshop and ImageReady for Web Work," for instructions on setting up the applications for Web work.

building the navigation menu

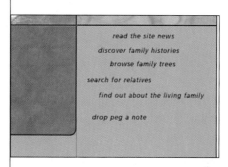

Adding the Menu

Most of the graphics for this design already exist in the file, but one more part of the design needs to be built: the navigation menu.

1. Use the Type tool to enter the first menu item. Do this for each item in the menu, creating a new Type layer for each item.

2. To align the Type layers, first select one in the Layers palette and then link the others to it.

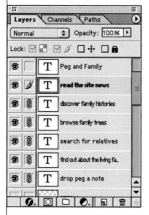

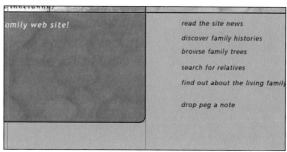

3. Then, choose Layer>Align Linked>Left Edges.

    The linked layers are aligned to the left edge of the selected layer.

4. To create uniform vertical spacing among the layers, while they are still linked, choose Layer>Distribute Linked> Vertical Centers.

    To adjust the spacing, unlink the bottom layer, shift it up or down, relink it to the others, and repeat the Distribute Linked command.

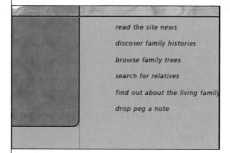

5. Use the Move tool to shift the list into its final location.

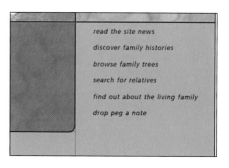

building the navigation menu

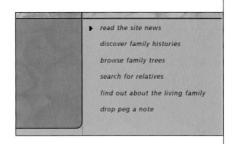

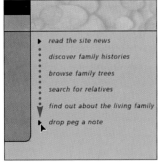

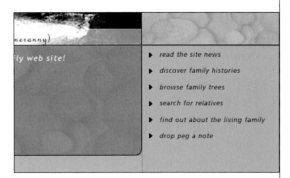

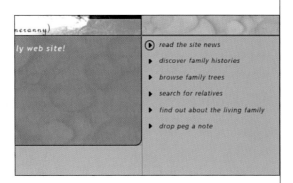

6. To add a graphic element in front of each item, I created a right-pointing triangular arrow. It is in the .psd file in a layer titled "arrow." Turn on the layer and move it to the left of the first menu item.

7. Make copies of the arrow layer for each item in the menu.

   To do this, drag the layer to the New Layer icon on the Layers palette. Do this for each copy needed. Then, select one of the layers and use the Move tool to drag it down to align with the last item in the menu (hold the Shift key as you drag so the arrow doesn't stray to the left or right). Then, link all the arrow layers and choose Layer>Distribute Linked> Vertical Centers. They should line up perfectly.

8. Next, turn on the Ring layer. This one-pixel stroke ring will become part of the rollover effects for the navigation menu. Use the Move tool to place it so that it circles the top arrow.

   You don't need to make copies of this layer because it can be moved to the other menu items when creating the rollover effects.

making graphics for an animation

9. All the navigation menu items are created and in place. To maintain an organized layer palette, put all these layers in a layer set. The easiest way to do this is to select one of the layers in the Layers palette, link the rest of the layers (for the menu) to it, and choose New Set from Linked from the Layers palette menu. Title the layer set, "Menu."

Building the Animation

The last of the graphic elements to build is an animation for the clover that appears next to the site title. The animation itself must be built in ImageReady, but Photoshop can build the graphics.

10. Make a copy of the layer by dragging it to the New Layer icon at the bottom of the Layers palette. Turn off the original Clover layer.

11. The new layer is selected. Press (Command-T) [Ctrl-T] to turn on the transform handles. For precision, use the numeric settings in the Options bar. Enter 72 in the Rotate window. Click the check at the end of the Options bar to accept the transformation.

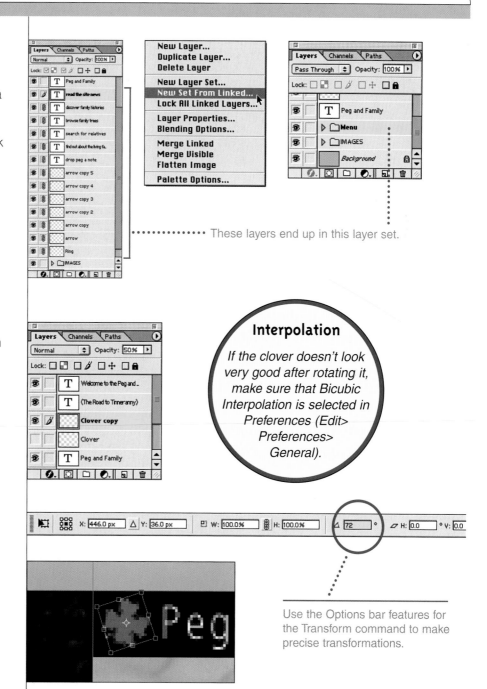

These layers end up in this layer set.

Interpolation

If the clover doesn't look very good after rotating it, make sure that Bicubic Interpolation is selected in Preferences (Edit> Preferences> General).

Use the Options bar features for the Transform command to make precise transformations.

making graphics for an animation

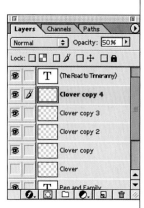

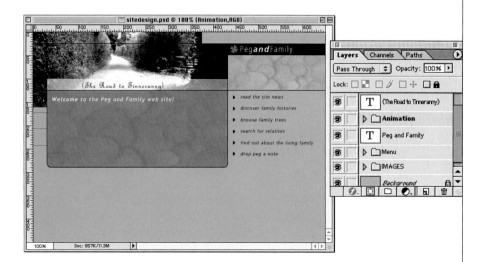

12. Make a copy of the rotated layer by dragging it to the New Layer icon, and then press (Command-Shift-T) [Ctrl-Shift-T] to rotate the new layer another 72°.

13. Repeat the previous step two more times to make a total of five clover layers.

14. Create a layer set for the clovers in the same way as you did for the menu items.

15. Turn on the original clover layer and turn the rest of them off. Also turn off the Ring layer.

    The importance of this step, returning the clover to the Normal state, is realized when creating the animation later.

    The graphics for the design are complete. The next step is to slice the design. Slicing could be done in Photoshop, but ImageReady's slicing features are expanded and more convenient.

    We've made significant progress at this point. Now would be a good time to save the file so you don't lose your work.

16. Click the Jump To ImageReady button on the bottom of the toolbox. It will take a moment for ImageReady to open and the file to be transferred.

Take a break . . .

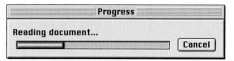

defining the slices

Slicing the Design

You should be in ImageReady now and ready for slicing. Slices for this document are relatively straightforward. Slices should be made so that the photographic images are separated from the graphic images, such as type and icons. Slices also must be made for any element that will have a URL or rollover effect attached to it. Finally, this design presents opportunities for creating No Image slices for areas of solid color.

Slice View Prefs

If the slice numbers and icons are in the way, turn them off by choosing Edit>Preferences>Slices and setting the Numbers and Symbols to None.

17. Select the Slice tool. Choose View>Snap To and make sure that the Slices option is checked; then make sure snapping is checked (on), too (View>Snap).

18. Drag the first slice from the upper-left corner down and to the right, as shown in this figure.

    Keeping the white bar and text on top of it in their own slice enables it to be easily replaced if necessary.

19. Make two more slices that include the leftover parts of the photograph not covered by the white bar. Then, make a slice to contain the white bar.

    As the slices are drawn, ImageReady creates auto slices for other parts of the design. Don't worry about those for now. We'll straighten them out later.

defining the slices

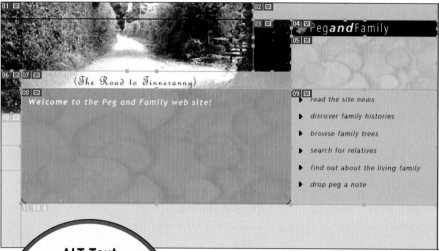

ALT Text

Enter text in the ALT box on the Slices palette to assign ALT text to the slice. This text appears in the event that the image does not load in the browser.

The challenge is to divide this slice into uniform slices and have the lines of text centered vertically within each slice.

20. Drag more rectangular slices to enclose

- The solid green area in the upper right

- The site title and black bar underlying it

- The two areas with the stone backgrounds

- The entire navigation menu area with one slice

Take stock of the current slices. The image should look like this.

21. You still have more slices to define. The clover animation should be defined in its own slice to reduce the file size. Zoom in and draw a slice around it and let the snapping effect guide the slice.

22. Also, the menu slice needs to be divided into separate slices. When building a menu such as this, it is best to create slices of equal size because they will be easier to replace if necessary.

23. You could simply use the Slice>Divide Slice command to divide the menu slice into the correct number of uniformly sized slices, but that command alone does not guarantee that the text for each menu item will be vertically centered within the slice.

defining the slices

24. Select the rectangular Marquee tool, zoom in on the menu, find the Info palette (Window>Show Info), and draw a selection from the baseline of one line of text to the baseline of the next, as you see in this image.

You want to know the exact distance between the lines of text. Read it from the Info palette.

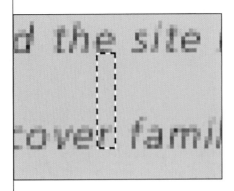

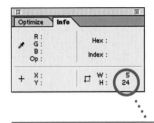

The height of the active selection is listed on the Info palette.

25. Multiply the distance by the number of items in the menu. The full menu slice should be that size.

24 pixels x 6 menu items = 144 pixels

26. Get the Slice Select tool, and select the slice surrounding the menu. Find the Slice palette (Window>Show Slice), and choose Show Options from the palette menu to reveal the slice dimensions. Change the vertical dimension (H) to the number calculated in the previous step (144 pixels).

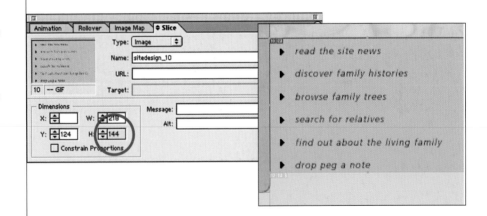

27. Choose Slices>Divide Slice. Check the Divide Slices Horizontally Into box and turn on the "slices down, evenly spaced" radio button. The slice divides into uniform slices in the window behind the dialog box.

To check the numbers, turn on the "pixels per slice" radio button and enter the value found in step 25. It should produce the exact same result.

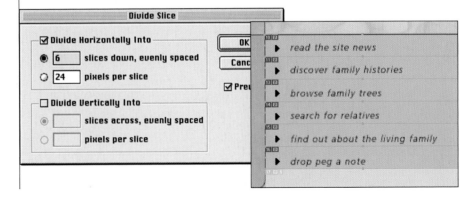

defining the slices

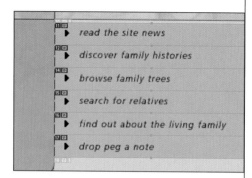

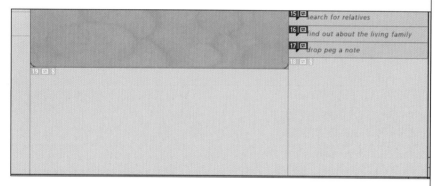

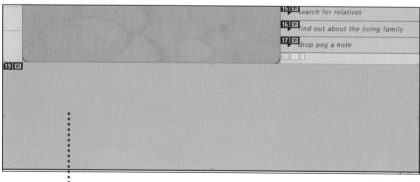

When you draw a slice across an auto-slice, the new slice takes precedence and the auto-slices are automatically readjusted so as not to create overlapping slices. User-slices, on the other hand, can overlap. See step 41 for just such a case.

28. All the slices for the menu are now selected. If necessary, use the arrow keys to nudge them up or down so the menu items are centered in the slices vertically.

29. The last slice issue to resolve is the bottom area of the design. Because there are no graphics in this area and it is covered by a single solid color, it should be defined by a single slice.

    Actually, the ImageReady document could be cropped to eliminate this part of the image and have the HTML document fill this area with the color. Leave it in for now because it helps to show how the page will look in the browser.

30. With the Slice tool, draw a slice around this solid area. The auto-slices that had been drawn here are redrawn to accommodate this new slice. Slicing is now complete.

    The rest of the slice issues, such as what to do with the auto-slices, can be taken care of when the file is optimized. Let's move on to creating the rollover effects.

adding the rollover effects

Rollovers

31. Find the Rollover palette (View>Show Rollover). When working with rollovers, it is very important to know which rollover state is current. Keep this window visible.

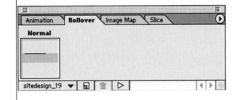

32. The Normal rollover state should be established before adding the rollover effects to any slices. Review the image on page 341 to make sure that the correct layers are turned on and off. The ring layer should be off.

33. Use the Slice Select tool to select the first menu slice. On the Rollover palette only a Normal state exists. Click the New State icon. The new state defaults as the Over state, which is what you want.

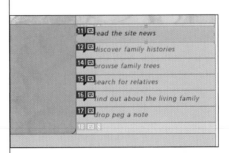

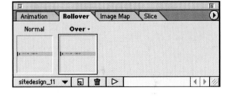

34. On the Layers palette, turn on the Ring layer. Then, use the Move tool if necessary to move the ring so that it surrounds the arrow next to the first menu item. You might need to turn off snapping for better positioning (Command-;) [Ctrl-;].

    Remember that the Ring layer is inside the Menu layer set. If necessary, unlink it from other layers before moving it.

    Play it safe and click the Normal state on the Rollover palette to help prevent the creation of unwanted rollover effects.

Use Caution near Rollovers

Make sure not to make any other changes in the Layers palette while you are editing a rollover state for a slice.

adding the rollover effects

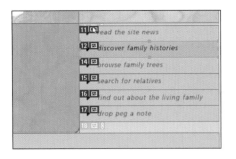

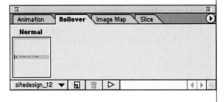

35. Use the Slice Select tool to select the next menu item slice.

The Ring layer is automatically turned off because you have switched to the Normal state of another slice. Notice in the Rollover palette that only a Normal state exists.

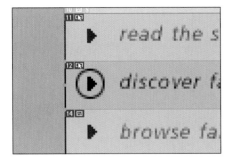

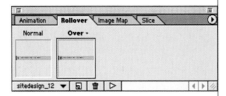

36. Again, click the New State icon to create the Over state, turn on the Ring layer, and position it (with the Move tool) over the arrow next to this second menu item.

37. Repeat this process for each menu item slice.

Be very careful about the order in which you perform these operations, and always be aware of which state in which each slice is selected.

38. When finished, click the Slices Visibility icon on the tool palette to turn off the slices; then click the Rollover Preview button. Move the pointer over the menu items to test the effects.

39. Click the Rollover Preview button again to turn it off.

adding the animated rollover

40. There is one more rollover to build—the one that includes the spinning clover animation. Get the Slice Select tool and select the slice that contains the site title, "Peg and Family."

41. Notice that this slice extends over the clover slice. To correct this, use the Slice Select tool to grab the left handle of the slice and drag to the right until it snaps to the right edge of the clover slice.

42. The Rollover palette should still be visible. Click the New State icon to create the Over state for this slice.

43. Click the Animation palette tab to bring it forward. Currently, only one frame exists. Click the New Frame icon to create a second frame.

44. On the Layers palette, open the Clover layer set. One of the layers is on, and the rest are turned off. Turn off the one that is on, and turn on the layer above it in the set.

    In the image, the clover should rotate 72°, or one-fifth of a rotation. If not, you've turned on the wrong layer. Find the right one and turn it on. Click back and forth between the first and second frames of the animation to see the clover rotate.

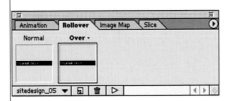

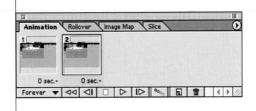

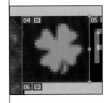

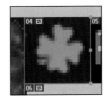

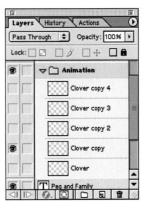

Do not be tempted to select the slice that contains the clover while building this animation. This type of rollover effect is called a *remote rollover*, which means that rolling over one slice causes changes in another.

adding the animated rollover

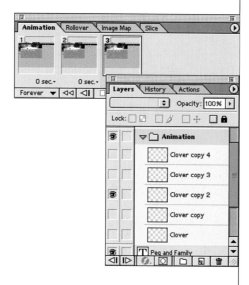

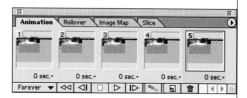

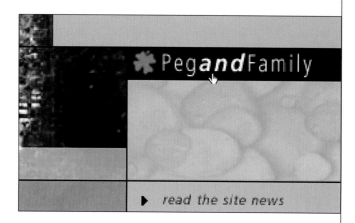

45. Select the second frame of the animation and click the New Frame icon again.

46. Back on the Layers palette, turn off the current clover layer and turn on the next clover in the order. Make sure it's the correct one—rotating another fifth of a rotation.

47. Create two more frames in the same manner, turning layers on and off, so that each clover layer is on (while all others are off) in one of the five animation frames.

48. To test the animation, click the Play button on the Animation palette. ImageReady's animation playback is slow and choppy, but it gives you a general idea of what the animation does. Correct any problems.

49. To test the animation as a rollover effect, click the Slices Visibility icon on the toolbox to turn off the slices; then click the Rollover Preview button. Move the pointer over the site title to start the animation.

50. When finished, turn off Rollover Previews, switch to the Rollover palette, and select the Normal state.

optimizing the slices

Optimizing

The graphics and effects are complete, and the file is ready for optimizing. The slices of this design can be separated into groups according to their content and functions. The slices within a group can be optimized with the same settings. Linking slices makes this operation quicker.

After moving this slice boundary down one pixel, the thin strip contains only one color and can therefore become a memory-saving No Image slice.

51. Before jumping into optimizing, take another look at the slices created earlier. Zoom in to make sure that the slice boundaries are exactly where you want them. A one-pixel difference can mean including extra colors or part of a photographic image in a GIF.

 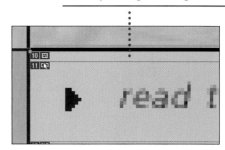

52. Get the Slice Select tool and select all the slices that contain photographic images. Use the Shift key to select multiple slices. Then, choose Slices> Link Slices. Later, the slices in this linked group will all become JPEGs.

A link icon is placed next to the slice number, and they are all made the same color.

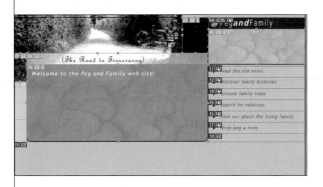

53. Then, select all the slices that contain only a solid color and link those slices. These slices will be made No Image slices. Link these slices using Slices>Link Slices.

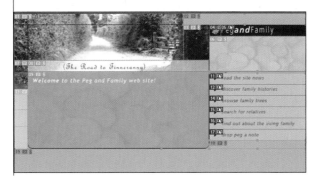

optimizing the slices

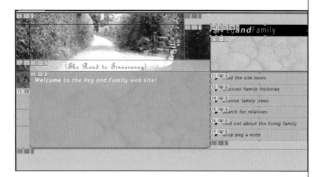

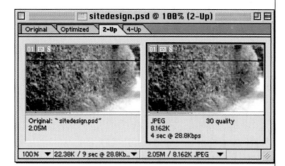

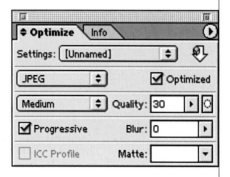

54. Finally, select the rest of the slices: those containing menu items, arrows, the clover, and the site title. Link them. These slices will be GIFs because of their flat areas of color, and because one of them contains an animation.

    Linked slices all have the same optimize settings. Changing the settings for one slice changes the settings for all.

55. Switch to the 2-Up view so you can see the original and optimized views at once. Use the Slice Select tool to select one of the photographic slices.

56. Find the Optimize palette and change the File Format to JPEG. Set the Quality to 30— this is a good general setting that produces a small file that doesn't sacrifice too much in quality. Turn on the Optimized option.

    All the linked slices receive the same settings. Although the 2-Up image at left shows only part of one of the JPEG slices, it's important to view all of them because the Optimize settings are being set for all the linked slices.

optimizing the slices

57. Select one of the menu item slices. Choose GIF as the file format on the Optimize palette. GIF is the best format for images that have sharp edges, such as those that exist between type and the background on which it lies. It is also the only possible choice for the clover slice because it is an animation.

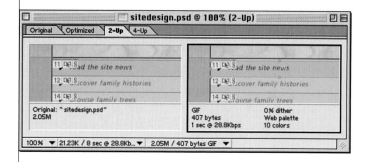

58. Set other GIF options: Palette to Web (which produced 11 colors in the Color Table via the Auto setting), and Dither to No Dither.

Notice that all the slices linked to this slice share the same Optimize settings.

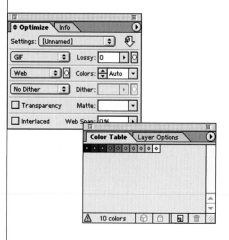

LINKED GIFS

The advantage of saving an image as a GIF is that you can control the color perfectly. But linked slices saved as GIFs share the same color table. This means that for all images to look good, some of the GIFs will contain extra colors in their color tables. This unnecessarily increases their file sizes. Sometimes, though, this can be a good way to force consistency across slices.

59. Select one of the slices that contains only the solid green. Find the Slice palette (Window>Show Slice) and choose No Image from the Type menu.

Making a slice a No Image slice does not make all linked slices No Image slices. Linking this group of slices is only a matter of organization.

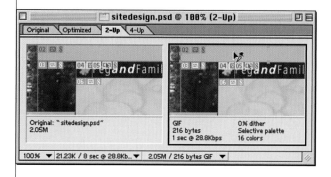

previewing and saving

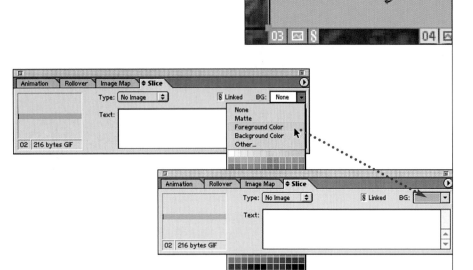

60. Get the Eyedropper tool and use it to select the color from one of these slices. The color becomes the Foreground color on the tool palette.

61. Return to the Slice palette and click the arrow next to the BG swatch; then select Foreground color from the menu. This sets the background color for the table cell that this slice becomes in the final HTML document, but it causes no visible change to the image. Repeat this step for all the No Image slices.

Previewing and Saving

Before previewing this file, you have one more thing to set up— the background color for the HTML page.

62. Choose File>Output Settings>Background. Click the Color swatch and choose Foreground color from the pop-up menu.

    As long as you haven't changed the Foreground color from the last step, this makes the background color of the Web page the same green as what appears throughout the design.

previewing and saving

63. To preview the entire design in a browser, click the Preview in Browser icon on the toolbox. The HTML file and images are opened in a browser. Test all the rollover effects and make sure the quality of the opti-mized images is adequate.

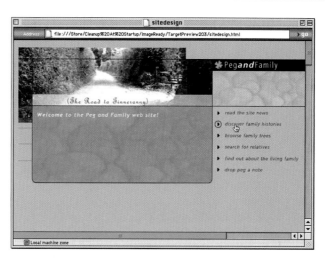

64. Return to ImageReady and choose File>Save Optimized. For Format choose HTML and Images. Select All Slices from the pop-up menu below. Click Save. The HTML file and an Images folder are saved in the selected location.

The HTML file can be opened in any HTML editor for further adjustments.

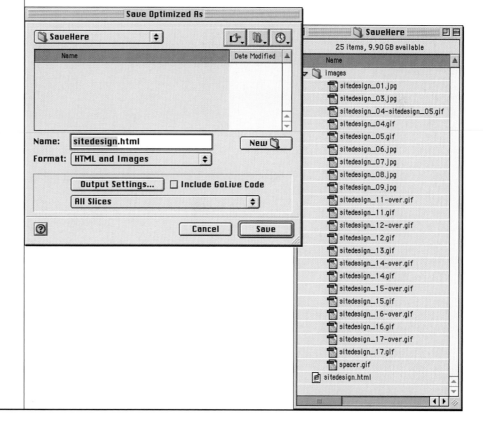

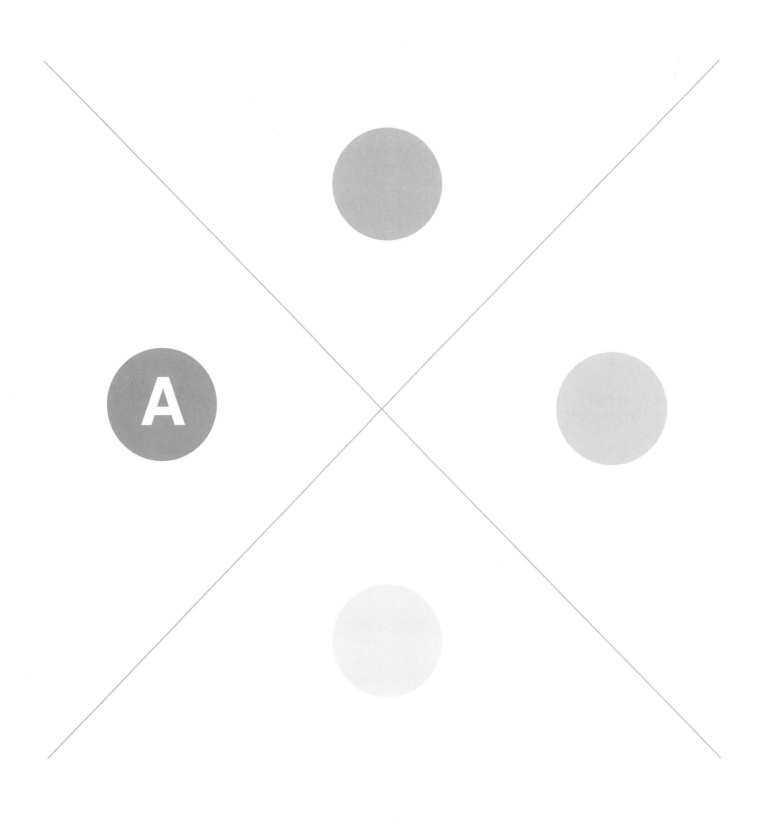

Web Resources

This appendix contains an extensive list of Photoshop links—
from official to commercial to personal there is a wide range.
The sites in the top-six list cover most issues, and the others
supplement specific needs.

The Top Six

A handful of sites stands out as the most useful. Try them first. Keep these sites bookmarked for use as references.

Web Developer

http://www.webdeveloper.com/

Everything you need. The one-stop source for up-to-date information on Web development with a section on Web graphics.

Hotwired's Web Monkey Site

http://www.webmonkey.com/

Magazine-style resource for all things to do with Web design.

WebReference.com

http://www.webreference.com/

A great general Web info site. Virtually everything is covered.

About.com

http://webdesign.about.com

Many areas discussing many aspects of Web design and Web graphics. Mostly article driven. Individual articles lead to links to other sites. Up-to-date and changing information.

CNET - Web Building

http://www.builder.com/

Click the Builder link in the navigation bar to go to the Web Building section, which is full of articles on Web design and graphics, including a Photoshop section.

Adobe

http://www.adobe.com/photoshop/

Photoshop's official site.

General Photoshop Sites

Adobe

http://www.adobe.com/products/tips/photoshop.html

The tutorial section of the official site.

Photoshop User

http://www.photoshopuser.com/

The online version of the magazine dedicated to Photoshop. Subscription holders only. The official site of the National Association of Photoshop Professionals (NAPP).

About.com: Web Graphics Section

http://www.graphicssoft.about.com/compute/graphicssoft/cs/photoshopweb/

Tutorials and tips for creating Web graphics.

Hotwired's Web Monkey Photoshop Crash Course

http://hotwired.lycos.com/webmonkey/98/20/index0a.html

Photoshop basics broken down in lessons. Not yet updated for Photoshop 6.

Planet Photoshop

http://www.planetphotoshop.com/

Bills itself as the "Ultimate Photoshop Site." There's lots of up-to-date information including, tutorials, articles, related product news, links to other resources, and a daily featured tutorial.

DeepSpaceWeb

http://www.deepspaceweb.com

Up-to-date tutorials, plug-ins, actions, and more, including Web issues.

Desktop Publishing.Com's Photoshop Tips and Techniques

http://desktoppublishing.com/photoshoptips.html

Links to many tips and techniques sites.

Special Edition Using Photoshop 6

http://www.ps6.com/

Richard Lynch's (author of *Special Edition Using Photoshop 6*) site, including a listserver of Photoshop issues.

The Pixel Foundry

http://www.pixelfoundry.com/

As the site states: "Tips, tricks, and resources for Web designers, photoshop users and graphic artists." Tips, forums, and background images.

The Photoshop Guru's Handbook

http://gurus.onlinedesignschool.com/

Tutorials broken down by user experience level.

Tips and Techniques

Jeff's Photoshop Tips and Tricks

http://www.geocities.com/SiliconValley/Way/9571/

A personal site with tips, actions, and links to many other sites.

Russell Brown's Tips & Techniques

http://www.russellbrown.com/body.html

Quicktime videos of various tips and techniques.

The Internet Eye Magazine

http://the-internet-eye.com/HOWTO/Photoshop.htm

A good, long list of useful techniques. Up to date for Photoshop 6.

PixArt

http://www.ruku.com/

Lots of tutorials divided according to the version of Photoshop being used.

Photoshop Web Tips Database

http://www.ex.ac.uk/~jastaple/photoshop/searchframe.html

A searchable index of sites with tips and techniques.

General Web Info Sites

The World Wide Web Consortium

http://www.w3.org/

The official site of the group that develops and promotes Web standards.

Web Developer

http://www.webdeveloper.com/

Everything you need. The one-stop source for up-to-date information on Web development, with a section on Web graphics.

Hotwired's Web Monkey Site

http://www.webmonkey.com/

Magazine-style resource for all things to do with Web design.

WebReference.com

http://www.webreference.com/

A great general Web info site. Virtually everything is covered.

About.com

http://webdesign.about.com/

Many areas discussing many aspects of Web design and Web graphics. Mostly article driven. Individual articles lead to links to other sites. Up-to-date and changing information.

CNET - Web Building

http://cnet.com/

Click the Builder link in the navigation bar to go to the Web Building section which is full of articles on Web design, and graphics including a Photoshop section.

Netscape

http://home.netscape.com/browsers/

Extensive information on the Netscape browser. Other parts of the Netscape site offer information on developing Web pages.

Bandwidth Conservation Society

http://www.infohiway.com/faster/

According to the site, "The goal is that this site becomes a resource for Web developers with an interest in optimizing performance, but still maintaining an appropriate graphic standard. The conviction (or perhaps hallucination) that there is a balance between a pleasing page and an economical, low-bandwidth delivery of that page."

Web Style Guide

http://info.med.yale.edu/caim/manual/contents.html

Articles on most aspects of Web design and site production, including color, file formats, GIFs, JPEGs, optimizing, image maps, and more from the authors of the *Web Style Guide*.

World Wide Web FAQ

http://www.boutell.com/faq/oldfaq/

Dated but useful and extensive general information about the World Wide Web.

Webtools

http://www.webtools.com/

A Byte.com site with Web info geared to professionals.

ZDnet Developer

http://www.zdnet.com/devhead/filters/homepage/

Another general Web development source.

Web Page Design For Designers

http://www.wpdfd.com/

A site that emphasizes design issues.

HTML Goodies

http://www.htmlgoodies.com/

Extensive HTML site that includes many topics dealing with graphics.

Creating Killer Websites

http://www.killersites.com/1-design/

Includes articles on color, file formats, compression, and more.

Actions

The Action Xchange
http://www.actionxchange.com/

Action Addiction
http://www.actionaddiction.com/

Photoshop Actions
http://desktoppublishing.com/psactions.html

Plug-Ins

Plug-ins.com
http://www.plugins.com/plugins/photoshop/

Has links to many sources.

Plugin Head
http://planeta.terra.com.br/informatica/pluginhead/

Has links to many sources.

File Formats

Image Compression and Optimization Software
http://webdesign.miningco.com/compute/webdesign/msubgraphicsopt.htm

A list of other useful applications for optimizing Web graphics.

JPEG FAQ
http://www.faqs.org/faqs/jpeg-faq/

Includes details about the format.

JPEG
http://www.jpeg.org/

The official site of the official group.

PNG (Portable Network Graphics) Home Site

http://www.libpng.org/pub/png/

The official home of the PNG format with everything you'd ever care to know about this format.

About.com

http://webdesign.miningco.com/compute/webdesign/msubgraphicsopt.htm

About.com's Image Compression and Optimization Software page has a rundown of utilities for compressing Web graphics.

Color

International Color Consortium

http://www.color.org/

All about computers, color, and consistency. This is the official home of the group that brought you color profiles.

Robert Berger's Explanation of Monitor Gamma

http://www.vtiscan.com/~rwb/gamma.html

An article that explains the gamma "effect."

PageLab

http://www.pagelab.com/

A quick animated tutorial about the basics of the hexadecimal Web-safe palette.

PaletteMan

http://www.paletteman.com/

A cool interface that enables you to set up a color palette of Web-safe colors. Some preset palettes exist.

Visibone

http://www.visibone.com/colorlab/

Commercial site selling color aids and including articles on Web color.

Poynton's Color FAQ

http://www.inforamp.net/~poynton/notes/colour_and_gamma/ColorFAQ.html

Detailed FAQ on color issues.

Yahoo! Color Links

http://dir.yahoo.com/Arts/Design_Arts/Graphic_Design/web_Page_Design_and_Layout/Color_Information/

GIF Animation

DefyTheRules

http://www.defytherules.com/

Probably the most you'd ever do with GIF animations. This site is intended to show off Adobe's products.

SmashTheStatusQuo

http://www.smashstatusquo.com/

Another Adobe site intended to show off their products—created by method.com.

Animation Factory

http://www.animfactory.com/ and *http://www.animfactory.net/*

A commercial site offering thousands of 3D computer-animated GIF animations for sale. Looking is free. Still graphics also available from animfactory.net.

GIF.com

http://www.gif.com/

A lot of articles on Web design issues plus free GIF animations, clip art, banners, and backgrounds.

Royal Frazier's GIF Animation on the WWW

http://members.aol.com/royalef/gifanim.htm

A somewhat dated site that still has good information about creating and displaying GIF animations on the Web. Examples are available.

Other GIF Animations Applications:

GIF Animator 4.0: *http://www.ulead.com/ga/features.htm*

For full-time animation nuts who want a fully loaded software package made just for them.

Animated GIF Artists Guild

http://www.agag.com/

The site for this guild has several galleries of GIF animations put here by many contributors.

Animation Library

http://www.animationlibrary.com/

Many animations, free for use on noncommercial sites, in many categories. There is also a tutorial for creating animations (using GIF Construction Set).

Animation Central

http://www.animation-central.com/money.htm

Free 3D animations.

Backgrounds

The Background FAQ

http://www.two4u.com/bg-faq/

Detailed information about background images and the HTML BACKGROUND tag.

Netscape's Backgrounds Page

http://home.netscape.com/assist/net_sites/bg/

Another site for basic information on backgrounds; examples are included.

Yahoo! Links

http://dir.yahoo.com/Arts/Design_Arts/Graphic_Design/web_Page_Design_and_Layout/Graphics/Backgrounds/

Has a list of sites offering backgrounds.

Absolute Background Textures Archive

http://www.grsites.com/textures/

Includes many free backgrounds.

Backgrounds Archive

http://www.backgroundsarchive.com/

Free site that takes contributions. Well organized by categories.

The Background Boutique

http://www.theboutique.org/

The site knows the meaning of subtle. The backgrounds here are all designed to add interest to the page without too much distraction. It has many categories.

Clip Art

The Graphics Library

http://www.graphicslibrary.com/

A limited set of free buttons and backgrounds.

ClipArt.com

http://www.clipart.com/

Links to sites with clip art, fonts, photos and Web graphics.

ArtToday

http://www.arttoday.com/

A commercial site with loads of stuff.

IconBazaar

http://www.iconbazaar.com/

Many categories of static and animated clip art.

GifArt.com

http://www.gifart.com/freeimages1.shtml

Lots of free stuff for those willing to provide their e-mail addresses.

Barnyard Graphics

http://www.angelfire.com/art/farmanimals/

When you've gotta have some livestock.

ImaGIF.net

http://www.imagif.net/

Free stuff: animations, buttons, and tilable backgrounds.

Stock Photos

GettyOne

http://www.gettyone.com/

A collection of stock photo collections searchable from this one site. Small comping images are available free for registered members.

Corbis

http://www.corbis.com/

Eyewire

http://www.eyewire.com/

Not just photos. There are also fonts, clip art, Photoshop tips, and more. It's a great one-stop design store.

Yahoo! Category

http://dir.yahoo.com/Business_and_Economy/Shopping_and_Services/Photography/Stock_Photography/

Fonts

The FontSite

http://www.fontsite.com/home.html

Fonthead Design

http://www.fonthead.com/

For Designers

http://www.fonthaus.com/

Garage Fonts

http://www.garagefonts.com/

Font Monster

http://www.fontmonster.co.uk/

1001 Free Fonts

http://www.1001freefonts.com/

Font Shop

http://www.fontshop.com/

Message Boards and E-Mail Lists

desktoppublishing.com's Message Board

http://www.desktoppublishing.com/photoshop/photoshoptalk.html

Post messages and read the FAQ from the desktoppublishing.com Web site without having to subscribe to a listserv or launch a newsreader. Visit Photoshop Paradise and download filters and plug-ins.

Photoshop Discussion List

http://lists.lyris.net/photoshop/

An active Photoshop discussion list.

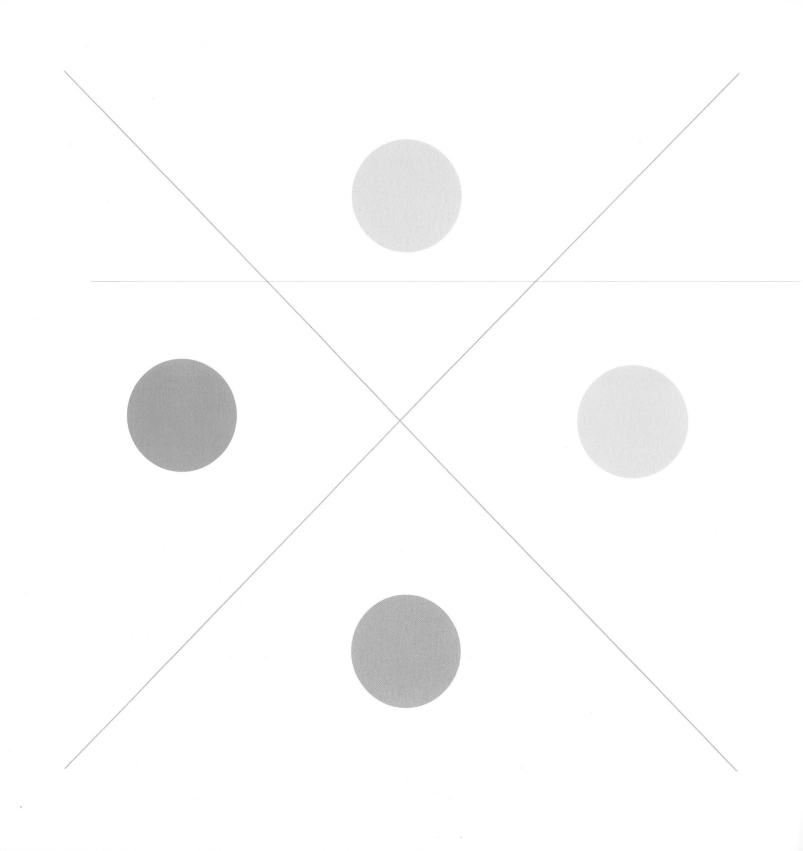

○ Index

A